The

MA...OOK

The Financial Times
MARKETING CASEBOOK

Second Edition

Levela Rickard and Kit Jackson

FINANCIAL TIMES
Prentice Hall

An imprint of **Pearson Education**

Harlow, England · London · New York · Reading, Massachusetts · San Francisco · Toronto · Don Mills, Ontario · Sydney
Tokyo · Singapore · Hong Kong · Seoul · Taipei · Cape Town · Madrid · Mexico City · Amsterdam · Munich · Paris · Milan

Pearson Education Limited

Edinburgh Gate
Harlow
Essex CM20 2JE
United Kingdom

and Associated Companies throughout the world

Visit us on the World Wide Web at
www.pearsoneduc.com

First published in Great Britain in 1997
Second edition published in 2000

© Pearson Education Limited 2000

ISBN 0273-63896-3

British Library Cataloguing in Publication Data
A CIP catalogue record for this book can be obtained from the British Library.

Transferred to digital print on demand, 2004

Typeset by 35 in $9^1/_2$/13pt Stone
Printed and bound by Antony Rowe Ltd, Eastbourne

Contents

Preface   vii

Acknowledgements   viii

1 Marketing Dynamics   1

2 The European Marketing Environment   8

3 Consumer Behaviour   16

4 Organisational Buying Behaviour   22

5 Segmenting Markets   28

6 Marketing Information and Research   36

7 Anatomy of a Product   44

8 Product Management   52

9 New Product Development   60

10 Price   68

11 Pricing Strategies   74

12 Marketing Channels   81

13 Retailers and Wholesalers   87

14 Communication and the Promotional Mix   95

15 Advertising   105

16 Sales Promotion   114

17 Personal Selling and Sales Management   120

18 Direct and Internet Marketing   124

19 Public Relations, Sponsorship and Exhibitions   131

20 Strategic Marketing   139

21 Marketing Planning, Management and Control   148

22 Services and Non-profit Marketing   154

23 International Marketing   162

Preface

Marketing is an activity that affects us all, consciously and unconsciously, throughout our lives. It lives with us at all times.

Above all, marketing is about communication. The skill is to make this communication as effective as possible – by whatever measure may be judged as effective. At its core, is the successful transmission of a message from one individual to another, and this embraces all human activity. It is no wonder that marketing is seen as such a wide and diverse discipline.

This Casebook serves to illustrate marketing activities, the good and the not so good, in the real world. It's foundation is articles drawn from the *Financial Times*, a publication widely regarded as providing impartial, factual reportage of world organisational activities, large and small, whether manufacturing, service or not-for-profit.

The structure of the book follows, in general, the format adopted in the second edition of Brassington and Pettit's, *Principles of Marketing*. For academic purposes, the Instructors' Manual accompanying this text also outlines links to Kotler's, *Principles of Marketing European Edition*. It may also be regarded as a 'Reader' and 'Workbook' for any student wishing to move from strictly theoretical consideration of the subject to a more practically based perspective.

Use may be made of the Casebook in a number of different ways.

The Marketing Practitioner – will find a series of articles that are interesting in themselves and which present a range of topical issues facing them in today's rapidly changing and evolving environment, together with thought provoking questions for them to consider.

The Marketing Student – will have before them a sequence of topic related real-life examples they can explore on their own, or in groups, which encourages them to discover the wider issues for themselves. It also serves to lead them through the subject in a logical manner, developing their expertise in an inter-linked way, building on the learning that has gone before.

The Academic – is presented with a 'potted' version of the topics covered in most Principles of Marketing texts together with a simple Instructors' Manual. Importantly, and new to this edition, is the index which is a significant feature in that it allows the academic to identify and select specific topic areas, and related questions and answers, that may, otherwise, cut across the foci of individual chapters. This facilitates the integration of topics across chapters, illustrating the inter-connections between the multifarious activities that we know collectively as 'marketing'. This feature transforms the book into a valuable resource both of cases and of related questions, bridging the gap between theory and practise.

Acknowledgements

Just like the Oscars, we would like to extend our thanks to many people for their consistent encouragement throughout this work.

To Sheila Wright, who pioneered the Casebook by writing the first edition, and who offered our services when a second edition was proposed. There were times during the process when we weren't quite so grateful!

To our mothers, Evelyn and Bette who believed in us and knew we could do it! An additional thanks to Bette who kept us supplied who home cooking.

To John Jackson, Kit's father who would have been proud of us.

To the staff at Pearson Education, especially Liz Sproat, who supported and 'pushed' us to bring it to publication.

Lastly but not the least to La Grand Champ, our French bolthole and the provider of silence and velvety black French nights which nourished the creative juices.

About the Authors

Levela Rickard is a Principal Lecturer in the Department of Marketing at De Montfort University specialising in International Marketing. A native of North Carolina in the USA, until coming to England she worked at the University of North Carolina at Charlotte and has been at De Montfort University for 12 years and is married to Kit Jackson. Her previous role at De Montfort University as Director of International Training for the Department of Marketing involved work with and in China, Indonesia, the Former Soviet Union, France and most notably in setting up De Montfort University's highly successful business school in Johannesburg, South Africa. Currently in addition to lecturing at both postgraduate and undergraduate levels she is responsible for the University's relationship with the Chartered Institute of Marketing.

C. S. (Kit) Jackson is a Lecturer in the Department of Marketing at De Montfort University specialising in Not for Profit Marketing and Product Management and Innovation. A long term resident of Leicestershire Kit, has worked in a senior management capacity with a number of companies in the textile sector with a special interest in sales, marketing and new product development. Having worked with De Montfort University for 7 years he has also been involved with international senior manager training programmes as well as lecturing at the postgraduate and undergraduate levels. Kit, a Chartered Textile Technologist (C. Text. ATI), is married to Levela Rickard.

1 Marketing Dynamics

'Marketing is the work of the devil and pure mind manipulation!' A direct quotation from a mature student when asked the question, What is marketing? The usual answer is something about selling, to which the joyous pedagogue can respond that selling is only a small part of the whole exercise and sometimes very little indeed, to the amazement of the gathered students.

The answer above concerning the devil and mind manipulation is, of course, apart from being a bit of a shaker, capable of a swift rebuttal, but it reflects a point of view which many hold to a greater or lesser degree. Perhaps it is a state of affairs which marketing professionals working either in industry or at the 'chalk face' would do well to address in a serious manner.

This chapter sets the scene, so to speak, for a discussion of the theory and practice of marketing as a discipline to be used as a tool of management, and especially a tool which should be central to the way in which any organisation thinks about itself and those with which it deals, internally as well as externally.

We are all affected by marketing throughout our lives, and to understand how it works and what it really means is to be enriched in a personal as well as a corporate sense. Let it also be said and acknowledged that things are done that hide under the mantle of marketing which have nothing to do with ethics, truth or fairness. But in its proper application as a servant supplying the eyes and ears of the organisation whether in a profit or a not-for-profit setting, ensuring the supply of goods and services at the right time, in the right place and at the right price focused on those members of the population who have the need, want or desire for such goods and services can only be of benefit to both participants in the transaction, the organisation and its customer. Much was said when it was proposed that marketing principles should be applied to, for example, the National Health Service in England. A large part of it was along the lines of 'I came into this profession to help people, not to make a profit.' Further study and application of the principles reveals that the core beliefs and theories of marketing, that one should find out what the customer wants and enable that satisfaction, are entirely compatible with the idea of helping people.

It is worth recounting the progression which has led to the current state of the art which, of course, did not spring fully formed from the brains of the marketing gurus. In the era of production-oriented companies, the drive was to produce as much as possible as economically as possible, generating profit through volume of sales. The next stage was to become product oriented and to concentrate on improving the product, sales being generated through improvement. Following came the sales era, when volume was generated by hard selling of the product, often with the use of heavy advertising expenditure. We then moved into the marketing era when the customer became the motivator and product was created to satisfy the customer, not the other way around. We are currently in yet a further development of this idea which is the socially responsible marketing mind set, where not only do we attempt to identify and serve the customer to our mutual satisfaction but also to achieve this by having respect for our neighbours and the wider environment. There is also now a detectable further development growing from the explosion in availability of cable, digital, satellite, and Internet sources of information, and the realisation that such knowledge is essential to secure a competitive edge.

So we are in a fast-moving world where only those who can respond quickly and effectively will survive. This chapter gives an outline of how marketing as a discipline fits within the broader organisational functions and starts to take 'the devil' out of the equation.

In order to successfully complete the tasks in this chapter you will need to be familiar with:

● marketing/business orientation;
● environmental scanning;
● marketing mix;
● branding.

Exposed links in the established value chain

Conventional ways of doing business are being turned on their head. Established companies will need to assess the damage, says Peter Martin

For an established company, the challenge posed by the era of digital business is this: what parts of your value chain does it make redundant – and how much does that damage your competitive advantage?

A company's value chain is the whole string of activities – from procurement to after-sales service – in which it engages to create and deliver its output to a customer. Successful companies usually have competitive advantages in a few important parts of the value chain. Digital business could turn that on its head.

'Where once a sales force, a system of branches, a printing press, a chain of stores or a delivery fleet served as formidable barriers to entry because they took years and heavy investment to build, in this new world they could suddenly become expensive liabilities,' say Philip Evans and Thomas Wurster of Boston Consulting Group. 'New competitors on the internet will be able to come from nowhere to steal customers.'

A bank, for example, which has established a substantial competitive advantage in a national chain of bricks-and-mortar branches may be threatened by the growth of online banking. Many of the routine transactions associated with banking can be carried out by a combination of automated teller machines, telephone call centres and direct access by the customer from home to the bank's central computers.

The potential threat is obvious, but that is only half the story. The task for traditional bankers is to assess how critical this loss of competitive advantage will prove to be. How many customers is it likely to affect? Do the bricks-and-mortar branches retain important advantages in customer acquisition and retention? How can the balance of costs and advantages of the two rival distribution systems – physical and virtual – be quantified?

Traditional businesses retain advantages: the social atmosphere of a bookstore; the reassuring presence of a physical bank branch; the personal relationship of a travel agent. Many customers value these advantages. On the surface, the answer to the question 'How much do these changes to the value chain damage your traditional competitive advantage?' may well be 'Not much'.

That may be to underestimate the impact, however. First, the minority will grow as customers who are uncomfortable with online transactions are replaced with new generations at ease with the technology. Second, even if only a minority of customers switch, that may still be enough to affect pricing.

Jed Dempsey, who runs the e-commerce investing activities of Orchid Partners, a private equity firm in San Francisco, thinks the arrival of cut-price electronic transactions will gradually force re-pricing of the whole range of the activities in an industry – even for those customers who still transact their business by conventional means. Thus, electronic retail stock-broking – by companies such as Charles Schwab and E*Trade – will put pressure on prices charged for conventional discount brokerage and possibly for full-service brokerage too.

The need to reassess pricing may be more complex than a simple across-the-board cut, however. In businesses where electronic delivery poses a threat, it will influence pricing in both directions. 'Almost all these businesses will have some segment that is still there at the original price – or even higher, since the cross-subsidy from other more routine transactions may have disappeared,' says Mr Dempsey.

Activities such as customer acquisition and service face the most obvious threats from digital business. But the more profound challenge from the new era comes when the whole value chain is undermined. This is most marked when the technological opportunities created by digital business combine with wider changes in the industry's operating environment and structure.

Take electricity. Until a few years ago, electricity was invariably generated, transmitted and distributed by vertically integrated monopolies. That remains the case for most of the developed world's consumers. But in some countries, the pattern has changed drastically, as a result of changes in regulation and the availability of cheap computers and telecommunications.

The first changes in regulation, in countries such as the UK, came as integrated monopolies were split into separate generation, transmission and distribution companies. But the really revolutionary change – already in place in Sweden and Norway and soon to happen in the UK – is only possible thanks to the era of digital business.

This is the splitting of distribution from supply, creating two different types of company: one which owns and operates monopoly cables to every home and business, the other which competes to supply customers over those cables with electricity bought from the generators.

In this sort of business, the traditional strengths of an electricity utility – reliability, technological depth, physical presence – may be less important than skill in managing customer relationships and spot-market trading.

Karl-Axel Edin, chief executive of Tentum, a Swedish electricity consultancy, thinks that, though some parts of this change could have come about without the digital era, 'new information technology helped to create and lubricate this market, and handle the individual customer relationships'. Because of digital business, he says, 'the electricity market works much more like a financial market'.

The task for managers in established companies is to see how the technological changes interact with other forces in their industry. In the entertainment business, for example, technological changes are reinforced by globalisation, a lifting of restrictions on broadcasting, and rapid concentration of large media groups.

The consequence, says Lawrence Wilkinson, one of the founders of Global Business Network, which links corporate strategists, is a change in outlook. 'People who have understood their businesses in format terms – 'I'm in the movie business', for example – increasingly have to look at themselves as performing a range of functions and choosing one in which they can be most competitive.' In the long run, he believes, they will have to focus on such functions as content creation, packaging, or distribution.

If traditional value chains are being splintered, will much of the competitive advantage migrate to companies that have particularly strong customer relationships? For example, will trusted retailers, such as Tesco, Migros, Carrefour or Wal-Mart, be able to move their brands into other industries such as energy supply or financial services, as some are already attempting to do?

Digital business removes much of the traditional competitive advantage of existing competitors in these fields. The retailers can buy the services they need, and rely on their customer relationships and brand names to create unassailable competitive advantages. In the most extreme version of this scenario, traditional suppliers will remain, but largely as profitless sub-contractors. The value added will migrate to the businesses that control the customer relationships.

This view risks over-stating the extent to which businesses genuinely have relationships with their customers. In many cases in which companies think they have relationships customers see only a stream of tiresome transactions. Even in the business that has tried hardest to create true customer relationships – retail financial services – many banks are growing disenchanted with their huge investments in customer databases. They are not providing the returns the banks had hoped for.

The unanswered question is how customers will balance the convenience of dealing with a single trusted intermediary in a range of purchases – from food to energy and financial services – against the dislike of giving any supplier too much information and power. John Hagel, of McKinsey's Silicon Valley practice, believes that companies can overcome this mistrust only by positioning themselves explicitly on the customers' side. He envisages the creation of 'infomediaries', businesses that make money by 'capturing customer information and developing detailed profiles of individual customers for use by selected third-party vendors'.

Whatever the plausibility of this forecast, it highlights the way traditional value chains are being transformed. Settled ways of doing business are unlikely to survive the era of digital business without challenge.

Source: Financial Times, 5 February 1998

1.1 In what ways might the Internet be described as heralding a new age of marketing?

1.2 Describe how financial institutions, which have heretofore depended on their 'appearance' (buildings and staff) for the dependable image of their services (the tangible aspects of an intangible process), can maintain their relationship with their customer in the face of the growth of Internet availability.

1.3 How would a company set about evaluating whether they have a successful relationship with their customers?

Article 1.B   **FT**

Diageo invites bidders for four drink brands

By John Willman

Diageo is putting four leading European drink brands up for sale as part of the continuing rationalisation of its spirits portfolio to focus on core global brands such as Smirnoff vodka and Johnnie Walker Scotch whisky.

The food and drinks group has asked Warburg Dillon Reed, the investment bank, to contact potential buyers to find out what price they might offer for the four, which include Cinzano, the number two vermouth globally.

The other three are brandies, which are the market leaders in their countries of origin but have made only limited impact elsewhere: Metaxa of Greece, Asbach of Germany and Vecchia Romagna of Italy.

Analysts believe the four drinks, which together sell more than 6m nine-litre cases a year, could fetch more than £300m. This would come on top of more than £200m raised by Diageo in two North American sales of Canadian whiskies, bourbons and other US spirits.

Diageo has recently put Cruzcampo, Spain's largest brewer, on the market and is expected to bank more than £350m from the sale. This would bring to almost £2bn the proceeds of disposals in the past year, which began with the sale of Dewar's Scotch and Bombay gin to Bacardi for £1.15bn in March 1998.

Diageo also announced yesterday it has sold four ouzo brands to Campari, the Italian company, for an undisclosed sum.

The four drinks put up for sale were acquired in the late 1980s or early 1990s by Guinness and Grand Metropolitan, the two companies that merged in 1997 to form Diageo. They bought them to boost their distribution networks in particular countries – and have been so successful that the national drinks have lost market share as consumers switch to their global brands.

Potential buyers are likely to be middle-tier drinks groups that need better distribution in selected European markets.

Source: Financial Times, 28 April 1999

1.4 Why would Diageo consider selling these successful brands, possibly to their competitors, and why would other companies consider buying them?

1.5 Marketing has created the idea of brand equity. Is the brand now more important than its parent company? Justify your response.

1.6 Customer needs are satisfied by the brand on the package. Provide your reasoned view of this.

1.7 Which elements of the marketing mix are mentioned in the article, and which are implicit and why?

Article 1.C FT

Sound way to survive among the big boys

Inventors of the first stereo headphones have remained in business by evolving as technology advances, writes Nikki Tait

Can innovators survive as niche players when their industries are dominated by multinationals? Ask John Koss, co-inventor of the first stereo headphones.

Forty years ago this month, two hopeful US entrepreneurs walked into Milwaukee's Hotel Wisconsin where a high-fidelity show was taking place. Mr Koss, now in his late 60s but still chairman of the quoted company that bears his name, and Martin Lange, his partner, were trying to enter the rapidly evolving music equipment industry.

'So we thought, well, let's build a portable phonograph,' recalls Mr Koss, who was playing trumpet with a jazz band at the time. 'And then to be different, we thought we'd use a set of nice stereophones, so people could have private listening.'

Turning this idea into reality was not easy. 'What happened was that there were no music phones available. Everything was communications equipment left over from the second world war, headphones for switchboard operators and language equipment.

'It didn't have the balance you needed for listening to music. There was really no excitement – like listening to music on the telephone.'

Undeterred, Mr Koss got his partner to install miniature hi-fi speakers in the type of headphones used by pilots. 'The fact is, we were using a much bigger surface than these (current) little things.

'But that gave the base, the balance and the excitement, even with those first ones. And it turned out that everyone at the show was nuts about the sound – except they didn't like the phonograph.'

So just as the Koss stereo headphone was born, the Koss phonograph bit the dust. Today, its inventor looks stoic. 'We were about 10 years ahead of our time,' he says, philosophically. 'Portable phonographs, boom-boxes and so on came on about the 1970s.'

But if timing on the portable phonograph was lousy, the stereo headphones were delivered into a highly receptive market. As Mr Koss points out, music was changing rapidly in the 1960s and volumes were getting louder.

College students in particular lapped up the new novelty: 'The kids at school, the only thing they wanted was a little school work and a lot of music.

'They had it in their dorms and they couldn't play it loud because they would rock the walls. So 'phones were the only way that they could hear it. Our timing was right.'

But Mr Koss's fortunes changed when large competitors, notably Sony, muscled in on its act. The company, formed with family money to manufacture the headphones had little patent protection.

It attempted to diversify, first into products like manual turntables and later into computer speakers.

Some hairy financial periods ensued and in 1984 Koss was forced into bankruptcy, re-emerging a year later.

But today, most of these peripheral activities have been pruned away, and Mr Koss's sons now run the business from the same modest Milwaukee headquarters that have housed the group for the majority of its corporate life.

And, in spite of the upheavals, Koss still leads the $120m-a-year high-fidelity stereo headphone market in the US. Michael Koss, chief executive, claims that the company's tailored focus and the fact that it manufactures locally allows it to be responsive to retailers' demands.

That, in turn, helps to combat some of the competition's size advantage. Sales last year were $40m, of which 87 per cent came from stereo headphones.

The younger Mr Koss also sees some opportunity for expanding sales overseas, especially in Europe, where the lack of uniform distribution and specifications has made the market tough to crack for a relatively small company.

'Even something as simple as the euro may help,' he says. 'As the EU becomes one market, you're going to see more cross-border retailing and that's going to improve our position.'

The Koss name, meanwhile, has been licensed to a couple of electronics companies, based in Hong Kong and Canada, who use it on a range of audio equipment, from speakers to car stereos.

This has boosted profits by more than $1m annually. The Koss share price has yo-yoed in recent years, but stands at double its mid-1990s level. The Kosses stress they have no plans to sell out.

But one important reason for Koss's survival may be because the technology has advanced significantly over the past 40 years.

'The first breakthrough was that we could get that big bass sound and the music sound. It's hard to remember if you weren't there, but when we brought the 'phones to the first show, nobody had heard stereo, and it's very exciting when you hear it for the first time,' says John Koss.

'But then as the technology grew, and we shot people up to the moon, the aim was to make the cone softer and make it do more, so that we could expand it.

'The metals and the magnets changed. It made a big difference to the way we could alter the sound.' By the late-1960s, the industry moved to electrostatic stereophones.

'The normal system is a cone, and a magnet that pushes the cone so that it vibrates. With electrostatic, there's nothing pushing, nothing to warp. It was a great innovation.'

And then, in the mid-1980s, there were the cordless phones, and a design that put two speakers in each earpiece. The dawn of the digital era, meanwhile, further improved the sound quality that stereo headphones could deliver.

'The better they got in cleaning up their act, taking the distortion out of the amplification, the better we were.'

Today, Koss's latest focus is on noise suppression. Mr Koss cites an all-too-familiar experience: 'Have you ever been on a plane, trying to listen to a movie which they've played once too often, where the head end of the music sound is about 25 years old?

'And then, to make matters worse, they've got a cheap pair of very inefficient headphones that you have to crank up to override the sound, so that you put all the distortion into them? Then you're supposed to hear what they're saying – it doesn't work.

'By using a noise suppression phone, you eliminate all this and you've got a very efficient result.' (The company's Quiet Zone system, which sells for just under $200, works by allowing the listeners to plug earphones into a small box. This, in turn, contains a microprocessor that registers the unwanted noise and sends out 'anti-noise' waves that are 180 degrees out of phase and counteract the offending buzz).

The same approach, Mr Koss adds, can help people who are slightly hard of hearing, and have problems with all the peripheral noise at parties or in a restaurant, although he admits that in this case the technology can become 'a little expensive'.

But he says: 'It's a personal interest. I came at this business from the music standpoint. Now we're trying to look at it from another point of view.

'It's fun to combine things we know about at one end of the spectrum with [things at] the other.'

Source: Financial Times, 24 November 1998

1.8 Use basic marketing techniques of analysis to explain how Koss nearly failed, and how they have now achieved success.

1.9 In order to maintain their position prepare an outline environmental scanning programme.

1.10 How would Koss be confident in their analysis, and what techniques should they employ to maximise the reliability of their analysis?

2 The European Marketing Environment

Imagine waking from your slumbers, the curtains are drawn, your clock has stopped, there are no clues as to time, temperature outside, whether the post has come or the cat came in last night – indeed a multitude of questions to which you have no immediate answers. The only way to orientate yourself is to go downstairs, draw the curtains, perhaps open the front door and have a good look around to see what the score is. Maybe then you start to read the newspaper to find out what is going on at home and abroad in an attempt to find out what may or may not be good or bad for your own personal circumstances, not forgetting to check the cat's food bowl.

An organisation is faced with the same dilemmas and questions but on a much larger scale, and with the big drawback that it only has the eyes and the ears which we choose to give it. This chapter deals with how we obtain the information the organisation needs in order to achieve its goals and strategy. Naturally, we do not call this exercise 'going and having a look', we call it environmental scanning.

Essentially the process is to construct a framework to look at the macroenvironment, usually outside our direct control and to assess how this might affect what we do, how we might do it and what action we have to take in the future.

The most commonly used tool is STEP analysis, an acronym standing for the four major external environmental influences which have to be considered in any planning activity; these are sociological, technological, economical and political changes. Because we exist in the modern world which exhibits an ever-increasing rate of change we must take account of these influences, evaluate them for how they may affect what we do and particularly how we can mitigate their detrimental effects, at worst, and, at best, to turn them to our advantage.

Without a detailed knowledge and understanding of the external environment the organisation cannot make decisions with any degree of certainty about their success. Imperial Typewriters of Leicester, England, were bigger than the Italian firm Olivetti in the 1950s, and always believed that they were so far ahead in skill and world-wide fame that silly things such as electric typewriters were an unnecessary waste of time. Olivetti very soon identified that word processing was going to sweep the market and moved to being leaders in electronic information capture. Imperial? Long gone, their factories divided into little units for small businesses and their name only remembered when someone turns up an old manual typewriter and becomes nostalgic for the good old days of typing pools and carbon paper.

Perhaps the most complex and demanding environment we are given to scan at this particular time is that of Europe. Since although the UK is part of Europe in many ways it is fatal to assume that what is acceptable or understandable in the UK will automatically be accepted and understood across the Channel (the English Channel, of course!). On top of this is also laid the overarching bureaucracy and regulatory mechanisms emanating from the European Commission itself. What is legal today may not be legal tomorrow. While there is a degree of tabloid-driven scaremongering about straight cucumbers and British bangers (sausages) being banned, the fact is that the rules are generally being made to establish a level playing field in terms of competition, minimum specified standards of quality and safety, fairness and truthfulness. We must know these rules, understand them, anticipate them and work within them. In modern Europe, purely nationalistic attitudes no longer work, as evidenced by a quote from an Italian cotton spinner, 'We don't think of business with England or France as being export trade, but just as normal hometrade'. Ignore a close understanding of Europe at your peril – it is not just our back garden, it is the front garden and the house we live in as well.

In a world-wide perspective these strictures are also true to the extent that an understanding of some 450 million highly developed critical consumers becomes an essential part of any organisation's business thinking.

In order to successfully complete the tasks in this chapter you will need to be familiar with:

- STEP analysis;
- environmental scanning/micro and macro;
- the European regulatory environment;
- the Pan European market.

FT

Europe digs up safety case over Asian excavator imports

Not all construction equipment from outside the EU passes its stringent standards.
Peter Marsh reports

Earlier this month, officials from the Brussels-based Committee for European Construction Equipment (CECE), a trade body for European-based manufacturers, visited a building site in northern England after a tip-off about a 'rogue' excavator.

With the consent of the machine's owner, who had imported it from South Korea, via a trader in the Netherlands, the officials inspected the digger and found it contravened several aspects of European Union health and safety legislation.

The visit was sparked by concern by the European-based construction machine manufacturers that up to 5,000 machines (mainly excavators, but including other products such as dump trucks, cranes and compressors) may have found their way into Europe over the past year from factories in Asia.

It is alleged that this equipment, valued at up to DM1bn ($607m), has been manufactured for use in Asian countries which lack Europe's strict safety rules for plant and machinery.

The machinery has been diverted to Europe because of lack of demand in domestic markets resulting from the Asian economic crisis.

Britain, Germany, the Netherlands and France are the main countries where the machines end up.

The claims have prompted European Commission officials to launch a preliminary investigation. The CECE is preparing a formal complaint to the Commission to enable it to take legal action against traders contravening the legislation.

The machine in the north of England was found by CECE officials to lack safety restraints and its hydraulic lifting mechanism was possibly dangerous. The owner was advised to withdraw it from use.

'The importing of these machines is increasing and we are seriously worried about the problem,' says Guy Raymackers, technical secretary of the committee.

During 1998, a total of about 95,000 new excavators and other construction machines were sold throughout western Europe, an estimated 10 per cent higher than last year. Most of these sales have been through dealers authorised by manufacturers.

The unauthorised machines, many of which lack the necessary 'CE' safety mark required for equipment used in the European Union, are sold at a 30–50 per cent discount.

This is done through what amounts to a 'grey market' involving unofficial traders.

The rapid growth of the grey market in the past year – in step with the acceleration of the Asian crisis, which has led to a big cut in building and infrastructure development in the region – has undermined pricing in the construction equipment business.

At the centre of the controversy are a variety of traders across Europe who import machines from Asia which do not carry CE marks. Attention has focused particularly on large auction groups, including Ritchie Brothers and Forke Europe, two North American-owned organisations which operate in the Netherlands.

These auctions act as the conduit into Europe for new and second-hand construction machinery, some of it manufactured in Asian factories.

At Ritchie's most recent auction a few weeks ago, some $60m of equipment was sold, including machines made by Korean companies such as Hyundai and Samsung.

Both auction groups warn buyers if the equipment being sold is not CE approved, saying it is up to the buyer to make sure the machines have the correct specifications for legal use in individual countries.

They say they cannot be held responsible for the equipment after it leaves their yards. 'We know who is buying our equipment, but not where it goes,' says Scott Forke, a manager at Forke Europe.

A second group of organisations in the import chain frequently gets involved after a plant operator has purchased his machine. These organisations belong to a network of unofficial 'CE approval' companies which have sprung up around Europe. They offer a service to machine operators bringing machines which do not have the required CE mark up to the required safety standards.

They might charge a customer some £2,000 ($1,200) for this service, adding features such as hand rails or seating restraints.

However, Malcolm Kent, chairman of the CECE's technical committee, and who works for the European division of Komatsu, the large Japanese excavator manufacturer, says that in many cases these agencies cannot do the work they claim is possible due to the depth and breadth of the CE legislation.

In some cases, it is alleged, a 'technical approval' company will offer to forge the necessary safety documentation required for a specific machine.

One problem for the CECE is gathering the evidence it needs to make a watertight complaint to the European Commission.

In the UK, the Health and Safety Executive (HSE), the government agency charged with workplace safety issues, has examined several machines after complaints from European-based manufacturers, but says it has found no evidence of equipment endangering operators or passers-by.

The CECE, on the other hand, says bodies such as the HSE lack the necessary expertise to make the proper checks.

While some observers argue the machinery manufacturers are concerned mainly about an influx of cheap equipment which is cutting into their margins, and that the safety issue is a red herring, the equipment producers insist they have a genuine case.

'We spend millions of pounds ensuring our products meet the safety standards,' says an official at JCB, the large British construction equipment maker.

'Other groups should not be allowed to sell machines which break the law.'

Source: Financial Times, 14 December 1998

2.1 Produce a STEP analysis for a manufacturer of such equipment, based in Asia.

2.2 What is your view of the issues discussed and what opportunities have emerged?

2.3 The purpose of environmental scanning is to identify change and plan accordingly. What steps might a European manufacturer take to deal with the Asian difficulties?

2.4 Identify the principal problems and suggest ways of countering their effects.

Article 2.B   FT

Exporters apoplectic at being placed in bananas firing line

Why us, ask European companies facing heavy losses and plant closures if the US goes ahead with penal tariffs on their exports in its trade war over bananas

Reporting by Kevin Brown, Paul Betts, James Buxton, Sathnan Sanghera and Christophe Jakubyszyn

European companies facing the threat of US sanctions are furious about the Clinton Administration's targeting of exporters who have nothing to do with Washington's dispute with Brussels about the banana trade.

Across Europe, companies making the 17 categories of goods selected by the US for penal tariffs say they are facing financial problems, job losses and factory closures if the sanctions go ahead.

Many are bemused by the proposed US action, which is designed to force the European Union to modify its banana import regime to remove alleged discrimination against Latin American fruit distributed by American companies.

Ernesto Gismondi, chief executive of Artemide, one of Italy's leading light fitting manufacturers, described the threat of sanctions against his sector as 'a return to the Middle Ages'.

Mr Gismondi said he could 'understand and sympathise with the US when they decide to impose sanctions on the export of Italian coral in retaliation for overfishing on their fishing banks, but this business over bananas is totally incomprehensible. Where we come in into all this beats me.'

While the punitive levies were unlikely to affect the company's Italian and other European activities, they risked having dire consequences for its US operations. 'Artemide won't close in Italy but our US company could go bust. The sad thing is that the US market is growing and offers good prospects after all the effort we have put in during the years when the US market was not doing well.'

Italian companies and trade organisations held a video conference 10 days ago with Ralph Ives, deputy assistant US trade representative, to ask him specifically why Italy would be so badly hit.

'He told us there were no special reasons,' said a trade official. 'Italy does not have big interests in the banana trade and is a market quite open to South American products. But Mr Ives said the US had chosen products that would not damage the US economy.'

Paper D'Art, a London manufacturer of printed cards, is one of many companies that have been shipping extra stock to the US in recent weeks to try to beat the proposed sanctions.

'Our exports to America don't provide a critical amount of income, but with a doubling of the duties our American distributor might well go out of business. We could lose him overnight,' said Mark Everdell, joint owner.

Paper D'Art and Paper Rose, a Nottingham-based printed card exporter, both said they were considering licensing production in the US instead of exporting. 'I would buy their bananas myself if they'd leave my company alone,' said Mr Everdell.

Thousands of jobs are at risk in Belgium, where the US action would hit the biscuit industry. 'The peak season of Christmas is behind, but the US challenge is a threat for the future,' said Bernard

Kreilmann, general manager of Delacre Belgium, which exports 20 per cent of its production to the US.

Some of the deepest anger is emerging among Italian and Scottish producers of cashmere sweaters. George Peden, managing director of Ballantyne Cashmere, Scotland's biggest cashmere producer and part of Dawson International, said the sharp rise in import duty was a serious threat to the company's shops in New York and Chicago, which trade as Cashmere Cashmere. Although he had rescheduled orders for the spring collection, the shops, which obtain 75 per cent of their stock from Dawson companies in Scotland, 'could be left with empty shelves' for the autumn collection.

The issue is of crucial importance just now, he said, because companies were taking orders for the autumn season and US customers needed to know where they stood. 'It's iniquitous that we could be made to suffer over a completely unrelated issue,' said James Thomson, who runs the Hawick Cashmere company, based in Hawick.

Italian trade officials said the cashmere sweater producers were already adapting to declining demand in Asia, Russia and South America, while the problem was compounded for Italy by strained relations with Turkey, another important market, over an unrelated political dispute.

The sanctions will also hit European subsidiaries of Asian investors. Malcolm Howes, sales director of Yuasa Battery UK, a subsidiary of the Japanese Yuasa Corporation, said the sanctions could cost his company millions of pounds.

'We have been having meetings for three days running to try to find a possible solution,' he said. Three years ago the UK company, which has a turnover of £60m, had no trade with the USA at all. But exports have grown rapidly and this year they have US orders for more than 1m batteries. These count for about 10 per cent of their sales.

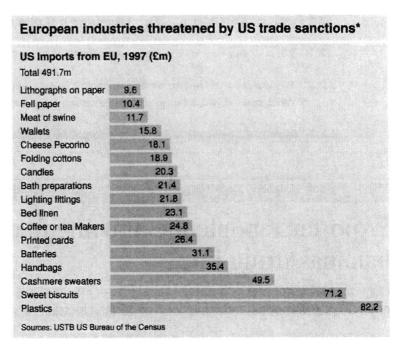

European industries threatened by US trade sanctions*

US Imports from EU, 1997 (£m)
Total 491.7m

Lithographs on paper	9.6
Felt paper	10.4
Meat of swine	11.7
Wallets	15.8
Cheese Pecorino	18.1
Folding cottons	18.9
Candles	20.3
Bath preparations	21.4
Lighting fittings	21.8
Bed linen	23.1
Coffee or tea Makers	24.8
Printed cards	26.4
Batteries	31.1
Handbags	35.4
Cashmere sweaters	49.5
Sweet biscuits	71.2
Plastics	82.2

Sources: USTB US Bureau of the Census

'If these sanctions go through then the work we have put into creating these exports will be completely wrecked,' said Mr Howes. 'The sanctions put our UK operations under pressure,' he said.

LVMH, the French parent of the Louis Vuitton luxury goods manufacturer, refused to say how it planned to deal with the sanctions, which could hit its €1.6bn sales in the US. However, the company is thought to be considering increasing shipments to the US before any sanctions come into effect, or switching some production to its small factory in the US.

Vince Bowen, managing director of Crabtree & Evelyn, a UK-based manufacturer and distributor of toiletries and food, said he was unsure which of the company's products would be hit by sanctions, despite being in the US all last week.

'If we can't export to America then within our group we will have to perform some balancing acts. If necessary, we will have to move our manufacturing from Wales to our site in America,' he said. 'It's all a bit silly.'

Source: Financial Times, 29 January 1999

2.5 Should Europe apply punitive tariffs against US imports? What is the likely outcome? (Use some desktop analysis of the trading figures to establish the potential.)

2.6 You are the commercial director of Fyffe's Bananas, a major growing transporter and distributor of bananas under their brand name. How would you use STEP analysis to establish the current and short-term future positions and how might the effects of a trade war be exposed and mitigated?

2.7 Why do you think that the US authorities chose the product categories they have and what other categories may become involved should the dispute continue?

Article 2.C   **FT**

Renault expected to drive hard bargain for Romanian car group

The French vehicle maker is the obvious candidate to buy 51% of Dacia, whose range is largely limited to a model based on the former Renault 12, writes Haig Simonian

Renault could mark a further step in its international expansion when final bids close today for the purchase of 51 per cent of Dacia, the Romanian carmaker, in eastern Europe's last big motor industry privatisation.

No details of the offer by the French group, which helped to launch Dacia in 1968, have emerged. However, Renault, which wants to use Dacia to develop a second, budget brand, is believed to have proposed an attractive mixture of cash and technical know-how to develop the group.

State-controlled Dacia is one of the biggest manufactures of vehicles in the former Communist bloc outside Russia. Output this year should rise by about 6 per cent to a record 106,000 units, says Constantin Stroe, general manager. The company has managed to remain profitable, in spite of collapsing exports and weak domestic demand, he says.

Mr Stroe, who has been with the company from its beginning, says Dacia should make about $5m–$6m this year, compared with $7m in 1997. That is a considerable achievement for an overmanned and inefficient car-maker whose range is largely limited to a 20-year-old model sold at rock-bottom prices in a country facing economic difficulties.

Dacia's most popular car is its 1310 – the former Renault 12. About 95 per cent of this year's output will be sold in Romania, where the cars retail for the equivalent of about $3,300. Such low prices have helped to maintain sales, in spite of the beleaguered economy, but the ageing product range and lower exports have convinced the company that its future depends on working with another car-maker.

'We are profitable, but the margin is very small,' says Mr Stroe. 'We have sacrificed margins to protect our market share. It's a difficult policy to follow – like tightrope-walking.'

Dacia had nearly 87 per cent of the domestic market last year. Although sales have fallen since because of rising competition and, until recently, plentiful cheap used-car imports, it still retains more than 75 per cent. Its dilemma is that its profits are insufficient to develop new models or replace decrepit machinery.

'Based on the way Dacia has kept going for the past nine years, we reckon we can only survive another four. We simply aren't making enough money to invest in a real new product,' says Mr Stroe. But while the company recognises it needs a partner to survive, potential acquirers have had mixed feelings. Mr Stroe says various leading car-makers have examined the group and requested the government's privatisation documents.

Most, however, have been put off by the likely cost and difficulty of revitalising Dacia – in spite of its resilience so far. 'We need to collaborate with a prestigious partner. But while that's easy to say, we know it's hard to do,' says Mr Stroe.

The main disincentive is Dacia's workforce. It had 28,000 workers last year – about three times the number Renault itself needed to build almost as many cars at its big Turkish subsidiary.

Finding alternative uses for surplus workers – and agreeing with the authorities on how to finance the restructuring – has been one of the biggest disincentives for potential buyers.

Mr Stroe says Dacia's managers and unions accept that jobs will have to go. He argues that it has already become more efficient: in 1989 Dacia had 7 per cent more workers, but built 21,000 fewer cars. In the past nine years, output has climbed from 288 cars a day on a six-day week to 453 a day on a five-day week.

'I realise we can't retain 28,000 jobs. But we have a reasonable trade union which appreciates the situation,' says Mr Stroe.

Hiring has been frozen and Mr Stroe sees scope for cuts through attrition. There may also be potential to expand the car parts industry around Dacia's base at Pitesti, 110km north of Bucharest. 'I'm sure the social problems won't block a solution,' he says.

That could make the company quite attractive to the right buyer. Most observers see Renault as the obvious candidate because of its links with Dacia and its interest in developing a lower-priced brand.

Dacia would provide a substantial production base, with trained workers and a big domestic market.

Moreover, monthly wage rates of about $160 before tax in the motor industry mean Romania even undercuts Poland, the Czech Republic and central and eastern Europe's other car-making countries when it comes to labour costs. And after 30 years in business, Dacia has a big customer base, creating strong demand for spare parts and, possibly, goodwill for new products.

Renault is playing its cards close to its chest. Executives in Paris admit their interest, but stress the time and money required to restructure Dacia.

While the company could soldier on with its existing cars for a while, the real challenge will be to develop a new car still cheap enough for buyers in the region. So while the French seem the obvious owners, there will be some hard bargaining before any deal is done.

Source: Financial Times, 7 December 1998

Article 2.D

Cashing in on an expanding market

As a vending machine giant, Azkoyen is poised to profit substantially from the advent of the new European currency

David White

The machines millions of Spaniards use every day when they buy cigarettes in a café or coffee in the office are more likely than not to come from Peralta, in the rural depths of the Navarre region.

Before the Azkoyen group started in a small way in the 1940s there was no manufacturing tradition in this area. But in the fields outside Peralta, just north of the River Ebro, a cluster of industries has since grown up, in many cases connected to the original venture.

Along with components suppliers, there is a direct rival in the same line of business, Jofemar, a specialist in tobacco and drinks machines set up by former Azkoyen employees and now its chief domestic competitor.

For three decades, Azkoyen was a small family-owned workshop. But it has since developed into a leading international manufacturer of vending machines and electronic change mechanisms, with a large portion of its shares now held by foreign institutions and a name that since the early 1990s has

become increasingly familiar in other parts of Europe outside Spain.

The company, with 800 employees and sales last year of Pta16.4bn ($115m), recently made it into Forbes magazine's list of the 100 fastest growing small companies outside the US.

One of the three other Spanish companies on the list – Viscofan, a sausage-skin maker and food group – also hails from Navarre.

Maintaining a majority share of its core market in Spain, Azkoyen is also a dominant force in Portugal and now claims to be the top supplier of cigarette dispensers in the UK. With marketing offshoots also in France and Germany, the share of sales going abroad has doubled since 1992 to over 30 per cent. Ricardo Armendariz, an Azkoyen director, says exports should make up between 40 and 50 per cent of the total within the next two or three years.

Few industrial sectors stand to be quite so directly affected by the introduction of the European single currency. Until now, different requirements for coin selection mechanisms have kept the European market fragmented along national lines, says Mr Armendáriz. The changeover to euro coins, due to take place in Spain and most of its European Union partners just over three years from now, promises to transform the industry.

Azkoyen is now poised to take a significant share of the business generated by the transition – substituting, adapting or reprogramming machines to take euros. Reckoning that there are between 9m and 10m automatic coin-operated machines in Europe, it has been building up capacity to meet the extra demand. From next year, it plans to be supplying equipment capable of operating and giving change in either existing currencies or euros, and of blocking the former when the old coins are phased out.

It was not always quite so hi-tech. Prior to starting the company, its founder, Luis Troyas, spent some time in Germany and came back to Peralta full of ideas about what could be done by machines. He called his venture Azkoyen after the name given to Peralta in the Basque language, also used by the local football team.

Early projects included potato and asparagus peelers, and an automatic cot for lulling babies to sleep. Vending machines only came later. The pace of change accelerated in the mid-1970s, when the company also began making coin selectors for games machines.

A 70 per cent stake was sold to a group of investors and the regional development agency. The company branched out into machines for hot drinks. The 1980s brought cold drinks, electronic technology, a deal to make mechanisms for pay-phones, a stock market listing, and diversification into catering equipment. Products ranging from ice-cube makers to coffee percolators are now made at a separate site outside Pamplona. By the same logic of market-driven expansion, Azkoyen now also does its own line in coffee beans.

Sales growth has been running at over 20 per cent so far this year and the total will have doubled over the last five years. Net profits have been rising recently at a more modest rate of about 9 per cent, reflecting the investment effort. The company has so far stuck to a policy of financing itself from its own resources rather than resorting to bank loans.

Source: Financial Times, 7 December 1998

2.8 Using STEP, analyse the current position of Dacia and Azkoyen, and compare their circumstances in a European context.

2.9 What advantages would there be both for Dacia and for Renault in such a grouping?

2.10 Considering the European regulatory systems, what advantages may be brought to Romania by such a linkage, especially since they are not members of the EU?

3 Consumer Behaviour

Now we come to consideration of the comment in Chapter 1, 'Marketing is pure mind manipulation'. Given the complexity of the machine we call the human being and therefore the consumer, to have an understanding of how people react to situations, marketing stimuli and offerings is at the very core of any attempt to market goods and services in any meaningful way.

Every individual is different and sees the world in a way different from their neighbour. Furthermore, each individual will probably change a number of their feelings and perceptions throughout the day, let alone a week, month or year. We all know that to visit the supermarket when hungry is to end up buying more food than we initially intended. We also change shape throughout the day, our waistline measurement increasing as the day progresses, so that a standard size 12 figure may have become a 13 or 14 by mid-afternoon.

We also have certain capacities for habitual behaviour, which may be evidenced by always shopping in certain stores, or buying certain brands of goods. This, of course, is where marketing attempts to reinforce this habitual nature by supplying the right marketing mix and especially by providing the product in such a way as to reinforce satisfaction on each buying occasion.

Marketers have been fond in the past of generating stereotypes of the ideal customer, but their very success in this has created a consumer who, having been exposed to choice, now wants more of it, demanding more and greater variety. The understanding of how consumers think and especially how they react is essential, but on top of this is the necessity for an understanding of how consumer attitudes are influenced, what influences them and how to discern, evaluate and put into action the appropriate marketing response.

Perhaps the most noticeable shift to be seen through the 1990s has been the growth in green issues and the response by organisations to this powerful force of public opinion, a force well understood by the Green lobbyists who have used their understanding of how to market very effectively to educate, inform and to shift consumers' perceptions and behaviour in a dramatic way. A further shift to be seen is the perception that marketers have of women and of women's perceptions of themselves. To look back at advertisements from the 1950s, 1960s and 1970s is to do so with something akin to embarrassment. To look back at advertisements from the 1980s and early 1990s is to be rather unpleasantly reminded of an age of rapaciousness. Women's roles have changed dramatically, and the old acceptance of the woman's place in society has been turned on its head, as witness, for instance, that research has shown that in 1998 48% of purchasers of DIY products were women, not just selecting the wallpaper for their husbands to hang, but buying the tools and the materials to tile or put up shelves themselves.

The contention might very well be then that far from being a mind-manipulating exercise, marketing is itself being manipulated and changed by consumers as a result of its own effectiveness.

In order to successfully complete the tasks in this chapter you will need to be familiar with:

- **the consumer decision-making process;**
- **motivation;**
- **Maslow's hierarchy;**
- **psychological influences;**
- **environmental influences.**

Tasteful campaign to counter a stale image

Rebranding showed that the group's staid reputation concealed values out of step with its customers, writes Peggy Hollinger

It was almost inevitable that J. Sainsbury's new advertising campaign would receive a lot of attention, given the spectacular failure last year of the 'value to shout about' promotion starring a loud-mouthed John Cleese.

But the company's management was still surprised by some of the comments that came from within. One store manager, present for the unveiling of the new campaign at a staff convention in Brighton, objected to one advertisement showing a divorced father introducing his children to a new girlfriend.

Surely this was not the sort of customer the supermarket wanted to be associated with, the manager suggested – little realising as he did so that he may well have made the most disastrous move of his career. 'That kind of manager is exactly the sort of person Sainsbury's does not want,' says one company adviser.

Yet the episode illustrates how Sainsbury's problems are more deep rooted than simply having a board that has appeared reluctant to modernise.

To the public, and some staff, the company is perceived to share many of the characteristics of the now unpopular Tory party – authoritarian, conservative and wielding a moral superiority out of step with the times.

Kevin McCarten, Sainsbury's marketing director, believes all that will change when the new brand identity, launched last month, becomes established.

The slogan, Making Life Taste Better, is not simply a catchy phrase to plaster across every store poster, he says. It was designed to remind staff why they are stacking tins on the shelf, or picking boxes of cereal in the warehouse.

'We needed a unifying purpose in this business which pulls all the people together,' he says. 'It is a clarion call for our people and a signal to our customers that we are giving them what they want.'

The campaign certainly conveys a fresher image of the group than has been seen for some time. The traditional dingy orange for which the company is famous has been changed to a mouth-watering clementine hue and matched with a rich blue. The advertisements – effective, if a bit mawkish in their attempt to pull a few heart strings – remind viewers that food plays a far more significant role in their lives than the drudgery of a shopping trip would imply.

'If we are going to change the brand, then we have to change fundamentally what we value and the way we work together,' Mr McCarten says.

The process of trying to find new cultural and brand identities began two years ago when Sainsbury hired 20/20, the design consultants. The first step was to identify what the company stood for, and how this was relevant to the future for a group that was finding it hard to hold its own against fleeter competitors.

While doing his research, Mr McCarten came across a photograph of one of the earliest Sainsbury stores, taken in 1908. Several white-coated sales assistants stand outside the open-fronted shop, where hundreds of chickens, geese and other fowl are laid out, perfectly spaced and identically positioned.

'That picture says we cared more about our products and the way we presented them than anyone out there,' Mr McCarten says. 'But we never lost touch with the fact that we were feeding the masses.'

As time went on, however, that strict approach began to cause problems. 'We established ourselves as clinical, methodical, rigorous, professional and very, very precise,' Mr McCarten says.

Those qualities, appropriate at a time when no one else seemed to have them, became less relevant in the 1990s when they were more widespread and had been adapted by rivals.

'The emotional attributes of our brand became increasingly old-fashioned,' he says. Society had moved from 'Margaret Thatcher to Tony Blair – more open, more apt to admit mistakes'.

Mr McCarten believes that while the photograph illustrates some of Sainsbury's core strengths – such as that rigorous attention to detail – equally, it highlights fundamental problems facing the group and its staff today.

'Think about what that store manager was told when the chickens were not lined up,' he says. 'He was told he was wrong. Others might have been told they shouldn't care if their chickens were lined up, or about conformity, but what mattered was selling with personality.'

Years of conforming to strict standards obscured the goal of retailing at Sainsbury's, he adds – serving the customer.

'If you told people at Sainsbury to sell with personality, they would think it was a great idea, but would not do it because other things get in the way,' he says. 'The way people put things on the shelves is influenced by all these constraints which have developed over the years, and customers feel that when they walk through the door.'

To shed those constraints, the company has embarked on what it believes will be a far-reaching programme of cultural change.

For example, staff are no longer called staff. Instead, as at rival Asda and US trend-setter Wal-Mart, they are referred to as colleagues.

Sainsbury has also embarked on a wide-ranging training programme, which has involved the board participating in customer discussion panels for the first time. Videos and brochures attempt to impress on all 'colleagues' the idea that whatever their job, they contribute to 'making life taste better' for their customers.

A detailed map has also been drawn up by 20/20 to be used from head office to store, showing how the company can affect every stage of the shopping journey, beginning and ending in the customer's home.

Meanwhile, more than 1000 jobs are being lost to eliminate some of the bureaucracy that it believes has hampered performance in recent years.

Finally, it comes as some surprise to learn that Dino Adriano, chief executive of the group who for years was also head of the supermarkets division, has spent more time in stores talking to staff and customers in recent months than he has done in years.

Management experts applaud such actions but say they must prove to be more than mere gestures if cultural change is to take hold. Jon Katzenbach, director at McKinsey, the consultants, has argued that top management must demonstrate that not only is it prepared to get stuck in, but that it too is willing to take personal risks to make the changes successful.

'Top management cannot leave to chance the development of the attitudes, skills, tools and approaches needed to steer through change,' he says. Middle management 'needs to believe that their leaders will stick at it even when the going gets tough'.

Changing the attitudes of a middle management fearful of new methods will be crucial to the success of Sainsbury's new brand image, and of the business itself. 'Management cause the problems,' says Mr McCarten. 'The people on the floor do not cause systemic problems. Top management has had to get in tune with the challenging and different culture of the people in the store.'

The marketing campaign, which focuses on real people and their everyday experiences, says it all, he believes: 'Changing the brand doesn't mean changing the ads and the colours. It is how we behave internally, how we act with each other.

'If we can change the brand in all its manifestations – the way the stores look, how colleagues interact – we can recreate a new Sainsbury's. Making life taste better is just the creative pull together of all that.'

Source: Financial Times, 29 June 1999

3.1 What is rebranding and how does this relate to consumer behaviour? Illustrate by reference to the article.

3.2 What analytical tools may be utilised to track changes in consumer behaviour? Prepare such an analysis from the article, and show how Sainsbury's reached their conclusions.

3.3 The consumer is not just motivated by price. What other factors have to be taken into account?

3.4 What segmental changes are referred to, and how might Sainsbury's address these?

Article 3.B   FT

Consumer power forces the food industry to modify its approach

Manufacturers and retailers are following Iceland's lead in banning GM ingredients from its products, writes John Willman

When Malcolm Walker, chairman and chief executive of Iceland, announced 15 months ago he was banning genetically modified ingredients from the frozen food retailer's own-label products, the reaction from the rest of the food industry was largely disdainful.

The most common response in public was that it was impossible, given the difficulties of separating GM and non-GM crops. Competitors sneered that Iceland had taken the step as a marketing ploy.

'You cannot equate a niche frozen food retailer with a supermarket as the quantities required are so different,' said Safeway, the fourth largest supermarket chain.

Today, Iceland's stance has become the norm as manufacturers, retailers and fast-food chains have lined up to declare their products are GM-free, or fast-becoming so.

Mr Walker's success in buying non-GM products has demonstrated the feasibility of his approach.

But yesterday's admission by Northern Foods that it was phasing out the controversial ingredients means one of the biggest defenders of the biotech revolution has conceded the day.

'We support GM foods in terms of safety,' said Jo Stewart, chief executive. 'But we have to take our lead from our customers, and our customers want non-GM foods.'

Northern Foods is an important scalp for the environmental groups campaigning against genetically modified crops.

Lord Haskins, its chairman, is an adviser to the prime minister who has been one of the staunchest supporters of the biotech industry.

Although his brief in Whitehall is to control the dragon of red tape, Lord Haskins has been prominent in his support for GM crops – as last summer when he launched a report on sustainable agriculture and rural policy.

Genetically modified foods could provide important benefits, especially to 'poor and hungry' people in third world countries, he said. 'The rich parts of the world do not need GMOs [genetically modified organisms] but they have greater appeal to the poor people of Africa than the rich people of Hampstead.'

Lord Haskins went on to say it would be 'very foolish to deny science, but we have to manage the science'. The truth is British consumers appear to be losing faith in scientists to protect their interests.

An ICM poll in yesterday's Guardian showed 40 per cent of people had no trust in what scientists, said on the safety of genetically modified food. Of the rest, 16 per cent had a lot of trust and the rest a little. The same poll found 56 per cent thought GM foods were unsafe to eat, more than double the percentage thinking them safe.

The findings are hardly surprising after six months of news stories in which scientists have been portrayed as divided over the merits of biotechnology.

Meanwhile a stream of opinion-formers have lined up behind the demand for a moratorium – from the

Prince of Wales to famous restaurateurs and distinguished food writers.

Those businesses prepared to stand up for genetically modified ingredients have dwindled, with even staunch defenders such as Tesco, the largest supermarket chain, and Unilever, the Anglo-Dutch consumer group, following competitors by going GM-free.

A Friends of the Earth survey last month showed 24 of the 30 largest UK food manufacturers were GM-free, while most of the rest were about to follow.

'For us, GM has been a pain in the neck,' Lord Haskins said last week. 'It has just been an added cost.'

Source: Financial Times, 9 June 1999

3.5 Illustrate from your own reading and experience how consumer behaviour has become more significant to all organisations. Relate this especially to essential marketing principles.

3.6 Iceland led the way in the process illustrated by the article. What may have prompted them to their conclusion (other than intuition)?

3.7 What have been the significant omissions on the part of the producers of GM foods, and how might they now address these failings?

3.8 Why might it be said that consumerism owes its existence to effective marketing? Justify your answer.

Article 3.C   FT

When climate care exploits a feelgood factor

Vanessa Houlder finds that climate neutralisation techniques are being seen increasingly in some quarters as a marketing tool

To purists, a 'green' product based on fossil fuels is an oxymoron. Fossil fuels emit carbon dioxide, one of the main greenhouse gases implicated in global warming. Reducing consumption is the only solution, in the eyes of many environmentalists.

But marketeers may have found a way round this problem. Since trees absorb carbon dioxide, it may be possible to offset the carbon dioxide emitted when a product is made or used by planting or preserving forests. This promise of 'climate neutrality' may be a useful marketing tool for targeting environmentally conscious consumers.

Several 'carbon offset' or sequestration schemes are underway. For example, Mazda has promised its customers that it will pay for five trees to be planted for every Demio car sold, which is enough to absorb carbon dioxide from a typical year's driving.

Another scheme has been introduced by Amerada Hess, a gas supplier. It has introduced a gas tariff called the 'climate care saver', which carries a premium of 10 per cent over the company's other tariffs.

Amerada Hess will pass on this premium – together with a one-off payment of £10 for each customer – to the Carbon Storage Trust, an independent organisation set up to plant trees on deforested sites around the world and invest in energy efficiency and renewable projects. The money raised will initially go to a number of reforestation projects around the world.

The trust, which has been set up by an academic at Oxford University, is negotiating to get its Climate Care label – which informs consumers that its manufacture or use of the foods and services contributes nothing to global warming – on a range of products and services including carpets, holidays and even bags of cement.

CST is convinced that investing in forests – with the promise of additional benefits of conserving wildlife – has marketing appeal. Market research suggests that consumers care about tree planting far more than global warming or cutting emissions through energy efficiency and renewable projects, says Mike Mason, director of CST.

Amerada Hess hopes that its Climate Care Saver tariff will offer an incentive for people to switch gas suppliers, over and above the prospect of cost savings. 'A lot of people just cannot be bothered to switch their gas supplier. It is just not interesting enough,' says Caroline Harper, managing director. Focus groups responded positively to the idea of the Climate Care Saver tariff, she says.

But there are risks attached to this project. One is that it fails to capture the imagination of the public, which lost much of its interest in green products after a surge of enthusiasm in the late 1980s.

More seriously, companies that get on the environmental bandwagon risk being accused of hypocrisy, particularly if some of their activities are deemed to be damaging to the environment. And there is a risk that carbon sequestration schemes could become controversial if problems emerge with poorly thought-out projects.

The main challenges with these schemes are two-fold: ensuring that the trees would not have been planted anyway and that their planting does not have knock-on effects that would reduce or cancel out the original benefit. For example, if a scheme that preserved a particular tract of forest merely shifted logging activity to another area. Furthermore, little would be gained by planting a forest that was later chopped down, with the result that the carbon dioxide stored by the trees was released into the atmosphere.

CST argues that the only way to preserve the trees it plants in developing countries is to pay local people a maintenance fee, equivalent to what they could earn by putting the land to another use. As a result, its carbon offset scheme is expensive: it costs $30 (£17.80) for every tonne of carbon, which is up to 10 times as much as some other schemes.

Another criticism of carbon sequestration schemes is that they are not long-term solutions. Critics assert that absorbing the world's CO_2 emissions would mean covering an area the size of France with trees each year. But tree planting is only a start, says Mr Mason. The CST is also committed to energy efficiency and renewable energy schemes, which would play an increasing role as the scope for tree planting diminishes.

CST has won support from several environmental groups for its thoughtful approach. Its steering committee includes representatives from the World Wide Fund for Nature and Forum for the Future. That said, the scheme will not find favour with all environmentalists. Some worry that the idea of offsetting emissions will lead to complacency and delays in actions to reduce them.

But persuading people to make drastic changes to their lifestyles is unrealistic, says Mr Mason. Moreover, making people feel guilty is counter-productive. People will only reduce their impact on the environment if they are allowed to feel good about the choices they make.

If this logic proves persuasive, many more companies will try to make their impact on the climate into a marketing tool.

Source: Financial Times, 29 September 1998

3.9   There are many influencing factors on the stages undergone in reaching a purchase decision. Apply these to the case above. Which stages may need special consideration in the light of the article? How might such considerations be addressed?

3.10   Social class and occupation are used as a means of identifying customer types. How relevant is this today, and why do we still use such descriptors?

3.11   Which general segmental criteria would be used to take account of environmentalists? Justify your answer and relate this to Maslow's hierarchy.

3.12   Favourable consumer behaviour results from detailed consideration of internal and external environments. Describe these, and relate them to consumer behaviour.

4 Organisational Buying Behaviour

Organisations have to buy resources, as do individual or family consumers, to satisfy needs, wants and desires. They are therefore as valid an area of marketing effort as the consumer, with a number of crucial differences. A consumer will purchase a tin of beans, not too strenuous a task with not too many decisions to be made, and even if the product fails (too few beans, poor flavour, more expensive than at the next shop) the implications both for the purchaser and for the supplier are probably relatively insignificant. 'Rotten beans these, shan't buy them again!' However, for the Supermarket Beans Buyer, who is buying not one tin but tens of thousands of tins over a long time span or contract, the significance of taste, quality, presentation, handling efficiency and so on is crucial. Poor buying in an organisational sense results in poor performance for the organisation as a whole. Efficient, effective buying increases the chance of success most positively. Clearly, the more complex the manufacturing or reselling operation for which the buying is being conducted (consider computer manufacture, car building or a supermarket's 20 000+ separate lines of merchandise), the more complex and interdependent become the buying decisions and how they are reached.

Characteristically, organisational markets have a number of features in common. Typically, there are fewer buyers and sellers than in a consumer market, and the buying decision is made with much more formality and the involvement of more people or organisational functions. This may be a combination of technical specification, delivery requirements, price etc. together with the element of risk associated with commitment of a large part of a company's resources. Quality control, finance, production, distribution, marketing, research and development are all interested to a greater or lesser extent in the decision chain and will have their own requirements and perceptions as to how these may be achieved. In large organisations they input their own requirements and use the buying function to co-ordinate all facets and find the ideal solution. It may also be that the buyer will choose to have the purchase confirmed and supported by as many others as possible as a personal safeguard.

From the above we can see that a true marketing orientation is essential in dealing with an organisational buying/selling market. A close understanding is required of the individual buyers, their organisations and how they work, alongside a knowledge of where the internal influences and influencers lie, in order to satisfy the customers' needs and wants precisely and repeatedly. The risk on both sides of the transaction can be significant. The buyer can risk poor sales, interrupted production or product failure, and the seller can risk the loss of a major customer. Both are going to understand the situation and attempt to alleviate the likelihood. On the plus side, though, it is possible to devise marketing mixes in an organisational marketing setting that are intensively personalised, with very often long-lasting relationships developed between buyers and sellers, and a complete understanding of what each needs from the business.

In order to successfully complete the tasks in this chapter you will need to be familiar with:

- **relationship marketing;**
- **relationship life cycle;**
- **organisational buying decision models;**
- **single/multiple sourcing;**
- **buying criteria/buying centres;**
- **Michael Porter's Five Forces;**
- **product innovation.**

Article 4.A FT

Clients worldwide respond to speedy signs of success

North Yorkshire components manufacturer is confident of continued growth, even if a downturn occurs. Sheila Jones reports

When a team of Nissan UK managers visited a small components manufacturer in North Yorkshire, they decided on the spot to award the company a supply contract.

'They liked the culture and the way we do things,' says Barry Dodd, founder and managing director of GSM Graphics in Thirsk. The company makes metal and plastic labels, control panels and assembled units, mainly for the car and electronics industries. Customers include General Motors, Ford, Saab and Akai Electric of Japan.

The company has grown rapidly and Mr Dodd believes it will grow next year, even in a downturn. GSM is increasingly adding value to its products by building more assembled units, as well as individual components. 'Customers are keener than ever to buy assemblies because it can save on their costs. We are adding value to the product, adding to turnover and profits and getting closer to our final customer,' he says.

Mr Dodd acknowledges there are signs of a wider downturn, with customers de-stocking and buying smaller quantities. But the company is still winning orders and recruiting. 'It's not that clever, we've been through a recession before. It's about fast delivery and responses,' he says. 'There is nothing unique about our products. We have many competitors, but our response times are so much faster than the others.'

The company gives a quote 'within hours' of a customer inquiry anywhere in the world. A German customer will receive a quote in D-Marks so they can compare with local suppliers and once an order is placed, 'we will deliver faster than their local dealer'. Payments go into a D-Mark account, which next year converts to a euro account.

Stock turnover is also rapid. 'There's never more than one week's supply of raw materials at any one time. It's in here and straight out of the door. Our own suppliers have to deliver to us within 48 hours or we are not interested.'

Output and profit per employee is among the highest in the industry, says Mr Dodd. GSM's relationship with Nissan, forged five years ago, has helped the company build those qualities. GSM operates the Japanese system of *kaizen*, or continuous improvement: of staff, products and processes.

'Actually, we have operated a continuous improvement system for years but we did pinch some ideas from Nissan when it became a customer,' says Mr Dodd.

Danny Griffiths, trim and electrics purchasing manager at Nissan Motor UK, says its supplier development programme starts with a commitment from the top of the organisation.

'If we can switch on senior management and underpin it with a sensible improvement strategy, we find that the management ethos changes,' he says. 'We will give them some tools and techniques, but they have to provide the sustainability.' At GSM, a chart shows the company's daily performance in terms of output, orders, delivery times, quality control and staff development. The company spends about 1 per cent of turnover on training, which is tied-in to the business development plan.

Decision-making is delegated through 16 team leaders who do the recruiting, decide work flow and 'pull in the raw materials they need for their orders'.

Every day, at 7.50am, managers and team leaders meet for a 10-minute briefing. 'We have a strict agenda and it finishes at 8am. If anybody rambles on, people will walk out,' says Mr Dodd. 'Communication is brilliant. Everybody knows what is going on. It works. We have virtually zero staff turnover.'

The company was created 20 years ago and has grown rapidly in the past 10 years. It employs more than 200 people at three sites. Turnover has jumped from some £750,000 in 1993 to about £10m this year. GSM has no borrowings and a positive cash flow. Exports account for 15 per cent of turnover and are rising. Last month, the company won a £1m contract to supply vehicle labelling for the new Saab 9-5.

Mr Dodd believes the group is well positioned if market conditions grow difficult next year. 'The culture is right,' he says. 'We're all going in the same direction.'

Source: Financial Times, 4 December 1999

4.1 What particular aspect of marketing is illustrated here? Show what special characteristics go to contribute to this aspect.

4.2 Organisational buying differs from consumer purchase in what important ways?

4.3 Outline what risks such a small company might run in developing business links with such large partners. Do the benefits outweigh the risks and how might they be managed and controlled?

4.4 Explain Kaizen and outline its principal advantages.

FT

Car groups start to squeeze component makers

Sell-offs replace period of expansion, writes Haig Simonian

After years of growing painstakingly through acquisitions, first at home and then abroad, US conglomerates such as ITT Industries elevated themselves into the first rank of the world's car parts makers. But a string of disposals suggests some are now dismantling their carefully assembled operations.

In recent weeks, ITT Industries and Cooper Industries, which also makes electrical equipment and hardware, have raised $5.5bn dismembering their automotive empires.

ITT raised $1.7bn selling its vehicle electrics division to Valeo of France. A further $1.9bn came through the sale of its braking activities to Continental, the German tyres group. Houston-based Cooper raised $1.9bn selling two automotive subsidiaries to Federal-Mogul, the fast expanding parts specialist.

More disposals may be on the way. AlliedSignal's surprise $9.9bn hostile all cash bid for AMP, the world's largest supplier of electric and electronic connectors, has sparked talk it might have to divest some businesses to raise money. AlliedSignal is a leading producer of turbochargers, brake parts and filters.

Uncertainty even surrounds Tenneco, a once sprawling conglomerate now focused on packaging and car parts.

Tenneco Automotive, its parts division, was widely tipped to buy ITT's brakes businesses until an eleventh hour withdrawal. Instead, Tenneco's parent company said it was examining spinning off its two subsidiaries' divisions.

The ITT and Cooper disposals would have raised few eyebrows had they been small or marginal operations. But the businesses were leading names in areas where consolidation had, apparently, reached its peak.

ITT's brakes business, best known for its German-based Teves brand, ranks alongside Robert Bosch and LucasVarity in the world's top manufacturers. Among the brands sold by Cooper were household names such as Champion sparking plugs, a market leader.

Three broad reasons explain the readiness to sell:
● Conglomerates such as ITT and Cooper are becoming concerned about profit margins in the motor industry. Components companies commonly report earnings equivalent to about 6 per cent of sales. That is about twice that of vehicle makers, their main customers. The discrepancy has prompted many vehicle manufacturers to target suppliers for price cuts. Fearless cost cutters, such as Jac Nasser, head of Ford's worldwide automotive business, have axed expenses internally and demanded similar sacrifices from suppliers.
● Vehicle makers have been demanding greater financial commitments from suppliers. Car and truck manufacturers have tried to save money by devolving product development work onto their component companies. Instead of being handed detailed technical drawings and told to submit bids, suppliers are now involved more closely in vehicle development.

The appeal for them is in winning exclusive, long-term contracts. With vehicles being produced globally, that could mean massive volumes. But a successful supplier would also be expected to invest heavily in research and development and, if necessary, in new capacity to supply its customer's plants just-in-time around the world.

● Sale prices for big components operations are looking full in historical terms. In May, Dana, a leading body parts specialist, paid about 10 times earnings before tax, depreciation and amortisation for Echlin, a braking and aftermarket parts group. That was comfortably above the margin of eight to nine times earnings common in the industry.

'The vendors have looked at their other businesses and decided they can get better returns on their capital,' says Greg Melich, motor industry analyst at Morgan Stanley in London.

John Riley, Cooper chairman, justified its decision, saying: 'Given the growth potential we see in our electrical products and tools and hardware segments, we believe that our shareholders would be better served by our focusing on and growing these core businesses.'

But while some companies have taken their parts operations to bits, the amounts they have raised shows there is no lack of buyers for such one-off opportunities.

Valeo's purchase will increase its sales by about a third to FFr45bn ($7.6bn), based on its 1997 figures. The deal will enable the French group, previously the world's 14th biggest parts maker, to expand its business with US and German carmakers – ITT's main customers – and reinforce its strong position in parts, such as wiper systems and electric motors.

Continental's $1.9bn bid for ITT's braking division, meanwhile, showed tyre manufacturers could pump up their low-margin businesses by moving into ancillary products. The step formed part of the tyre-maker's long-term strategy to supply entire automotive 'corners', including tyres, brakes and ride components, as part of the broader trend in the motor industry towards providing modular assemblies.

After the acquisition, Continental's sales will be divided equally between tyres and other components: before, tyres accounted for about 70 per cent.

Federal-Mogul's move appeared equally astute. The group, which has been growing frenetically through acquisitions under Dick Snell, its chairman, will expand its limited presence in braking and lighting and develop its lucrative aftermarket side. Sales should climb from more than $5bn to Dollars 7bn – closer to Snell's $10bn goal by 2002.

'It's a win-win situation. The vendors are pleased to get out, and the buyers think they can do better out of the businesses by leveraging their costs over much bigger volumes,' says Mr Melich.

Source: Financial Times, 2 September 1998

4.5 What buying criteria does this article illustrate for the car-building components? What other criteria should be considered?

4.6 How might you position the component manufacturers on the relationship life cycle and how could other aspects of relationship marketing be utilised by both supplier and customer to achieve the objectives of both parties?

4.7 What do you think lies behind Federal-Mogul's acquisitions when others are divesting? Economy of scale is only one facet of this move.

4.8 Relationship marketing and Porter's Five Forces are closely associated strategically. How?

Article 4.C FT

Building equipment makers dig out a healthy export trade

Excavators may lack glamour but Europe's manufacturers are finding a lucrative market for them in the US. Peter Marsh reports

For makers of some of the world's biggest machines, producers of construction equipment generally lack the cachet of industries such as cars or computers. But in recent years western Europe's manufacturers of excavators, graders and other types of building machines have emerged as one of the region's most successful exporters.

Last year, according to estimates by Off-Highway Research, a London-based consultancy, construction equipment manufacturers based in western Europe exported to non-west European countries roughly a quarter of the 136,000 machines which they produced. With imports running at an estimated 10,000 units, that leaves a healthy trade surplus, worth some $4bn, with the rest of the world.

According to David Phillips, managing director of Off-Highway Research, the favourable export trend is likely to continue for the immediate future, driven mainly by strong demand in the US – the destination for roughly half of all west European exports of this equipment.

Further statistics from Ifo, a German research institute, show that companies based in the European Union account for nearly 40 per cent of world trade in construction machines and related equipment for mining and quarrying. This is a relatively high figure and one, which, against the trend for much of European industry, has edged up slightly during the 1990s.

Within western Europe, demand has also been substantial in the past year. According to Off-Highway Research, 118,000 construction machines were sold across the continent last year, compared with 105,000 in 1997. This year, sales are likely to stabilise at this level, according to industry projections. Exports from western Europe to south-east Asia have never comprised a big part of the western European industry's sales activities. As a result, business has been little affected by the region's financial crisis.

According to Off-Highway Research's figures, JCB, Britain's biggest construction equipment company, is western Europe's biggest net exporter of these machines in units, selling 10,870 outside the continent last year. In second position is Caterpillar of the US, the world's biggest maker of construction machines, which has several European factories.

John Patterson, JCB's chief executive, says his company is building its first non-UK factory in the US state of Georgia to take advantage of the booming market.

New Holland, in which Fiat of Italy owns a majority stake, is planning to step up US exports by increasing production from a German plant which it took over at the end of last year when purchasing Orenstein & Koppel, a leading German machinery maker. The company intends to increase annual production from the Berlin site from 2,000 machines to

3,000 in the next five years, with a large proportion destined for North America.

This plan involving O&K is likely to stand, in spite of the merger announced recently between New Holland and Case of the US, a rival construction equipment maker. The merger will create the world's third biggest producer of construction machines, and the second largest maker of farm tractors, after Deere of the US.

According to Off-High Research, Case is a net importer into Europe, selling 1,100 machines into the continent last year on top of those produced in its European plants. However, these figures do not include Fermec, a UK-based subsidiary of Case, whose net exports from Europe last year totalled 1,944.

Komatsu of Japan, the world's second biggest construction machine maker, considers the US an important export market for some of the machines made at its three European plants.

Putzmeister of Germany, a specialist construction machinery maker and the world's largest producer of concrete pumps, last year sold roughly a third of its DM800m (€409m, $421m) production in the US.

Source: Financial Times, 9 June 1999

Construction equipment

Net exports from western Europe 1998 (units' 000)

JCB (UK)	10.87
Caterpillar (US)	7.47
New Holland (Italy)	5.98
Fermec (UK)**	1.94
Komatsu (Japan)	1.74
Schaeff (Germany)	1.28
Liebherr (Switz)	1.24
Manitou (France)	0.84
Volvo (Switz)	0.77
O&K (Germany)***	0.24

Source: Off-Highway Research
* Exports minus sales in western Europe from plants outside the continent
** Owned by Case of the US *** Owned by New Holland

4.9 Illustrate the buying decision model with regard to the purchase of construction equipment.

4.10 What factors have European manufacturers taken into account in their approach to the US market?

4.11 How might JCB defend their position in the USA, and what might they do to expand their market position?

4. 12 Which elements of the marketing mix do they employ in this market and how?

5　Segmenting Markets

Market segmentation is at the very heart of all that marketing aspires to bring to the organisation when developing its strategy and aiming to succeed. The process can be applied equally to organisational markets or consumer markets, although the type and manner of its execution will vary.

Essentially we are trying to describe our ideal customer, the one who most nearly fits our capabilities, and then to discover as much as we can about this customer. Perhaps one day we may be able to target and design a marketing mix for every customer, but until then the process is to identify groups of people with the same or very similar needs and wants, desires and aspirations, around which we can design our product in all its dimensions. Accurate, clear and realistic segment description is the lodestone around which the alchemy of the marketing mix is performed. Fundamentals to be considered are the make-up of the population by age, sex, and financial capability, how it thinks about itself in the context of family, work, leisure, nationality and personal perception. This becomes especially important as the move towards increasing harmony within the European setting takes place. We are now in a marketplace with 400 million consumers, a relatively well-developed and financially and politically stable bloc, which yet throws down even more challenges to any organisation attempting to exist and compete within it. Surveys have shown that there are strong national feelings, which do not always react easily to pan-European products or offerings. French people think about the world in a different way from Germans or English or Spanish, each geographical area has different traditions in food, dress, domestic habits and income levels, all overlaid by differing aspirations, family structures and preferences.

This leads us to consider that there is a paradox, which we must be careful of acknowledging and allowing for. This is that we must conduct diligent segmentation and analysis and accurate targeting in order to achieve our aims and yet at the same time we must avoid overdoing it otherwise we run the risk of overfragmentation of a market, leading to loss of segment viability in terms of ability to serve and sufficient quantity to obtain economies of scale. As always, there are exceptions, most notably in the high-class, high-quality exclusive and very expensive luxury goods market – for instance, the antique watch company which sells wristwatches for up to £60 000 each, and has a world-wide connection of customers, almost all known by name and as friends of the owner. This is a segment as valid as that of the frozen fish finger, but highly specialised and not for the average or above-average local, national or international manufacturing company.

Segmentation, at best, is the equivalent of searching for and finding the Holy Grail and, at worst, is an accident waiting to happen, and it all depends on an honest, clear, and rigorously conducted analysis, carried through with conviction and belief. Nothing less will suffice.

In order to successfully complete the tasks in this chapter you will need to be familiar with:

- segmentation criteria;
- geodemographic segmentation;
- psychographic segmentation;
- marketing mix;
- brand loyalty;
- SWOT, STEP and portfolio analysis.

Article 5.A   FT

Bidders steer a course towards coveted lists of affluent motorists

The membership of the RAC and AA should be an entry to cross-selling, but achieving results may not be easy, says Charles Batchelor

The car is not the luxury it was when motoring organisations like the AA and the RAC were established around the turn of the century. But car owners still represent the more affluent section of society.

'Market research indicates that members of breakdown organisations tend to be in the higher socio-economic groups,' the Monopolies and Mergers Commission said in its report last February into the bid by Cendant, the US marketing group, for the RAC.

The access provided by the membership lists of these organisations to the relatively well-heeled forms a key attraction for many of the commercial bidders circling what up to now have been mutual organisations.

The RAC has been a potential target since last April when plans to split its motoring services from its two members' clubs were made known. It has been joined this week by the larger AA which is considering a move away from a membership structure.

In retrospect, it is surprising it has taken so long for the demutualisation wave that began to sweep through the building society movement in the late 1980s to reach the roadside emergency services.

Unlike building societies, which were spurred by competition from banks, motoring clubs faced little competition. Small rivals including Europ Assistance and Mondial were dwarfed by the established organisations.

But that is all changing. The AA's 9.2m members and the 5.5m at the RAC are an attractive market for companies selling motoring, holiday or insurance-related products, particularly if potential customers are approached through a brand they trust. That, at least, is the theory.

Cendant, whose £450m bid for the RAC was effectively barred by the competition authorities, had hopes of cross-marketing a range of services to RAC members.

Some, including its Avis car rental and PHH fleet management arms, were motoring-related while others such as its holiday timeshare businesses could also be expected to appeal to well-off members.

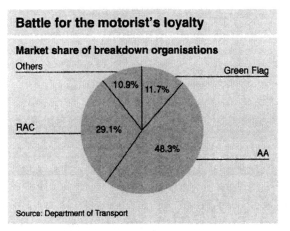

Battle for the motorist's loyalty

Market share of breakdown organisations

Others — 10.9%
Green Flag — 11.7%
RAC — 29.1%
AA — 48.3%

Source: Department of Transport

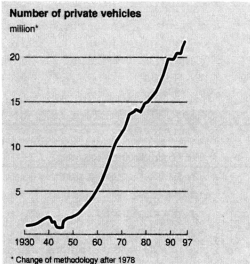

Number of private vehicles
million*

1930 40 50 60 70 80 90 97

* Change of methodology after 1978

Cendant has withdrawn but cross-marketing is clearly an attraction for bidders such as Centrica, the gas-distribution group, and Lex Service, the vehicle leasing and distribution company. Centrica is attempting to build a 'household services' business from scratch grouped round its Goldfish loyalty card and home insurance activities.

The membership lists of the RAC and the AA should provide a ready-made entry to the world of cross-selling. However, achieving results may not be easy.

'Developing cross-selling is one of the greatest challenges of modern marketing,' says Mark Pavan, head of PR3 Mapa, a marketing strategy consultancy. 'The profit opportunities often blind people to the practical difficulties.

'It revolves round IT issues and managing the database, putting people into meaningful groups. There is a spread of AA members from students to pensioners, from the wealthy to the poor. The building societies had to make huge investments to get better information on their customers.'

For potential bidders such as Ford, the cash-rich motor group suggested as a suitor for the AA and the RAC, there is a different rationale. Ford wants to develop the company as a consumer services business, tapping into the after-sales market including servicing, repairs and insurance.

It is attracted to the higher return possible in businesses such as Kwik-Fit, the specialist replacement parts group acquired this month.

But there are sceptics who say the AA is very different. 'Acquiring the AA means you buy the roadside rescue network which is a lot of operational infrastructure,' said one analyst. 'By comparison Kwik-Fit is like a standard dealer network.'

The third group to have shown an interest in the RAC are financial groups such as PPM Ventures, part of the Prudential financial group; BC Partners and Nomura. Their plan would be to extract more value from the business by backing managers with a more commercial approach and then selling on at a profit.

The AA has become more focused under John Maxwell, its director-general, selling its retail shops to concentrate on the quality of service to motorists. Group pre-tax surplus doubled to £40.4m in 1997, the most recent period available. The RAC, meanwhile, increased pre-tax profits by 45 per cent to £24.7m in 1998.

Both organisations are adopting a more commercial approach but the financial bidders believe scope exists to extract more value from the businesses. Whichever strategy prevails, a link with a more leisurely age of motoring will have been severed.

Source: Financial Times, 23 April 1999

5.1 Explain why volume sales are only one measure of worth of a segment to an organisation.

5.2 Such customer data as discussed in the article requires a system of evaluation to maximise its value to the organisation. What bases could be used and how would such information be used to create integration of organisations' functions?

5.3 Construct an outline marketing plan illustrating how the information and resulting segmental descriptors would influence the choice of marketing mix components.

Article 5.B   FT

Males boost use of cosmetics in Europe

Men turn to skin care and women return to colour, reports John Willman

Growing use by men of skin care products, fragrances and other toiletries and a return to colour cosmetics by women have contributed to the biggest growth in sales for the European cosmetics industry since the beginning of the 1990s.

Sales of cosmetics and toiletries reached €43.7bn ($45bn) in the European Union last year, 6.4 per cent up on 1997, according to figures to be published in London today at the annual meeting of Colipa, the European industry body.

Country-by-country figures provide material for those fond of national stereotypes. The French, for example, are the highest spenders per capita, buying €140 of cosmetics and toiletries a year, compared with an EU average of €117. This puts them on a par with Americans and only slightly behind the Japanese, who are the highest spenders globally.

French consumers spend a higher proportion than the average European on perfumes, cosmetics and skin care. But they spend less than average on hair care and general toiletries such as soap, shower gels and deodorants.

Despite the unromantic view of the English, UK consumers also spend more than average at €121 per head a year. The British spend a higher proportion on cosmetics and toiletries but less than average on perfumes and skin care.

Germany is the biggest European cosmetics market, with sales of €9.7bn, which puts it third globally behind the US and Japan. But Germans spend a lower proportion on fragrances and decorative cosmetics than average, and more on general toiletries.

Bottom of the league table are Portugal and Greece, spending an average of €71 and €83 a head last year. Scandinavian countries also spend less than average in the Colipa figures – which exclude

duty-free sales, more important in these high indirect tax countries than elsewhere.

EU per capita spending on perfumes, cosmetics, skin and hair care products and other toiletries mirrors growth in income and has reached the same level as that on bread, says Colipa.

'Most consumers now see such purchases as an essential part of the weekly shopping basket,' says Udo Frenzel of the German industry, who heads the Colipa taskforce that collects the data.

Make-up – an eighth of the total – produced the biggest growth last year, up 11.3 per cent, as fashion moved away from colourless, natural products back to colour cosmetics. The biggest category is toiletries, with more than a quarter of the market; it rose 5.2 per cent last year.

Growth last year was the highest since the start of the decade, when the reunification of Germany

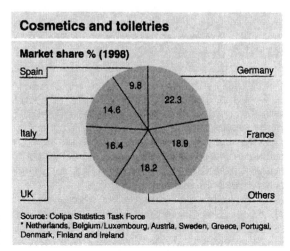

Cosmetics and toiletries

Market share % (1998)

Spain 9.8
Germany 22.3
Italy 14.6
France 18.9
UK 16.4
Others 18.2

Source: Colipa Statistics Task Force
* Netherlands, Belgium/Luxembourg, Austria, Sweden, Greece, Portugal, Denmark, Finland and Ireland

boosted sales. It was similar to the increase in the US market, which is now worth slightly less than the combined EU total.

Own-label sales remain stable but are not growing, in a market driven by the innovation offered by branded products.

The market is dominated by large companies such as L'Oreal of France, Unilever, Procter & Gamble and Wella of Germany. But the European cosmetics industry also includes about 2500 small and medium-sized enterprises, according to Colipa.

Source: Financial Times, 25 June 1999

5.4 You are the marketing manager for a toiletries manufacturer. Devise a marketing plan to exploit the change and growth shown by the article, clearly illustrating the development of the targeting strategy and techniques, and the resulting marketing mix to be employed.

Where luxury is an addiction

This exclusive event is where the finest watchmakers meet to compare notes and display the quality and flair of their new designs, says Michael Balfour

The ninth annual Salon International de la Haute Horlogerie (SIHH) opened in the Palexpo exhibition halls in Geneva on April 22 and continues until April 29.

This event is for the watch trade only, unlike next week's much larger Basel Show, and is devoted entirely to the values of fine watchmaking. Exclusivity is the watchword of the organisers, and there are just 17 specially invited exhibitors presenting new models and future plans.

This international showcase is under the presidency of Franco Cologni. He comments: 'The SIHH is not only a commercial event, but a meeting point between manufacturers who guarantee the extreme quality of their products, and distributors who are the privileged vectors of the brands' images. This is the reason the SIHH has been so successful for nearly a decade, and it will remain our philosophy in the years to come.'

To this end the promotional activities of the Association Interprofessionnelle de la Haute Horlogerie, under the guidance of Eugen Maier, secretary-general, are of increasing importance.

Of this year's exhibitors, seven are newcomers. They have moved from the Basel Show, and include for example, Breguet, bearing the name of probably the greatest watchmaker ever to engage in this trade.

Breguel is now wholly owned by Investcorp, and, under Jean J. Jacober, the chief executive officer, marketing is being sharpened up and new models are coming on stream. The familiar engine-turned dial and moon hands are present on its new Classique for gentlemen. There are also two new automatic chronographs, the tonneau-shaped Héritage and the round stainless steel Type XX Transatlantique.

New double rotor movements are housed in the new deluxe wristwatches of Perrelet, and this brand has discovered the marketability of beautifully presented limited editions, such as Old Rose (100 pieces only).

Another new exhibitor is Bovet, which flourished 177 years ago and is now handsomely back in business. It is showing the Fleurier de Bovet, a lady's gold and diamond pocket watch.

Audemars Piguet arrives in style, to the manner born since 1875. They are presenting the Jules Audemars Tourbillon Minute Repeater Split-Second Chronograph, a mechanical masterpiece, combining scientific, technical and artistic skills of a very high order. Collectors should note that there will be just 15 made.

Audemars Piguet are also unveiling their Canapé Tourbillon; there will be 25 of these. Limited editions are also found on the elegant booth of Girard-

Perregaux. They include the SF Foudroyante (no accelerator needed for selling the 750 pieces of this Ferrari 70th anniversary piece), the Vintage 1999 automatic Column-Wheel chronograph, and the new F1-048 (1,000 pieces).

Daniel Jean-Richard is another debut exhibitor with a limited edition, under the tutelage of Luigi Macaluso (owner of Girard-Perregaux). It is showing the Gold TV Screen Chronograph (25 pieces), and also a larger version of it, alongside the three model Bressel line.

Roger Dubuis of Geneva completes the new 'guest list' at the SIHH, and discloses his season's novelties for the company's traditional limited world distribution. One of the particularities of Roger Dubuis is its cases fashioned from palladium, and the Sympathie range demonstrates their appeal.

Daniel Roth is showing the automatic Papillon. This jump hour, with a most original dial layout, is limited to 110 pieces each in 18 carat white and pink gold, and 30 in platinum.

The Vantage and Masters collections demonstrate the art of fine watchmaking, and so does the Back-timer, by fellow exhibitor Gerald Genta. These two companies are associated with Singapore-based The Hour Glass and combine some of their essential functions with no loss of individual identity.

Parmigiani Fleurier is another high class watch-maker, and Michel Parmigiani and his able team will be unveiling the automatic Basica, the Crono Rat-trapante (10 pieces only), the tonneau-shaped mechanical eight-day Ionica, and the Torus Quantime Perpétuel.

The other SIHH exhibitors are part of the Vendôme Luxury Group. Whether there will be a combination of some of their long-established individual operations remains to be seen. The odds are greatly against such a development, but normal business housekeeping of course continues.

Piaget, for example, has recently acquired control of its north American retailing and distribution from Movado. Under Francis Gouten, chief executive officer, Piaget has brought more beautiful timepieces to Geneva. The eight-day Emperador marks Piaget's 125th anniversary (50 pieces), and its Altiplano is an ultra-thin model with the Piaget signature unusually at 3 o'clock.

Cartier is unveiling its Collection Privée, the best of the best. It includes a 25-piece edition of an automatic pink gold Pasha with a day/night indicator, another Pasha in white gold with a tourbillon movement bearing the intertwined Cartier double C logo, and an ultra-thin mechanical Santos-Dumont in platinum or yellow gold (small model in gold only).

Cartier is also enjoying a success among horological cognoscenti with the large Officine Panerai brand from Italy. Cartier also has Baume & Mercier under its wing. This year two limited edition Cape-Land chronographs are displayed. Each is numbered with a year of the present millennium, but number 2000 is in platinum and not for sale.

Vacheron Constantin is pleased with the new 245 in its Les Complications collection. This automatic for gentlemen comes in white or pink gold and has a transparent back.

The exhibition list is completed by Alfred Dunhill (with its Longitude Millennium watch) and Mont-blanc (showing a 75th anniversary limited edition Meisterstuck) in the Espace Luxe within the SIHH halls. This sector looks likely to expand in the next few years.

More than 5,000 invited visitors from 150 countries are expected. Each one is, to quote a 17th century expression, a 'luxurist', professionally addicted to the 'luxuriance' of the timepieces here.

Source: Financial Times, 25 April 1999

5.5 Clearly describe the market segments illustrated in this article.

5.6 What particular aspect of segmentation is especially demonstrated? Suggest the appropriate media and promotional approaches which would be most likely to be effective in successfully targeting and positioning such segments.

5.7 Describe the influences which affect the innovation of products in niche markets of this type and how these relate to their segmentation activities.

FT

Credit unions aim to fill void left by banks in financially excluded communities

Simon Buckby reports on the expanding role of the not-for-profit co-operatives

Jean Williams is pleased the tower blocks on her estate in Leicester are finally being pulled down. The chair of St Matthew's tenants' association says the council should then 'make that space nice for the rest of us on the estate. After that, we want the maisonettes turned into houses'.

These are just a few of the improvements she would like. 'They should close both the betting shops and several of the pubs, because they just attract trouble.' But the most urgent problem is debt, and she hopes others will find an answer to this in credit unions.

Part of the problem areas such as St Matthew's have faced is they have been left without access to banks as more than 600 branches closed in the past five years. In recognition of this 150 community leaders from across Britain will today meet Eddie George, governor of the Bank of England, and Howard Davies, chairman of the Financial Services Authority. They will discuss a new code of practice for banks working with financially excluded communities.

Based on income per head, St Matthew's is technically the second poorest estate in Britain, but it is surprisingly free of vandalism. Ms Williams puts that down to 'the excellent agencies we have working here and the wonderful forum where tenants can discuss issues with them'. Based at a one-stop shop on the estate, these include a housing officer – who cleans off graffiti as soon as it appears – community workers, a policeman, an ersatz job centre and Dr Angela Lennox, the local GP.

'With the tenants, we have done a lot to provide services on the estate,' said Dr Lennox, 'but debt is a real problem. Now we are thinking of setting up a credit union.'

Credit unions are not-for-profit financial co-operatives, owned and run by their members. By saving money together, the members create an asset pool from which to make low-cost loans. Although they have been around since the 1850s, and are developed in the USA, Canada, Australia and Ireland, they are small in Britain.

Steve Finnigan, president of the Association of British Credit Unions, sees an opportunity for expansion. 'As building societies abandon mutual status, credit unions can step into that role. We can teach our members to budget and manage their money, encourage savings and offer loans they couldn't otherwise get from official sources.'

In fact, official sources are almost unknown on estates such as St Matthew's. Few residents have a bank account – not least because they are seen as a risk by financial institutions. There is a 50 per cent annual turnover in its 4,500 residents and many are refugees who speak little English. The estate has the highest unemployment rate in the country, with 80 per cent dependent on welfare benefits. Many tenants are in arrears with rent, or cannot pay debts to loan sharks.

Patricia Hewitt, a Leicester MP and Treasury minister, believes that where banks have moved out, credit unions can put a floor under the socially and financially excluded. 'We have one of the most competitive and sophisticated financial services sectors in the world – but some people are still missing out. Without fanfare, credit unions have been doing invaluable work. We are determined to encourage the sector.' Hence she is proposing to allow credit unions to borrow from banks.

This is music to the ears of the Alliance and Leicester, which is involved in examining the potential for a credit union in St Matthew's.

'We don't yet know what form it could take, but we are working with all the local stakeholders,' said John Noble, head of community affairs. 'We can help with the business case, the legal framework, running software and so on.'

Alliance and Leicester's involvement could also help overcome some of the problems faced by other credit unions. A recent report by ABCUL concluded many had failed because of too much stress on social objectives with too little attention to economic management. 'They need to be operated more like a professional financial service,' it said.

Peter Tattersall, a local credit union development officer, said: 'We have the advantage of including Alliance and Leicester as well as St Matthew's established one-stop shop, which could be a base from which to build. But it won't work without the support of the residents.'

There are promising signs: credit unions are common in the Caribbean, so the large community of Montserration refugees is keen. So is Jean Williams.

'Lots of people here are in debt. I am told a credit union can help. If so, let's try it,' she said.

Source: Financial Times, 23 April 1999

5.8 Explain how segmentation by the main banks may have led to the growth of such organisations as credit unions.

5.9 Conduct a STEP analysis from the bank's point of view, paying attention to public and governmental reaction to the situation revealed. Some outside research into the topic will be necessary.

5.10 Describe how the banks could reposition their offering to take a positive part in this significant area of activity. SWOT analysis and segmentation analysis will be employed together with portfolio analysis.

6 Marketing Information and Research

Consideration of marketing at almost any level leads inevitably to the realisation that we are going to require hard information and facts before any useful decision making can be undertaken. This information and fact-gathering process involves a set of decisions all its own, since the manager will have to define who to ask what questions, under what circumstances and based on what sample of the population. The aim is to reconstruct the real world in a scientific manner so that statistical analysis can draw out the facts and construct a virtual world where experimentation can take place to reveal nuances of behaviour, likes and dislikes.

A number of processes may be involved before a recognisable structure or set of behaviours emerges which is meaningful in terms of the problem being addressed. It is essential, of course, that the problem to be investigated be precisely defined and that all those involved in the research should be well aware of their expected contribution. Indeed, it may very well be that some elementary research will be necessary in order to define the problem successfully. For example, a manufacturer may be experiencing falling sales. Problem: falling sales. Answer: find out why the sales are falling. Is it competition, quality, change in consumer/customer buying habits? In fact many possibilities may be involved. Having identified in a broad sense why the problem exists it is then possible to devise a research methodology to secure a solution to the problem.

Research can be secondary (desk-based), primary, or a combination of the two, which can be used in an exploratory, a descriptive or a causal setting depending upon the purpose for which it is designed.

Market research as an activity is best used as the major component in a fully integrated marketing information system whereby information is drawn from all manner of sources on a continuous basis. This information is gathered, collated and distributed throughout the organisation in a way which informs all interested functions and individuals. New ideas or trends may then be investigated, using research, to home in on specific areas that bear further investigation. This exercise may be conducted wholly in house, or parts, especially the research itself, may be entrusted to outside contractors, who will often devise and execute the sampling programme and questionnaire construction and conduct interviews where required.

It should be said, of course, that none of this effort and expense is worth the paper it is printed on if not conducted with utter probity, truthfulness, warts and all, and in an ethical setting mindful of the interests of the public who may be involved as well as the interests of the client firm. Market research, properly conducted, reveals the facts. How the organisation reacts to and uses these facts is, of course, the crucial question.

In order to successfully complete the tasks in this chapter you will need to be familiar with:

- secondary and primary research techniques;
- marketing information systems;
- research evaluation;
- sampling sizes and methods;
- branding concepts.

When an inspector calls

'Mystery shoppers' are used to identify troublespots and motivate staff, says Gillian Upton

During a hotel stay, have you waited more than three rings before the phone was picked up, not been referred to by name, found hairs in the bath or failed to receive a message?

If you're paying more than £250 a night, these lapses are serious. A hotel's safety valve is staff training and, failing this, customer complaints. A third check is the annual and anonymous visit by the hotel inspector. The inspector's report is then used as a training exercise for all staff.

Hotels also use the services of a so-called 'mystery shopper', usually a hotel colleague, to come and stay. In these ways, staff and management correct problems before guests experience them.

'Using the services of an inspector is a motivator. We wouldn't want to come in on a score lower than the previous year,' says Brian Hladnik, deputy managing director of the five-star Landmark Hotel in London.

At the three-star Jarvis Hotels group, staff know that disgruntled guests have a hotline to the chairman from their bedroom and attend focus groups throughout the year.

All hotels have their reputation to maintain but deluxe hotels, in particular, have to justify their rates. The more deluxe the property the more nit-picking the inspection.

Inspectors checking any of Preferred Hotels, a marketing association of 125 deluxe hotels in 25 countries, answer 1,600 questions on each hotel during a two-day, anonymous stay. These generate 5,000 plus points. If a hotel fails the inspection in two categories – service and condition of the building – it goes on six months' trial, at the end of which is a second inspection. A second failure means a quick exit from Preferred.

'We look at things most people don't even think of,' claims Peter Cass, president and chief executive of Preferred Hotels. 'We believe our inspection is the toughest in the industry.'

Preferred uses an outside audit company, whose inspectors reveal their true identity only after checkout. A debriefing with the hotel's general manager and senior staff follows.

David Smith, (not his real name) is an inspector. A former general manager of a luxury London hotel, he travels the US and Asia, for 12 days each month, inspecting three, four and five-star hotels, never using the same hotel twice.

'It should be a pleasure but it's difficult to relax and enjoy the luxury,' he concedes. The room check forms the smallest part of the inspection and work begins as soon as he enters the hotel entrance. The check-in procedure alone generates 100 questions. The concierge is another obvious target. Popular with business travellers, variable in quality and too often gratuity-dependent, the concierge desk will be asked by Mr Smith for anything from an aspirin at an odd time of day to requesting a notary to sign a legal document after offices have closed.

'Four years ago concierges weren't that good,' says Mr Smith. 'Today, they're having to provide a full service, not just theatre tickets, and must not expect a gratuity.' Demand has forced hotels to double staffing levels, extend working hours and make them more proactive.

Mr Smith also samples the restaurants and bars for over-attentive, intrusive service, doesn't tip staff occasionally to check for scowls and orders room service to see whether staff are helpful in suggesting what to drink with the food order and how long it takes to arrive. He checks whether a message arrives under the door within 20 minutes and the cleanliness of the food trolley when it arrives with breakfast.

There are 165 questions in the bathroom and bedroom, which means a 45-minute check for debris under the bed, stains on a valance, dusty curtains, dirty or difficult to use phones, a hunt for the hairdryer, empty minibar, hair-strewn pillows, old towels and any plumbing problems.

'I'm a lot less friendly in terms of cleanliness in the bathroom,' says Mr Smith, 'It's a "No" for a hair in the tub, the water has to be instant, the shower easy to use.'

'At the end of the day, though, it depends on whether you get your faxes and messages,' believes Mr Smith. 'Is the message under the door within 20 minutes and is the message light illuminated on your phone?'

The criteria is more relaxed in a resort property and standards vary globally due to cultural differences. In America, housekeeping staff are trained to make eye contact with guests; in Asia that would be discourteous. Mr Smith still finds service in French hotels grudging and much better in Germany.

Off duty, Mr Smith's preference is to stay in a midrange hotel which is achieving something special and pay rather less than £250 a night.

Source: Financial Times, 7 December 1998

6.1 As a 'virtual customer' how does the mystery shopper contribute to an organisation's understanding of its customers' perception of the organisation? Describe the type of research this represents and give examples of its application.

6.2 How and why could the mystery shopper technique be an important component of Internet marketing? What kind of research does this technique represent?

6.3 What advantages does the mystery shopper bring to staff training, product development and management?

6.4 A number of accommodation and restaurant guides exist (e.g. *The Michelin Guide*, *The AA Guide*, etc.) with an inspectorate system to evaluate existing and potential entries in their publications. Should they be viewed as a promotional aid and therefore paid for by the establishment? What are the benefits and the potential problems which may be encountered?

Net enables companies to filter flood of information

Web-based business applications can bring together knowledge management functions with e-commerce and e-business applications, says Tom Foremski

The internet is having a great effect on how companies handle their knowledge management requirements as they make use of inexpensive internet-based technologies to develop applications that can turn a flood of information into useful knowledge.

By using standard, web browser-like interfaces, companies have a wide range of options in terms of using internet-based software or more expensive groupware applications to link corporate databases with web-based resources.

The main challenge, however, is deciding which options to use and how to organise the information and collect it in the most effective way. And as companies build their web presence and use it to interact increasingly with customers, additional challenges surface in how to manage that relationship.

Terry Wilcox, managing director of Silknet Software UK, a vendor of knowledge management software, says: 'Today, more and more consumers are turning to the internet to interact with companies.' In this environment, companies are finding it increasingly difficult to know who their customers are and to offer the personalised service that these customers still demand.

'The companies that are ahead of the game are using knowledge management to keep track of their individual customers' personal preferences, buying patterns and service needs.'

Silknet provides a range of web-based business applications that can be used for bringing together knowledge management functions with e-commerce and e-business applications.

The internet is also rapidly becoming the main communications medium for linking users of groupware products such as those from US-based IBM subsidiary Lotus Development and US software company Novell with its Groupwise product. Lotus, for example, has added a raft of internet-related features in a big upgrade to its groupware products in Release 5 of Notes and the Domino server.

Notes R5 uses a familiar web browser-like navigation model which saves on user training costs. Features include Notes R5 Headlines, a page that brings together corporate information with information from outside web sites.

Lotus Domino R5 Server software allows corporations to host collaborative web-based business applications such as those for customer relationship management, interactive self-service, and supply chain management.

Michele Deziel, Lotus's general manager of web application development, says: 'With R5, we have improved our highly productive development environment to offer a leading edge, standards-based toolset which broadens the scope and decreases the time to market for global collaborative web applications.'

Knowledge management has a very broad definition and although it includes well known applications such as Lotus Notes and Domino, it can also be represented through applications such as corporate intranets which use internet technologies to link staff and give them access to key information, and also allow companies to capture knowledge from their staff.

The natural progression here is the development of corporate portals that bring together the internal intranets with the knowledge resources available on the internet.

Corporate portals combine corporate information with web-based sources of information and e-mail in one window. Corporate portals are similar, in these respects, to the leading portal web sites such as Yahoo and Excite but are tailored for a company's staff.

US market research company Delphi Group predicts a big rise in the building and the use of corporate portals over the next two years within large so-called Global 2000 corporations.

Hadley Reynolds, Delphi's director of research, says: 'Portal development is a necessary second stage in the maturing of corporate intranets and an indicator of the tremendous promise of this medium inside the organisation.

It is transparent now that the rapid spread of intranets has initially perpetuated the challenges of information silos, bottlenecks, and backlogs that were the problems in the first place.'

Delphi's research shows that 55 per cent of organisations surveyed have portal projects under way. Another 17 per cent had production sites up and running at the beginning of 1999, while 38 per cent are evaluating, planning, or piloting portal implementations.

Corporations which do not currently have portal work under way plan to deploy portals late this year and next year.

Delphi expects that by the beginning of 2001, nearly 90 per cent of larger organisations will have moved into portal deployments, with 80 per cent showing corporate portals in production mode.

The next step beyond corporate intranets and portals is to actively manage the information generated and turn that information into knowledge that is useful to the corporation. Consultancy Cap Gemini, based in France, has developed a concept which it calls an 'Everybody Information System' (EIS) where the goal is to control what can quickly become a glut of information and automatically tailor it to the needs of specific staff members.

Geoff Smith, Cap Gemini business manager for knowledge transformation services, says: 'EIS is like the perfect hostess, tirelessly going round the party with the observation that "You really must talk to Mr X. You have so much in common!"

'It is going to take some getting used to, having an electronic gossip listening in on your every word, but if we accept that we need to constantly build new knowledge-based relationships that add value, then staying in the kitchen at the global info party is no longer going to be acceptable.'

Other companies believe that effective knowledge management revolves around the creation of specialised web sites targeting key industry segments.

UK-based JBA Holdings, an enterprise software company, has helped sponsor several portal web sites that focus on specific industry segments such as the clothing and footwear and vehicle industries.

Mike Gove, electronic marketing manager at JBA, says: 'With integrated marketing, attraction and involvement of branded partners and management of quality information, portal sites will soon be recognised as the ideal channel for industry knowledge management.

'The vertical sector sites will be shaped by the industries' needs and wants and therefore will be able to provide information that is relevant, easily accessible and in real-time. The future of portals sites is optimistic. I can not see how any company can afford not to be involved or linked to an industry-specific portal site.'

Source: Financial Times, 28 April 1999

6.5 The manipulation of such information enables organisations to understand their customers more competitively. What effect could this have on the advertising and direct marketing industries?

6.6 How would you expect the communications possible via the WWW to enable more effective product development and innovation?

6.7 Explain why the filtration activity as mentioned in the article should be undertaken by the marketing function within the organisation. How does this filtered information prove to be of value throughout the organisation?

Return on investment is difficult to quantify

The measurement of the value of intellectual capital or knowledge may be one of the key factors for business success in the next century, says Philip Manchester

Knowledge management is a hard concept to define, even for some of its most eager proponents. So it should be no surprise that the task of measuring the business benefits of a knowledge management programme is equally difficult.

Measuring the Value of Knowledge, a report by Business Intelligence, the UK research company, sums up the problem in a quote from Philip McPherson, a consultant and emeritus professor of systems engineering and management at London's City University.

'The status of information management is undermined in practice because it is difficult to ascribe value to information and knowledge in conventional accounting terms,' he believes.

Business Intelligence's report also states that it found no convincing evidence in its research that organisations performed any genuine analysis on the return on investment of their knowledge management programmes.

The report also notes: 'The widening gap between the market and book value of companies (which is over ten times in many knowledge-intensive companies) raises questions about the relevance of traditional measures and accounting methods.'

Hard though it may be, the measurement of the value of intellectual capital or knowledge looks set to be one of the key factors for business success in the 21st century.

Establishing Business Benefit from Knowledge Management, a briefing paper by management consultancy PA Consulting Group, notes, for example: 'It has become conventional wisdom that the organisations that will thrive in the next decade and beyond are those that understand the value of their intellectual assets and work actively to increase the return on those assets.'

PA Consulting advocates a 'holistic' approach to measurement that establishes the 'link between knowledge management and the cost and revenue levers of the business'.

The intangible nature of knowledge and its role in enabling a corporation to perform means that the only feasible measures of success tend to be anecdotal.

In the same way that the concept of what knowledge is tends to differ in every corporation, the impact of a knowledge management programme is likely to manifest itself in a number of different ways.

Skandia, a Swedish-based financial services company, is widely acknowledged as one of the pioneers of measuring knowledge and the impact of knowledge management. Starting in 1991 with the appointment of the world's 'first director of intellectual capital', Skandia has evolved formal methods for measuring and reporting intellectual capital.

Skandia is using a technique called the Intellectual Capital (IC) Index to try and track the ebb and flow of intellectual capital over time – aimed both at providing managers with an indicator of change, and external analysts with a quantitative measure of company performance.

The results of the project are significant – not the least of them being that Skandia has risen from number 300 to number three in its market sector in just five years.

At the practical level, the project has delivered several benefits from better reporting of its 'intangible assets' to shareholders and a redefinition of the role of financial controller to 'intellectual capital' controller.

Other organisations have been able to identify different benefits from their knowledge management programmes.

Tony Roberts, senior data management specialist at Nortel Networks, acknowledges the problem of measuring business benefits in his company's installation of Livelink from Canadian-based Open Text.

He goes on to say, however, that some benefits have become apparent: 'It is very difficult to assess tangible benefits when implementing a knowledge management strategy, but so far many business benefits have been achieved.'

Streamlined work processes, reduced foreign travel and reduced e-mail traffic are examples of the benefits which Mr Roberts describes. It has also helped speed up the bureaucracy involved in taking on new employees.

'We have created a process using Livelink's workflow capability where all the departments involved are attributed a task. The hiring manager can initiate the recruitment process and the service request all on the intranet, allowing human resource co-ordinators to track and manage any potential bottlenecks.'

The Strategic Management of Knowledge and Organisational Learning Consortium, an industry-wide body with members drawn from many different areas of business, has researched several organisations' experiences of knowledge management programmes. Despite its elusiveness, measurement of business benefits is high on the agenda. General Motors of the US, for example, began a transformation in the early 1990s with a programme based on the development of 'intellectual leadership' which aimed to ensure that decisions were market-led and that the environment let people learn from mistakes – either their own or others.

One key element of GM's programme is the inclusion of a formal process where the actual results of decisions are measured and compared to expected results – with built-in processes that allow for changes if the results do not come up to expectations.

Dow Chemical implemented its programme with the specific aim of deriving measurable value from intellectual property.

This involved the 'active management' of its patent portfolio to generate new business and also increase licence fees. Following the success of this approach, Dow Chemical says that its focus has since shifted to 'know-how', supported by a significant investment in technology infrastructure and tools.

Steelcase, the world's largest office furniture manufacturer, re-positioned itself in a stagnant market by changing its focus, based on better use of its knowledge of productivity in the office environment.

By taking architectural design and ergonomics into account, US-based Steelcase has been able to build more appealing products, improve its market share and generate bigger profits.

Bill Miller, Steelcase's vice-president of research and development, notes: 'For us to deliver value to customers, we have to deliver knowledge.'

Source: Financial Times, 28 April 1999

6.8   With the availability of information in such large quantities the possession and evaluation of processed data forms a major component of the marketing information system. Suggest an outline structure of how this might be practically managed, and how such information could be disseminated throughout the organisation.

6.9   In what kind of research does such information become an important component, and how would this lead to more accuracy in the conducting of the other main strand of research?

6.10 It has been said that the wealth of available information, and the ability to process such information in an increasingly effective way, will replace traditional interviewing techniques. Justify this statement, showing how this might be achieved.

Article 6.D   FT

WPP adopts new brand research tool

By Alison Smith

WPP, the marketing services group, will today launch a new method of brand analysis that will strengthen its involvement in running its advertising, public relations and research businesses.

WPP's increasingly hands-on approach contrasts with the attitude of other big marketing groups, such as Interpublic and Omnicom, which allow their businesses a large degree of autonomy.

The new method of analysis is based on a study, known as 'Brandz', that drew on interviews with 70,000 people about 3,500 brands in seven countries including the US, the UK and China. The study, which has cost $6m (£3.5m) so far this year, was aimed at analysing consumer loyalty and predicting changes in market share.

The introduction of the analysis is a further example of WPP's eagerness to increase its role in directing its businesses. Last year the group was the driving force behind a plan to combine the media operations of its J Walter Thompson and Ogilvy & Mather advertising agencies.

Eric Salama, strategy director, said the analysis was part of a plan to add value 'from the centre'. 'We've worked with people from the operating companies in the past year and it's been a very co-operative effort.'

The launch in New York will emphasise how the Brandz methodology can both identify strengths and weaknesses and indicate how consumers will react to changes in a brand's positioning or use of media.

Mr Salama said the research tool was needed because businesses were not only looking to expand into new countries but also to offer an increasing variety of services. 'Many companies are also look- ing at sponsorship deals and affinity partnerships. For that they need a more rounded and detailed picture of brand loyalty and perceptions around the world.'

The study measures brand strengths include a 'bonding' score – the percentage of consumers in the brand's target group who feel 'emotionally and rationally' committed to it – and a 'voltage' score – the brand's success at converting people who are familiar with it into people who want to use the product or service.

The study identifies eight types of brands, such as olympic brands, fading stars, cult brands and 'little tigers', which have significantly below average presence, but significantly above average bonding scores. It covers 50 categories, including entertainment providers, cars, cereals, fast food and airlines.

The conclusions suggest that even strong global brands can see significant variations in their appeal in different countries. For example, Nike's bonding score was 53 in the US and 26 in the UK, while McDonald's scored 25 in the US and 42 in the UK.

Source: Financial Times, 5 October 1998

6.11 The article demonstrates how market research, environmental scanning and consumer behaviour are all part of a marketing information system. What other components may be involved, and how do they help the organisation to secure and maintain competitive differentiation?

6.12 'A brand only exists in the mind of the consumer, has no instrinsic value of its own.' Rebut this statement, and explain the concept of brand equity, and the part that market research plays in maintaining such value.

6.13 Global marketing makes use of 'broad-brush' segmentation, dealing with countries as segments in their own right. Explain how market research contributes to this notion, and the particular measures and characteristics that will be taken into account.

7　Anatomy of a Product

We can now turn our attention to the object of all our desires, the product. Naturally, on closer examination, we find that this is a complex area, which requires a clear understanding by the marketer in order to be successful in creating and developing products which meet customers' needs in all respects. Many separate disciplines are involved in designing, engineering, researching and bringing to a prepared market a product which satisfies both parties to the transaction, the customer, on the one hand, and the manufacturer or supplier of the product, on the other. As if this did not pose sufficient questions to answer we also have to consider the nature of the product. In fact, what is a product?

In a sense the answer is clear since the product forms the core of the transaction and is that which provides the mutual satisfaction gained by the transfer of ownership as between one party and the other for a satisfactory consideration or payment in some form. One party relinquishes something of value in exchange for something else of agreed value, usually, but not always, money. But what about an insurance policy? The customer is expected to part with substantial sums of money against the promise from the company that they will redeem the policy at some time in the future against the eventuality of certain circumstances occurring, either time related or life related or both. Nothing of any intrinsic value changes hands. We enter here into the realms of service-based products, which are covered in more detail in Chapter 22.

Put simply, the customer has an offer made to him or her which he or she accepts or rejects, and this offer may be as the result of a product made available in such a way as to create an impulse purchase decision at one end of the buying spectrum. At the other end of the spectrum the purchase decision may be made as the result of extensive research on the part of the customer. The difference may be typified as being the difference between buying a tin of beans, which may be done frequently with little effort being made to compare and contrast, and the decision to buy a motor car or capital machinery or an audio system, where the implications of making a mistake are greater and therefore require greater consideration.

How the marketer deals with identifying the similarities and the dissimilarities in constructing the product, its packaging, design, performance, target customers and quality issues, having made the distinction between durable, non-durable and service products, is the subject of this chapter.

Identifying the correct message and image, what makes a brand so valuable and how we may best use it as part of the product offered are also addressed, especially in the light of the recently accepted convention that a brand has an accountable value and may be given this value as part of the assets of a company.

The marketer can be described as the conductor of the whole performance, bringing all the instruments into harmony to provide the right product, in the right form at the right price in the right place with the expected performance and quality characteristics to satisfy the customer (and often the customers' customer as in the case of a retailer).

In all this we are reflecting the modern attitude to sales, which is that we should be customer oriented rather than product oriented, and indeed should be intent on developing relationships with our customers to make use of their 'lifetime' value, rather than going for the quick sale. The product and our precise interpretation in it of our customers' needs, wants and desires are the crucial elements that drive us to success.

In order to successfully complete the tasks in this chapter you will need to be familiar with:

- **levels of products;**
- **purchasing decision process;**
- **product mix;**
- **product line, length, depth and width;**
- **branding/brand equity;**
- **environmental analysis.**

Article 7.A   **FT**

Still waiting after all these years

Richard Donkin clings fervently to his hopes of owning an open-topped Morgan four-seater

Many years ago I drove my wife's bright yellow Triumph Spitfire sports car in the south of France on our honeymoon.

We felt a million dollars on the French roads where the Spitfire was a comparative rarity. Nevertheless, I could not suppress a feeling of deflation and envy as we approached the Italian border and drew up behind a white, open-topped four-seater Morgan Plus Four. For posing and style there was no contest. It had to be a Morgan.

I decided we had to have one even though there was a seven-year waiting list. The Spitfire was barely parked in the driveway before I had signed a £100 cheque for the deposit on the Morgan and sent it to a dealer in Manchester. We couldn't afford one at the time but I was sure we would be moving up in the world within seven years.

In the meantime we settled for a Golf GTi, which in 1979 had the same rarity value in the UK the Spitfire had in France. But it wasn't real poseur material, providing instead a dangerous invitation to a youthful driver. The Golf ended life embedded in a wall of Caphouse Colliery near Wakefield.

With a year of the waiting period to go, the dream was fading fast. A larger house, a new roof and a baby had exhausted any surplus finances. The deadline came and went. Volkswagens made way for Volvos as the family expanded to four.

People tried to warn me off. Why on earth buy such out-of-date engineering built around a wooden frame? The answer was always the same – because it looked good. That honeymoon image of the stylish young couple in their white Morgan continued to haunt me.

Another year went by. Still no word from the dealer. I tried ringing. No answer. The dealership had gone into liquidation. The dream was shattered. In some ways it came as a relief.

The family expanded into people carriers. The Morgan did not expand. There is still a waiting list although these days it is down to nearer four years and the deposit is £250.

The Malvern-based Morgan Motor Company, which has made a virtue of slow incremental change, responded to increasing waiting lists by upping production from about 410 a year in the 1980s to 486 in 1997. In February it was improved from 10 to 11 cars a week. It has a target of reducing waiting lists to two or three years but don't hold your breath.

In the meantime there is bad news for those, like me, who have been hankering after a four-seater. Production of four-seaters has been suspended because of difficulties complying with new European vehicle approval standards.

Four-seater production is to resume next month.

There is also a better system of deposit-taking these days. Every deposit handed to a dealer is recorded by the factory and an order number allocated so potential buyers can be traced should a dealership collapse. That said, deposits, as ever, are not refundable.

I have the impression that long after people carriers have made way for New Age buses Morgan will still be making cars for a market where a shortage of supply helps to generate demand.

Part of the appeal is the car's simplicity. The basic Morgan 4/4 is so named because it has four cylinders and four wheels.

The problem for me is the more old-fashioned Morgan appears – the factory switches off its telephones at lunchtime because 'it's the only time they can get any work done' – the more I warm to the company.

It stands for a set of values that have all but disappeared. Our last four cars have been automatics and I have become de-skilled in motoring terms.

One day, many years from now, I might sign another hopeful deposit cheque. The rear seat might just have room for a zimmer frame.

Source: Financial Times, 18 April 1999

7.1 Morgan cars exist because the company understands it's customer clearly. Discuss.

7.2 Given that the company's products are produced in low volume, do they have the scope for increasing profits by (a) increasing volume or (b) increasing the margin? How will this affect the brand?

7.3 Is the Morgan experience relevant in a modern customer-oriented business situation?

Article 7.B   FT

Flying high with cheap frills

Low-cost airlines are offering deals to woo business travellers, writes Gillian Upton

When is a low-cost airline not a 'no-frills' airline? When it adds frills. Business travellers, who have taken enthusiastically to value-for-money air travel, are being offered packages more commonly associated with mainstream carriers.

In the wake of increased competition and aggressive price-cutting from mainstream airlines such as KLM uk, three no-frills airlines are changing tack. Virgin Express is increasing legroom and is contemplating the launch of a frequent-flyer programme; Debonair is introducing a business-class section next week; and Go, owned by British Airways, is wooing the business traveller.

To date, the attraction of no-frills airlines has been based on price. Forget the more convenient departure points (in the UK, that means finding Luton and Stansted airports instead), convenient scheduling or many creature comforts. EasyJet, Ryanair and Debonair undercut the leading carriers by as much as 70 per cent on high-volume routes.

Ryanair, the most profitable of the no-frills airlines, has witnessed passenger numbers soar on the

Dublin-London route, from 1m in 1996 to 4m today. Numbers on the Birmingham-Dublin route have trebled in 2½ years. 'There's no reason why the Dublin route should be so popular. It's the fare that's responsible,' says Michael Cawley, Ryanair's commercial director. It's hard to argue with a one-way London-Dublin fare of £19.99.

Virgin Express claims that since the start of its Brussels-Barcelona route three years ago its competitors have not lost a single passenger. 'We're making more people fly,' says David Huttner, the airline's promotions manager.

Debonair's business class, called ABC, is to be launched on October 27. It will give passengers more privacy during the flight; a fully refundable, flexible ticket; a free bar; a snack; and dedicated check-in desk. The ticket price will remain as much as 40 per cent below the average business-class ticket price.

Debonair, based at Luton airport, north of London, launched just over two years ago and went into profit for the first time four months ago. It set itself slightly apart from its low-cost competitors by offering more seat comfort, a drink in-flight and a simple frequent-flyer scheme.

Virgin Express's plans for a frequent-flyer programme rest on finding a formula that will not raise ticket prices. More definite is Virgin's plan to remove seats in order to make more legroom for passengers, although no start date has been set.

Go has been targeting business travellers with a print advertising campaign. It has also announced a range of price cuts on European flights. Fares to destinations such as Rome and Lisbon fall to £60 return.

The prices have been cut from Go's standard European air fare of £100 and will be available only on Tuesdays, Wednesdays and Thursdays from tomorrow until December 10.

Other low-cost airlines are standing firm, although EasyJet, which markets itself on lowest price, no catering and direct sell, has introduced a £10 charge to allow passengers to transfer from one EasyJet flight to another. This is effectively a concession to the business traveller, who needs more flexibility.

Attempts by Virgin Express and Debonair to move upmarket are being viewed by some as the beginning of a consolidation in the sector. Consolidation has been seen in the US, where the failure rate of low-cost carriers has been 85 per cent since deregulation. Sir Michael Bishop, chairman of British Midland, believes there will be casualties. 'Larger airlines will react and start to put the squeeze on them.'

Source: Financial Times, 19 October 1998

7.4 Offering 'frills' defeats the object of budget airlines. Discuss.

7.5 How should budget airlines react when the larger operators begin to 'squeeze' them?

7.6 Budget airlines grow a market rather than poach customers. Discuss the validity of this perspective.

Article 7.C FT

Satellite mobile phone venture drifts out to a distant orbit

Shift in global standards and reduction in the size of handsets and charges has sidelined $5bn project, writes Christopher Price

It started with the wife of a Motorola executive wanting to phone home from a Caribbean beach. Yesterday it was left to an embarrassed management to explain to investors – some of whom have now launched legal action against the company – how the Iridium dream went wrong.

The $5bn project, which launched the world's first hand-held satellite mobile phone service in November, has failed to attract enough customers and generate sufficient revenues to avert Iridium breaching its banking covenants.

The company has blamed poor marketing and

technical difficulties. But the departures of the finance director last month, and Ed Staiano, vice-chairman and chief executive, last Thursday, suggest something more fundamentally wrong.

When the idea of a mobile phone that could telephone anywhere was conceived, the burgeoning cellular market was beset by technical limitations, differing international standards and high tariffs.

Iridium's service partners and other strategic investors became shareholders in the project, offsetting some of the risk to Motorola, the founder. Crucially, the service partners would also be responsible for marketing, sales and billing.

The company joined the Nasdaq stock market in 1997 and, buoyed by ambitious forecasts by analysts, as well as Iridium's own flow of positive announcements, the stock rose from its $22.50 IPO price to more than $70 a year later.

Iridium's target markets were business travellers, industries in difficult environments, such as oil and gas exploration, and developing nations.

Unfortunately for the company, the telecoms market had changed when it came to launch almost six months ago.

Different standards still divided the US and the rest of the world but Europe, and increasingly countries outside the region, had found a common platform in GSM, the European standard for cellular telecoms.

Agreements between GSM operators have seen a raft of roaming agreements that have enabled mobile phones to be used across international borders. At a stroke, it also undermined the 'use-anywhere' benefit promised by Iridium.

Technology has driven other changes in cellular telephony. The size and weight of phones has been shrinking at a rapid rate. At the same time, power and functionality have increased. The Iridium phone, on the other hand, weighed and looked like a small house-brick.

And while terrestrial cellular call rates and phone equipment costs have fallen as dramatically, Iridium came to the market with call charges as high as $7 a minute and handsets selling for about $3,000.

Iridium believed it could rise above these changes because of the global roaming benefit of its service and because its service partners had a vested interest in seeing Iridium prosper.

They were wrong on both counts. First, the group's $140m advertising campaign failed to communicate the service's basic benefit. Second, some service partners complained they had not been trained how to market and sell the service, others that consumers were confused about what Iridium did.

In addition, in a highly competitive mobile market, few service partners felt compelled to advertise and market a service they viewed as superfluous to their business.

Finally, software problems with the handsets meant that supplies only began to become freely available earlier this year.

The result was that by the end of the first quarter of this year, five months after the service launched, there were just 10,000 subscribers.

Motorola, which holds a 20 per cent stake, has pledged to ensure the company survives. Iridium has sent its Washington-based directors out to the field to explain the Iridium message to its service partners and to underline the need for resources for sales and marketing.

However, the Iridium fiasco casts a longer shadow. Globalstar Communications and ICO Global Communications are due to launch rival satellite phone services over the next 18 months.

The stock price of all three companies has crumbled in the wake of Iridium's problems – a serious development if, like ICO, you still need to raise some of the $3bn your system costs.

Both rivals are likely to be taking a stern look at their own business models, which differ little from

Sales figures confirm investors' and analysts' fears

Iridium yesterday said it had attracted just over 10,000 customers and revenues of $1.4m since launching the world's first hand-held satellite mobile phone service in November, **writes Christopher Price**.

The figures confirmed the worst fears of investors and analysts over the disappointing performance of the group.

To meet its banking covenants, Iridium was supposed to achieve targets of some 30,000 subscribers and $30m of revenues by the end of the March quarter.

John Richardson, acting chief executive officer, said: 'Clearly, we have a great deal of work to do to improve our marketing, distribution and sales activities all over the world.'

He said the company was now involved in tailoring the products, which include paging and messaging services, to better fit areas of identified market demand.

Most significantly, there would be 'reconsideration of product and service prices', indicating that Iridium's much-criticised pricing model was likely to be revised.

Iridium's, except perhaps in cheaper call rates. Wall Street analysts, who have remained relentlessly positive about the industry, are quietly removing their 'buy' recommendations, in the short term at least.

Meanwhile, Iridium executives will be focusing their minds on how to get their subscriber numbers up. They had better be quick – with the Iridium satellites only having another five years of power left, they will soon have to start thinking about raising the next $3bn to replace them.

Source: Financial Times, 27 April 1999

7.7 How did Iridium's marketing strategy fail?

7.8 What elements of the competitive situation acted against Iridium?

7.9 'It's all the fault of the marketers, who should have foreseen the problem.' Defend or disagree with this statement.

Article 7.D   FT

What a good name adds up to

Richard Tomkins reports on a method of putting a value on brands and reveals the leaders, laggards and non-runners in the resulting world league table

Which is the world's most valuable brand? The answer is less clear now than it was two weeks ago, when Coca-Cola was so far ahead of the rest that it looked unassailable.

In spite of its fumbled reaction to a health scare over its products in Europe, Coca-Cola is probably still ahead of the pack. But research to be published today shows that the crisis is jeopardising billions of dollars' worth of shareholder value.

According to Interbrand, the international branding consultancy, the Coca-Cola brand was worth $83.8bn (£52bn) before the scare started – far ahead of Microsoft, the world's next most valuable brand, at $56.7bn.

How much less is the Coca-Cola name worth today? Raymond Perrier, brand valuation director in Interbrand's London offices, says recent events should be seen in the context of a product that is 113 years old and sells in 200 countries. 'It would be foolish to say it hadn't been affected,' he says. 'But I don't think it's been affected by a huge amount.'

Even so, the Interbrand survey serves as a timely reminder that the financial risks of a big product recall can go far beyond the cost of writing off a few hundred dollars' worth of lost sales.

At the time Interbrand did its calculations, the value of $83.8bn attributed to the Coca-Cola brand represented nearly 60 per cent of the company's market value. In other words, the brand was worth more than all the company's offices, manufacturing plants, distribution systems and other assets put together.

'Brands are significant assets which companies need to manage carefully because they add value to the underlying business,' says Mr Perrier. For a company such as Coca-Cola, that sounds like understatement: the brand almost is the business.

Interbrand says its league table, called The $1 Billion Brands, is 'the most comprehensive ranking ever' of brand values. It attempts to put a financial value on an asset that is rarely included in company balance sheets.

The biggest obstacle to this kind of exercise is the difficulty of separating the value of a company's brands from that of its other intellectual assets, such as its patents, technologies, skills and distribution systems.

'Although there is general agreement that the existence of brands can have a beneficial impact on the earnings of a company, there is less agreement on the reliability for valuing brands in the balance sheet,' notes the Oxford University Press's *A Dictionary of Accounting*.

Even so, Interbrand – part of Omnicom, the US advertising group – has developed a methodology that is recognised by auditors, tax authorities and stock exchanges in many countries, and which has been used to value more than 2,000 brands worldwide over the past 12 years.

The Interbrand method treats the brand as an intangible asset that generates an identifiable stream of earnings over the years. Once that idea is established, the brand value can be defined as the net present value of the future profits.

For each brand, Interbrand uses publicly available financial data to estimate the operating profits likely to be generated over the next five years by products carrying the brand. (A notional 2½ per cent growth rate was assumed for subsequent years). It deducts a capital charge – a notional 8 per cent return on the cost of capital employed – and a 35 per cent tax charge to arrive at a figure called economic earnings.

Interbrand then calculates the brand's contribution to those earnings by applying a 'role of branding' index to the earnings figure, based on its own analysis of the role played by brands in different product sectors and geographical markets.

Finally, a discount is applied to the earnings to reflect the amount of risk involved. A long-established brand with a strong market position and wide geographic spread, for example, receives a lower discount than a small newcomer in a fast-evolving sector.

This last factor explains why, in spite of all the hyperbole about the internet, new technology stocks emerge as relatively weak brands that do little to justify their relatively high stock market valuations.

Amazon.com, for example, only scrapes into the rankings at number 57 in spite of its costly efforts to become the best known brand on the internet. Yahoo! is at 53 and America Online, the only other internet brand in the rankings, is at 35.

In contrast, most of the world's 10 most valuable brands are well established names such as Coca-Cola, Ford, Disney and Marlboro. The only top-ranking companies less than 25 years old are Microsoft, in second place, and Intel, at number seven.

Interbrand's method of calculation means some notable brands are absent from the table. The private companies that own the Levi's, Mars and Lego brands do not provide sufficient financial information; figures for the CNN cable television channel and Time magazine cannot be stripped out from those of Time Warner, the parent company; and

Banking on a ranking
Top 60 global brands by value

Brand name	Country of origin	Industry	Brand value ($m)	Brand name	Country of origin	Industry	Brand value ($m)	Brand name	Country of origin	Industry	Brand value ($m)
1 Coca-Cola	US	Beverages	83,845	21 Heinz	US	Food	11,806	41 Colgate	US	Pers. care	3,568
2 Microsoft	US	Software	56,654	22 BMW	Ger	Automobiles	11,281	42 Hertz	US	Car hire	3,527
3 IBM	UA	Computers	43,781	23 Xerox	US	Office equipmt	11,225	43 Ikea	Swe	Housewares	3,464
4 General Electric	US	Diversified	33,502	24 Honda	Jap	Automobiles	11,101	44 Chanel	Fra	Fashion	3,143
5 Ford	US	Automobiles	33,197	25 Citibank	US	Fin. services	9,147	45 BP	UK	Oil	2,985
6 Disney	US	Entertainment	32,275	26 Dell	US	Computers	9,043	46 Bacardi	Cuba	Alcohol	2,895
7 Intel	US	Computers	30,021	27 Budweiser	US	Alcohol	8,510	47 Burger King	US	Food	2,806
8 McDonald's	US	Food	26,231	28 Nike	US	Sports goods	8,155	48 Moët & Chandon	Fra	Alcohol	2,804
9 AT&T	US	Telecoms	24,181	29 Gap	US	Apparel	7,909	49 Shell	UK	Oil	2,681
10 Marlboro	US	Tobacco	21,084	30 Kellogg's	US	Food	7,052	50 Rolex	Switz	Luxury	2,423
11 Nokia	Fin	Telecoms	20,694	31 Volkswagen	Ger	Automobiles	6,603	51 Smlrnoff	Russ	Alcohol	2,313
12 Mercedes	Ger	Automobiles	17,781	32 Pepsi-Cola	US	Beverages	5,932	52 Heineken	Neth	Alcohol	2,184
13 Nescafé	Swit	Beverages	17,595	33 Kleenex	US	Pers, care	4,602	53 Yahool	US	Software	1,761
14 Hewlett-Packard	US	Computers	17,132	34 Wrigley's	US	Food	4,404	54 Ralph Lauren	US	Fashion	1,648
15 Gillette	US	Pers. care	15,894	35 AOL	US	Software	4,329	55 Johnnle Walker	UK	Alcohol	1,634
16 Kodak	US	Imaging	14,830	36 Apple	US	Computers	4,283	56 Pampers	US	Pers. care	1,422
17 Ericsson	Swe	Telecoms	14,766	37 Louis Vuitton	Fra	Fashion	4,076	57 Amazon. com	US	Books	1,361
18 Sony	Jap	Electronics	14,231	38 Barble	US	Toys	3,792	58 Hilton	US	Leisure	1,319
19 Amex	US	Fin. services	12,550	39 Motorola	US	Telecoms	3,643	59 Guinness	Ire	Alcohol	1,262
20 Toyota	Jap	Automobiles	12,310	40 Adidas	Ger	Sports goods	3,596	60 Marriott	US	Leisure	1,193

Source: Interbrand

organisations such as Visa, MasterCard and the BBC do not generate economic profits in the conventional sense.

Also absent from the table are airline brands, because of the difficulty of separating their value from that of take-off and landing slots. And only brands that generate a significant proportion of their profits outside their own country are included.

One interesting aspect of the table is that it is heavily dominated by US brands. Mr Perrier says this is partly because the large US market acts as a springboard for companies with global aspirations, and partly because the US has been in the brand management business for longer than other countries. 'A lot of the earliest successes in creating brands came out of the US, and still today, a lot of our models of what a brand is like and how a brand should be developed is based on US expertise,' he says.

Mr Perrier also notes that the financial services sector is very poorly represented in the rankings in spite of its heavy spending on advertising. 'The great failure of financial institutions has been their inability to create any relevant differentiation for themselves, other than at the edges.'

Mr Perrier says most of the new brands in the rankings – Intel, Nokia, Ericsson and Yahoo! – have broken through because the categories in which they compete are new. 'It seems to suggest that launching new brands into established categories, and getting substantial value out of them, is a lot more difficult than launching new brands in new categories,' he says.

'So the game of new brand development is much more one of finding new market opportunities than simply launching brands against established players.'

Source: Financial Times, 22 June 1999

7.10   The marketer's aim should be increase the value of the brand. Discuss.

7.11   Why should it be more difficult for the financial institutions to achieve major brand value?

7.12   Coca-Cola need have few worries concerning their recent product recall, as their brand is too valuable/powerful to feel the effects. Evaluate this statement.

8 Product Management

Products have a life in much the same way that natural organisms have a life. They are born, they grow, they become mature and they eventually decline and die. Of course, products have one major difference from, for example, human beings or cabbages, and that is that since they are a wholly man-made object they have no capacity for performing any of the functions of life in a literal sense. All aspects of a product's life, from its very existence in the first place to the time and circumstances of its demise, have to be controlled or managed.

The successful control and management of a product leads to maximum profit over the longest possible time. This can only be achieved by an understanding of the product life cycle (PLC) and the clear linking of the life cycle stages in the PLC demand different techniques and strategies to achieve the most satisfactory result.

This understanding also leads to the successful interlocking of management tasks when dealing with a number of products at different stages in their life cycles, enabling the effective planning of product development effort, range building, and withdrawal of products at the most appropriate time, securing the smooth flow of revenue. Although we may draw a neat PLC curve, in theory few products conform to smooth progress from development to introduction, growth, maturity, decline and final deletion. In the real world we want the curve to be steeply upward at the start, leading to a long period of maturity, and indeed some products by dint of successful product management continue to exist in a state of maturity and even growth for considerable periods of time, sometimes over generations, as witness Coca-Cola and McDonald's. This happy state is achieved through careful monitoring of performance, introduction of modifications as and when necessary by reference to the customer, and well-thought-through promotional campaigns.

However, the normal situation is for a product to be suitably refreshed, modified and promoted, but still to face a time when it no longer supports the effort and expense involved in its maintenance. Effective management is able to foresee this event and make the necessary preparations, both to organise the withdrawal of the product in a way to cause as little upset as possible among its loyal customers, and to introduce replacement products to ensure the continuance of the organisation. This management task uses many of the core theoretical marketing tools, and will certainly involve environmental scanning, market research, perceptual mapping, alongside such old warriors as SWOT. Unless we fully understand where we are, where we want to be and how we aim to achieve this state, then we cannot successfully manage our products to achieve our goals, both personally and in a corporate sense.

In order to successfully complete the tasks in this chapter you will need to be familiar with:

- perceptual mapping;
- product;
- product line extension;
- brand management.

Article 8.A   FT

Heinz soups up its old image

Alison Smith looks at the food group's efforts to make its products stand out from the crowd on the supermarket shelves by redesigning the packaging

As Andy Warhol showed, images of soup tins can be used to striking effect. While he featured the white-and-crimson Campbell's cans in his print-making, the classic bright red packaging of Heinz tomato soup also has an iconic quality. Like the turquoise of the baked beans can with its black keystone, it prompts instant recognition.

But not all the brand's packaging is as clearly recognisable. Now Heinz is trying to bring coherence to the appearance of the 100-plus soups, pasta meals and beans it sells in the UK alone.

Redesigning the packaging for convenience meals is an early stage in the company's efforts to make more sense of its vast worldwide portfolio of brands and to focus on those with greater strength. This approach received fresh impetus at the end of last year with the appointment of William Johnson as president and chief executive. It is still in its infancy: across eight categories, including weight control, frozen foods, sauces and convenience meals, the company has a plethora of brands and – in many cases – several depictions of the same brand.

Jones Knowles Ritchie, a London brand design consultancy, was appointed to produce the new convenience meal designs, and has since been appointed to work on re-presenting the company's tomato ketchup as a global brand.

Nir Wegrzyn, managing director of jkr, says consumers are changing so fast that what they would have found acceptable very recently may no longer be effective.

'Even three years ago, people would go into supermarkets with shopping lists and spend longer getting their groceries. Now they buy on impulse: they react and move along the supermarket aisle within an average of four to five seconds.'

This means that packaging design has to be clear and hard to copy. For familiar and everyday products, consumers must feel instantly comfortable with the new version.

In the case of the Heinz redesign, the detailed alterations to the three central products of tomato soup, baked beans and spaghetti might well escape casual shoppers. More substantial changes have been reserved for the variations on those themes which strayed further from original designs. Most strikingly, the range of 'Chef's special' tinned pasta meals such as ravioli, macaroni cheese and spaghetti bolognese – in orange, bright green and brown respectively – are being packaged with a yellow background and a red keystone which derives more closely from the classic packaging of the 1920s and 1930s.

According to Nigel Clare, managing director of Heinz's European grocery division, the changes that appear on the shelves were possible only because of changes within the organisation. Until this initiative, managers of individual sub-categories had been able to make their own decisions on packaging based on how best to promote individual products, and without having to pay too much regard to a consistent presentation of the brand.

'This created a lot of confusion on the shelf, and perceived difference on the shelf between Heinz and other brands was short-lived,' says Mr Clare. 'The end result of this redesign process is that every single one of those managers is aligned to the values of the brand in terms of design and consumer communications.'

The project also meant a change in how the design agency worked. Mr Wegrzyn says: 'This was the first big account where we took our designers away from their computers, and made them draw ideas to put to the client. We found this was an effective way of getting the focus on the ideas for the design rather than on details of what the finished version could look like.'

The sheer scale of the Heinz operation – it has more than half the canned soups and canned pasta markets in the UK and sells 1.5m tins of baked beans each day – means that several millions of the newly designed cans have been sold since they began appearing in stores last month. But sales alone will not answer the two deeper questions prompted by the change.

The first is whether the coherence of the new designs can prevail across the convenience meals category. The redesigned 'Big Soup' cans are maintaining a different look from other soups – most notably by being presented in a dark green background instead of the trademark red – on the basis that they are directed at a different audience.

Equally, the 'Heinziness' in the design of character-based canned pasta shapes aimed at children is slight compared with the emphasis on Barbie, Action Man or the Teletubbies. It is not hard to envisage that managers of new products might similarly argue that their innovations are aimed at different markets and should have the impact of modified designs.

The second question is how widely, through its different categories, Heinz will spread its return to more traditionally grounded designs and the emphasis on the keystone which has become its emblem. Although the company says it is looking at its food services (the products it supplies to hotels and pubs), it adds that there are 'no plans yet' to extend this to other Heinz categories such as infant food.

Yet the brand values expressed by Mr Clare – simplicity, consistency and security – are equally appropriate for the Heinz tins and jars for babies, and the packaging of the baby feeding range has the same lack of brand imprint identified as a flaw in the convenience meal design.

So while the canned groceries redesign is a sensible step, Heinz still has a long way to go in harmonising and consolidating its brands. Without further and faster moves in that direction, its classic boast of '57 varieties' may yet come to sound like an admission of failure.

Source: Financial Times, 2 October 1998

8.1 Identify the benefits that Heinz expects to gain from this redesign.

8.2 What dangers have to be considered and planned against when changing a brand's distinct and well-known packaging design?

8.3 Construct a perceptual map, placing four of Heinz's brands against two branded products from other manufacturers and two supermarkets' 'own brands', and identify what segment each may be aimed at.

Article 8.B

FT

New-style quality is just a fiddle

Old-style excellence got a bad name, says Tony Jackson. The aim should be provide a product consistently and make it the best you can

'[We] offer our customers', said the UK retailer Marks and Spencer last month when warning of falling profits, 'attractive prices and unbeatable quality.'

One does not want to pick on poor old M&S, which is going through a rough patch these days.

But the term 'quality' is one of the most abused in the business lexicon. What exactly does it mean?

Our grandparents would have been in no doubt. Quality meant excellence: a thing was the best of its kind, and that was that. A Stradivarius violin had quality, a tinker's fiddle did not.

In the business world, however, the word has acquired an unrecognisably different meaning. As defined by the American statistician W Edwards Deming some 50 years ago, quality means consistency, a lack of defects.

As such, it has no connection with the first meaning at all. Take the ultimate expression of business quality these days, the so-called Six Sigma programme. This aims to reduce defects to the improbably small level of 3.4 parts per million.

But a defect means only a result lying outside a specified range. The product can still be rubbish, but it must be consistent rubbish. As someone puts it in the Spice Girls' film *Spice World*, 'that was perfect, girls, without actually being any good'.

Whatever happened to the first definition? Shortly before the first world war, the US journalist Negley Farson visited the industrial heart of Britain. What struck him, he wrote, was the almost arrogant display of quality. A brass column or banister would be solid brass. In America, someone would have devised a way of saving a few nickels by hollowing it out.

Wind the tape on 50 years or so, and a different picture emerges. Around 1970, legend has it, a group of investment analysts visited a world-famous UK engineering company.

They posed the usual questions of their trade: about margins, stock turns, balance sheet ratios and so forth.

The company's executives seemed honestly puzzled. They did not see the relevance of all this, they said. Their products were the finest in the world. Why all this nit-picking about numbers?

Rolls-Royce, the company in question, duly went bust in 1973. The trouble about old-style quality, it seemed, was that it pandered to the worst kind of supply-driven management.

The engineers would make the product to the highest possible standard and price it accordingly. If the public were Philistine enough to turn it down, so much the worse for the public.

And so old-style quality got a bad name in business circles. It was all very well for artists to produce uncompromising masterpieces. The job of companies was to please the market.

Further damage was done by the rise of Japan. When Japanese cars, toys and television sets first reached the market in the US and UK, local manufacturers dismissed them as cheap trash.

Initially, so they were. But under the teaching of Edwards Deming, the Japanese were learning about the second definition of quality.

It then began to dawn on western customers that while Japanese cars might be tin cans, they did not keep breaking down, as did both British and American cars.

In time, of course, Japanese cars stopped being tin cans, and became stylish and comfortable vehicles instead. That is, they achieved old-style quality as well. As western manufacturers discovered to their cost, that was in some respects the easy bit. New-style quality was harder.

At this point, let us go back to M&S. We can imagine its executives getting restive by now. After all, they would not claim to sell the world's best suits or boeuf stroganoff: for that, you would go to Saville Row or a three-star restaurant.

But neither would they accept that their quality lies in mere consistency. One would expect a pair of M&S shoes or knickers to be the stated size, and to be efficiently cut and stitched. But one would also expect them to look and feel nice: to exhibit, in other words, a degree of quality in the older sense.

Thus quality acquires overtones of a third meaning: that of value for money. This is not an absolute concept. If I am selling a badly-pressed CD of unpopular songs from the 1960s, I do not confer quality on it merely by ensuring it is cheaper than any comparable CD. To qualify for this meaning, the article must be of a certain standard; and it should convey a sense, not of outright cheapness, but of being sold at a fair price.

Even so, this is slippery ground. The US fast foods group McDonald's, for instance, talks of its 'high quality food'.

But at 99c or 99p, its hamburgers are as close to absolute cheapness as any inhabitant of the developed world could reasonably desire.

They are also highly consistent. Eat a McDonald's anywhere around the world, and the result will be roughly similar – a logistical feat which is not be to be sneered at.

But as anyone who has eaten a really good American hamburger can attest, a McDonald's is also a long way from quality in the original sense. At best, it is a statistical Six Sigma job, with standard fries on the side.

McDonald's, like M&S, has had its ups and downs in the past year or two. Perhaps what is needed here is a slightly different view of quality: one which aims at consistency, but at the same time tries to achieve an old-fashioned type of excellence.

When Negley Farson was in Britain all those years ago, he worked briefly as a salesman for a Manchester engineering company which claimed to make the best chain in the world. When he received an inquiry from a prospective US customer, he instructed the works – in the usual American way – to make up a special sample.

The boss promptly appeared in Mr Farson's office, 'half out of his mind with rage', and banged the offending sample on the desk. 'Every foot of my chain', he shouted, 'is just as good as every other foot'.

Doubtless the company in question went bust in its turn. But Mr Farson's boss was ahead of his time.

Find out what people want and provide it consistently: but at the same time, make it the best you can.

It sounds a tall order. But in today's markets, customers are in charge. And why should they accept any less?

Source: Financial Times, 29 December 1998

8.4 How can the possession of an internationally recognised quality certification (e.g. BS 5750 or ISO 9000) affect customer satisfaction?

8.5 What techniques may be employed to ensure that the product achieves maximum possible customer satisfaction?

8.6 How does a brand identity help or hinder the search for customer satisfaction? Identify situations from both sides of this discussion.

Article 8.C   **FT**

Apple takes a fresh bite at the PC market

Roger Taylor on the iMac computer's appeal to design-conscious consumers

It comes in a translucent blue, futuristic conical case, is reviving the fortunes of Apple Computer, and could be pointing the way for the world's manufacturers of personal computers.

It is the iMac, a consumer computer costing $1,299 which has produced reactions from wild applause to raised eyebrows among the rest of the industry. This week brought the first fruits of that daring when Apple announced full-year profits for the first time in three years and said 278,000 iMacs had been sold in the six weeks since it was launched.

Apple, the company that introduced the personal computer in the 1970s and then revolutionised software in the 1980s by replacing computer instructions with simple 'icons' and a mouse, is now a minor player in an industry dominated by the rival Wintel standard.

But the early success of the iMac shows that Steve Jobs, the Apple founder who returned to rescue the company two years ago, retains his innovative flair.

It also suggests that other PC manufacturers may have to pay more attention to computer design and ease of use – the two prime characteristics of the iMac – if they are to attract technologically unsophisticated buyers.

In much of northern Europe and the US, the computer market is increasingly saturated. Every business has computerised and 40–50 per cent of households have PCs.

The need to upgrade machines and the development of the multi-PC household is keeping industry growth at about 10 per cent a year. But manufacturers are failing to make much of an inroad with the half of the population that does not yet own a computer.

Significantly, 30 per cent of iMac owners appear to be first-time computer buyers. So what is different about the machine? Certainly not its operating system, which breaks no significant new ground.

The most obvious change is the flair of its external design, being heavily emphasised by Apple in an advertising campaign with slogans such as 'Chic. Not Geek'.

But the real innovation is its 'plug and play' ease of use. For example, it comes in one piece, cutting down on the external wires that need attaching. And it has a 'universal serial bus' which allows printers and other devices to be plugged into any available socket. The computer will then sense its presence and reconfigure itself accordingly.

US PC ownership

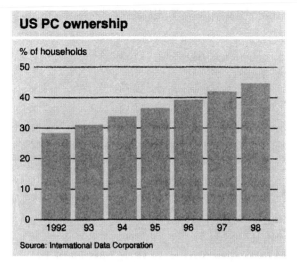

% of households

Source: International Data Corporation

The technology behind the bus has been around for some time and is generally available, but most computer builders still insist on selling machines with a full range of differently shaped plugs to ensure every possible printer and peripheral can be attached. Apple has sacrificed that ability in return for the certainty that when you have the right printer there is no fumbling around at the back of the machine wondering how to plug it in.

Similarly, speakers are built into the machine, rather than outside it. This means you cannot upgrade them, but it means two less wires to get confused about.

The lack of a floppy disk drive also annoys computer enthusiasts. But Apple argues that most people buy computers to get on to the internet or to play games. They do not need a floppy drive and will be grateful not to have to worry about one.

There are already signs of other companies moving in a similar direction. In August, Intel, the computer chip manufacturer, unveiled a prototype of a blue triangular computer and urged the industry to move in new directions.

Emachines, a Californian-based joint venture between two South Korean companies, has announced plans to launch a 'space-age monoputer' in four months' time. Monoputer is industry jargon to describe computers that come in one piece, such as the iMac. Emachines says its device will be available in 'magnesium', or coloured plastic.

To some, the sudden interest in colour is a distraction from the serious business of building beige computers. Compaq, the world's largest maker of personal computers, has no plans to start making its machines in pastel shades. Asked if he thought the iMac would have any influence on his company, Earl Mason, Compaq's chief financial officer, replied with a gruff 'No'.

But Andy Grove, chairman of Intel, which provided much of the underlying technology for the iMac, has complimented Apple on pointing the way forward for the industry.

Brian Halla, chief executive of National Semiconductor, the big chip manufacturer, believes the iMac is an important step in getting a broader range of consumers online, in preparation for the day when services such as banking, shopping and even telephony are delivered via computer networks.

However, analysts believe far greater changes are needed before the computer becomes ubiquitous. Bruce Stephen, PC analyst with IDC, the industry research group, does not believe there will be a real breakthrough until companies come up with genuine appliances – devices that are as easy to operate as a toaster or a microwave oven. Something you take out of the box, plug in and know how to use instinctively.

Mr Stephen predicts it will be several years before such 'information appliances' start to make an impact on the market.

Apple has no plans to move further away from the traditional computer market. Fred Anderson, chief financial officer, points out that the company has just gone through a painful period of retrenchment, cutting its product portfolio from 15 to four. But he says the company will continue to surprise with innovative design.

Early next year, it is due to launch its latest product: a cheap notebook aimed at the education market. Mr Anderson says it will be different. Who knows, maybe green?

Source: Financial Times, 17 October 1998

8.7 What role, if any, do you think the exterior design of a computer has in the purchase decision? Explain your answer.

8.8 The successful introduction of the iMac illustrates what type of demand from the market? Use the PLC model to substantiate your view.

8.9 Show why portfolio analysis led the Apple Corporation to produce iMac.

Article 8.D   FT

BBC plans Teletubbies joint venture

Corporation agrees deal with Japanese toy maker. By John Gapper

The BBC is to design and market cuddly toys for the first time as part of a global effort to make more money from merchandising based on its programmes.

The corporation has struck a deal with Tomy Company in Japan for toys based on its *Teletubbies* programme for young children.

The BBC has moved to take control of design and manufacturing of Teletubbies dolls, watches and backpacks for the Japanese market.

BBC Worldwide, the commercial arm of the corporation, intends to design its own merchandise – and commission Asian manufacturers to make it – for new products including its forthcoming children's programme *Tweenies*.

Under the deal with Tomy, one of the world's largest toy makers and distributors, BBC Worldwide will design the toys and commission their manufacture based on firm orders from Tomy, which will then distribute them.

Teletubbies, made by the independent production company Ragdoll Productions, will appear on television in Japan for the first time today under a deal signed with TV Tokyo, Tomy, Amuse Video, Shogakukan and Showa Note.

The initiative follows efforts by private sector companies that make and sell children's programmes to gain more revenue from merchandising. In the US market, merchandising revenues can outstrip those from programme sales.

Until now, the BBC has gained a margin of only about 5 per cent to 8 per cent of the trade value of merchandise from its programmes because it has licensed rights to other companies to design, make and distribute the goods. It hopes to double this margin by controlling the initial part of the sales process, which will allow it to contribute more to programme making. It also believes it can improve the quality of some of the merchandise.

Jeff Taylor, BBC Worldwide's director of global marketing and brand development, said that after paying rights holders from its 5 per cent to 8 per cent margin, it had been left with only about 2 per cent to put into programmes. It had also been concerned about maintaining quality. 'We do not just want to slap badges on any old products. We want products that reflect the values of the programmes we make, and of the BBC.'

Tomy is to take on the risk of over or underproduction of merchandise – a key risk in the toy market – since the BBC will only commission the manufacture of batches of toys when it has letters of credit from Tomy.

Mr Taylor said that *Teletubbies*, which is shown in 70 countries, had given the BBC more credibility with toy makers and distributors.

Source: Financial Times, 5 April 1999

FT

Teletubbies earn £32m for BBC commercial arm

Programme brand is corporation's most successful children's property.
By Cathy Newman

The BBC will no doubt give Tinky Winky, Dipsy, Laa Laa and Po a big hug. Revenues from the Teletubbies reached a record £32m in the last financial year, according to the annual report and accounts to be published by BBC Worldwide, the corporation's commercial arm tomorrow.

Revenues generated by selling the Teletubbies programme, videos, books and other merchandise around the world beat BBC Worldwide's own internal forecast of £29m, and were well ahead of last year's sales of £23m. The brand is the BBC's most successful children's property ever.

BBC Worldwide will also report this week that its cashflow has reached £81m, up from £75m the year before. That money is passed back to the BBC to supplement the corporation's £2.2bn annual income from the licence fee.

The record cashflow contribution is likely to revive controversy about the BBC's commercial activities. Critics question why the BBC is entitled to licence fee income when it also collects healthy profits from its commercial division.

Teletubbies, which was created by the independent production company, Ragdoll Productions, was launched into Asia and Europe in localised versions during the year. The programme can now be seen in 120 countries and territories in 20 languages. Other best-selling programmes internationally include *The Life of Birds, The Human Body, Vanity Fair* and *The Planets*.

BBC Worldwide is expected to unveil sales of £446m, and a 67 per cent increase in profit before tax to £20m for the year to the end of March.

The annual report will also disclose that Rupert Gavin, chief executive, was paid £249,000, which included a bonus of £50,000 in partial compensation for loss of earnings following his departure from British Telecommunications.

Mr Gavin joined BBC Worldwide last July and is charged with quadrupling BBC Worldwide's cashflow by 2006. That would see Worldwide increasing its contribution to the BBC from 5 per cent to 10 per cent of total funding.

Distribution of BBC Worldwide's wholly owned and joint venture channels grew from 115m to 230m homes around the world. Programme sales to joint venture channels and the global success of brands such as the Teletubbies, led to a rise in payments by BBC Worldwide to contributors such as writers, musicians and Equity artists of 23 per cent to £64.4m. In addition, payments to independent producers and co-producers increased by 50 per cent.

BBC Worldwide has two significant joint ventures with Flextech, the UK pay-TV group, and Discovery Communications, the US cable television giant.

Source: Financial Times, 22 June 1999

8.10 Why should product management, as reflected in the above articles, be important to a not-for-profit service organisation such as the BBC?

8.11 What opportunities can be exploited to extend the Teletubbies brand? Which techniques would best suit this line?

8.12 Place Teletubbies on their PLC and explain what options there are for this product's PLC to be extended to maintain its profitability for as long as possible. You may wish to compare this with the brand extension apparent in the Muppet characters.

9 New Product Development

In any consideration of managing a product or range of products, the case of new product development (NPD) inevitably raises its head. Any organisation that has the desire to grow and improve must have a system to bring forward new products to refresh or replace the offering currently being made to their customers. This must be achieved in the full knowledge of the implications behind such an activity, and most particularly the dangers inherent in change.

Accepting that change is forced upon us by the level of activity by others in any area of undertaking, and that therefore there is risk in not developing new product, the proper and effective management of NPD has as one of its aims the reduction of risk related to failure. As a simple rule of thumb, the more inventive the product development, the higher the risk of failure for all sorts of reasons ranging from the sheer cost of such an activity to the blow to a company's image and self-esteem should failure ensue. But the rewards can be enormous and can achieve superiority over rivals. Conversely, the less the invention content, the less the risk and probably the fewer the absolute rewards.

It follows then that if we are to be invention based we must possess the skills to translate such ideas into appropriate applications and effective commercialisation. Such a process might be best described as innovation. We therefore have the possibility to consider innovation as a technique in its own right, ranging from subtle changes (e.g. pack size or colour) to radical changes based on an understanding of the customer and how we might best provide something which supplies maximum satisfaction to the customer and to the organisation. We might even choose to adopt a follower mode, merely copycatting our competitors' NPD and selling on a cheaper price base, especially since we have had little or no research expenditure.

All these choices and all points between are available to us, and must be considered in some depth, with a particular regard being given to monitoring and control of developments as they proceed through the system, being ever prepared to stop such development if it begins to look unlikely to succeed. More than this, we have to be in a position to make changes to a product even after launch as we learn the lessons to be derived from exposure to the real world, and we can only achieve this by continuing evaluation of performance and customer perceptions. This surely demonstrates that NPD is not only continuous but also circular in aspect, the very act of new product development generating the need for product and new product development, *ad infinitum*!

In order to successfully complete the tasks in this chapter you will need to be familiar with:

- external macro/microenvironment;
- product life cycle;
- research and development management;
- consumer behaviour;
- new product classification;
- new product failure;
- new product development (NPD) process.

Article 9.A

FT

Bigger can be better . . . as well as faster

The days of departments being scattered around various buildings are coming to an end. Manufacturers are reaping the rewards of working under one roof, writes Haig Simonian

A new competitive benchmark has crept into motor industry talk. Rather than output, profits, or even their vehicles' performance, executives are starting to brag about the size of their technology centres.

Two of the largest have been taking final shape in recent months. In Guyancourt, on the western outskirts of Paris, 150 hectares of farmland have given way to a group of low-lying buildings forming Renault's new Technocentre.

Just south of Stuttgart, a similarly grandiose project is taking shape at Sindelfingen. There, Daimler-Benz is building a new headquarters for its car design and development work.

The two centres have much in common. Renault's Technocentre, which claims to have been the biggest building site in Europe, will eventually house 7,500 engineers, designers and supplier staff. Daimler-Benz's centre, though more compact, will have about as many on site when it fully opens in 2000. With the design team already installed, most of the new arrivals will come during next year.

Both complexes symbolise carmakers' determination to accelerate product development times and cut costs by concentrating and co-ordinating R&D much more efficiently than in the past.

Renault's FFr5.5bn Technocentre brings together the group's entire car development staff, formerly split between numerous Parisian locations. Daimler-Benz's DM1.3bn complex is as ambitious: the new site will eventually house personnel previously split between 18 sites. Separately, the company is centralising its 3,000-strong engine, gearbox and axle R&D activities at a second, smaller plant at Untertürkheim.

Approached via an artificial lake and fountains which would not look out of place at Versailles, the shallow slanting columns of Renault's Technocentre are far more striking than Daimler-Benz's more sober complex. The Germans have, however, allowed themselves a little more levity in the fan-shaped design centre styled by Italy's Renzo Piano, one of Europe's best known architects.

Whatever their external differences, the hearts of both centres are much the same. Both have beehive-like buildings housing the platform teams for their products. Unlike the functional structures of the past, this is where designers, engineers, manufacturing specialists and finance and marketing men come together in single platform or product groups. Renault even underlines the matrix nature of the teamwork work by calling this part of its complex the 'hive'.

Daimler-Benz, by contrast, refers to its centre as the 'city of short cuts', to emphasise the interconnection between different activities and the ease of access for those working there. 'We will become much faster in processes – although speed for itself was not our first aim,' says Helmut Petri, the group's head of passenger car development. 'Product development has already got 30 per cent faster, but we see scope to do more.'

Renault hopes the advantages of bringing together so many people on one site will eventually help to save FFr1bn a year on its R&D budget. Product development times are expected to be reduced to 36 months by 2000, eventually falling to 24 months.

Both centres exemplify an accelerating trend in the motor industry as carmakers try to concentrate their R&D activities and move from sequential development work in functional departments to 'simultaneous engineering', where the processes involved in developing a new model are conducted in parallel to save time.

The real model for the latest generation of design and R&D centres has been Chrysler's technical centre at Auburn Hills, north of Detroit. Now the group's headquarters after the construction of an adjoining 15-storey management tower, Chrysler's site pioneered the concept of grouping employees in multi-disciplinary teams rather than keeping them in functional departments.

Like Guyancourt, Chrysler's decision to build on a greenfield site also provided room for extensive outdoor facilities. Natural light is always useful to stylists, who often maintain not even the most powerful supercomputer modelling can beat seeing a planned new car in the daylight. For engineers, too, greenfield complexes offered scope for big adjacent test tracks. That simplifies logistics, and, incidentally,

should help to keep prototype products further away from the prying lenses of unwanted photographers.

Daimler-Benz, however, decided to shoehorn its new centre on spare land adjacent to the massive Sindelfingen works. 'We thought of going for a greenfield site, but eventually decided to put it next to the factory,' says Mr Petri. 'Conceptually, we wanted to shorten the distances.'

Whether brownfield or green, the most striking similarity between the French and German centres is that both boast an actual production line on site – still something of a novelty. The production facilities, although obviously far short of a full-scale factory, are meant to replicate the conditions of the shop floor where a new model will be built.

A history of botched launches across the industry bears witness to the wisdom of trying to get the job done properly from the start. Motoring history is littered with examples of carmakers having to add expensive changes, much slower ramp-ups to full production, or even costly recalls as debugging has had to be postponed to final production rather than the development stage.

'It is much better to make the changes at an early stage than only when the car goes into production,' says Patrick Le Quément, Renault's head of styling and quality. Renault is already reaping some of the benefits: full volume production of its new generation Clio compact hatchback, launched earlier this year, was reached within three months, compared with seven-and-a-half for the earlier Mégane.

Source: Financial Times, 3 December 1998

9.1 What specific characteristics of NPD are revealed in the article?

9.2 What particular benefits flow from such an integrated development process, and how might the consumer benefit?

9.3 Should NPD be industry based rather than company based? If not, why not?

A new generation of business

The Baylis radio manufacturers have extended and honed their commercial edge, says Meg Carter

The Freeplay wind-up radio, which uses technology devised by British inventor Trevor Baylis and was developed primarily for use in Africa, has become one of the best-known 'against the odds' product development stories of recent years.

Much less is known, however, about the company that was set up four years ago to manufacture and market the Freeplay radio: Cape Town-based BayGen Power Group. No longer a one-product company, BayGen is pioneering a range of self-powered technologies for use in developed and developing countries worldwide.

'We want to build a new industry for portable, self-powered consumer electronic products,' says Rory Stear, joint chairman and chief executive. 'We have developed our own technology and in the future we want to develop relationships with other inventors for new, naturally powered products.'

The Freeplay uses a spring storage mechanism which enables the generation and storage of electricity from human energy without the need for mains electricity or batteries. Although granted the licence for Mr Baylis' technology exclusively and in perpetuity, BayGen is developing different self-power technology in partnership with General Electric of the US.

The company has an exclusive licence to develop illumination, audio and toy products using a chemical-energy storage system conceived by GE, which now holds a one-third interest in the company. GE has also agreed to pay BayGen a share of revenues from other uses of the technology. That, with additional technology developed by BayGen's research and development team, will drive the company's business forward, Mr Stear explains.

'All our research and development is focused towards making future generations of products smaller, lighter and cheaper,' he adds. A Freeplay radio to be launched in January utilises both the Baylis' spring and GE's chemical storage systems and will be able to fit into the palm of a hand.

'We are looking to joint venture and licence our technology – like Intel or Dolby. Our ultimate goal, however, is to develop a stand alone, all purpose self-powered generator.'

Since the first Freeplay was launched in January 1996, BayGen has launched a second and third generation wind-up radio and a wind-up torch. The company is developing prototypes of a broad range of other self-powered products including a mobile phone generator, a land mine detector, a global positioning system and a computer.

BayGen is also working to incorporate self-power generation into a digital radio receiver for WorldSpace, the US digital radio group. WorldSpace plans to beam several hundred digital radio stations worldwide using three dedicated satellites, the first of which was launched last month.

The radio will be used to bring the digital age to people living where batteries and mains electricity are in intermittent or short supply. 'We have the ability to power the sets, but digital transmissions pose a particular problem as they consume power at three times the rate of conventional broadcasts,' Mr Stear says. 'We are now well-advanced in developing the Freeplay energy generation system to be three times more powerful.' The digital sets will also incorporate a solar panel.

To emphasise the company's broadening interests, BayGen will trade under a new name, Freeplay Group, from January. The aim is to associate the 'Freeplay' trademark with a variety of products that use self-generated power and to underline clearly the company's commercial ambitions.

BayGen needs better commercial positioning to satisfy its growth plans, Mr Stear explains. 'There is a danger in positioning ourselves as an aid company,' he say. 'We are not "do gooders". We are determined and commercially focused'.

Although the original Freeplay radio was aimed at aid agencies for use in the developing world, aid sales so far have represented only a small percentage of business. By developing joint ventures and partnerships with other organisations, the company hopes to develop its technology to produce newer, smaller and cheaper products.

Developing countries – where benefits of self-powered products tend be greatest, because power supplies are often intermittent – will remain an important focus, Mr Stear says. 'Strategically, this will be very important for us in the long run.' He expects sales in these markets will represent about 30 per cent of BayGen's business within the next three years.

However, during the next 12 months, BayGen will focus on distribution in the US – which now accounts for half of its sales – and in continental Europe. The UK market already accounts for a further 25 per cent of BayGen's sales. Important to the company's success will be research and development, Mr Stear adds. BayGen, which will turn over an estimated $20m when its current financial year ends next March, is re-investing 7 per cent of its income in R&D. 'For a company our size, this is an ambitious investment programme,' he says. 'But we are determined to make this new industry – self-powered consumer products – our own.'

Source: Financial Times, 21 December 1998

9.4 How might Baygen harness the power of the environmental lobby to secure their progress?

9.5 Calculate the development capital available to Baygen through their revenue. Do you think this will be sufficient to enable their progress? What other alternatives may be available to them?

9.6 What dangers might exist for Baygen in focusing so closely on one basic idea? How far should they diversify?

Article 9.C　　　　　　　　　　　　　　　　　　　　　　　　　　　**FT**

Futuristic menu for the kitchen

Thomas Barlow takes a look at why media-related researchers are focusing on ovens, dishwashers and refrigerators

What do kitchens have in common with radio, television, and the internet? In the Media Lab at the Massachusetts Institute of Technology, kitchens, perhaps surprisingly, have become the focus of 'media-related' research.

First, Joseph Kaye, a British-born student, invented a button-less and instruction-less microwave oven, which fixes cooking times by reading the barcodes on food packaging. Now, a team of research staff is working to create what they ambitiously call 'the kitchen of the future'.

There, food is tagged to enable radio-frequency identification, shopping is automated, and countertops are programmed to help you weigh ingredients and talk you through recipes. The research is still academic, even 'pie in the sky'. But that it is taking place at all – especially in such a place as MIT – hints at a wider phenomenon: kitchens have become a focus for innovation.

Consider only a few of the most recent products to hit the market. In cooking technology, there is the Flashbake oven: the first household oven to come out of Silicon Valley, and the first oven based on visible and near-visible light, producing traditional oven cooking quality at microwave speeds. Cliff Adams, chief executive of Quadlux, which manufactures the oven, calls it 'the first innovation in cooking since the microwave'. The oven has been available for a few years in the commercial cooking market, and the first household version became available in the US on December 1.

In dishwashing, the hot news is the dishwasher-in-a-drawer. Developed by the Australian company Fisher & Paykel, this will probably turn out to be the first of many products aimed specifically at the growing market of one- and two-person households. The smaller design also reflects an industry-wide drive to improve efficiency.

Super-efficiency is the principal design feature of Maytag's washing machine, the Neptune, which Maytag claims will save, on average, 6,000 gallons of water a year compared with conventional machines. Frigidaire has created an efficient and remarkably quiet dishwasher called the Precision Wash.

At the very least, most brands now offer a delay-start option to run machines at off-peak times to take advantage of lower energy costs.

In refrigeration, there is nothing quite so revolutionary. But Klondite makes a refrigerator with glass panelling so you can see what's inside. Sub Zero has engineered a refrigerator in a drawer. Frigidaire makes a big thing about the built-in water filtration system that comes with their refrigerator: so effective that it removes the giardia parasite, which can cause diarrhoea.

Maytag has introduced something that seems so obvious, it is a wonder no-one thought of it before. They call it the elevator shelf: you twiddle a knob and one of the shelves in your fridge adjusts up and down.

In cookware, things have never looked better for the consumer, says Hugh Rushing, executive vice-president of the Cooking Manufacturers Association of America. Non-stick pans, once seen as disposable, now frequently come with a lifetime guarantee. Stainless steel cookware is now commonly layered, with aluminium or some other high-conductivity material sandwiched on the inside to improve heating times. And Hemo, based in the West Midlands, has made cooking safer with an ovenproof phenolic plastic that stays cool to the touch during cooking.

What has sparked this flurry of innovation? One of the problems faced by manufacturers of kitchen appliances is that product lifetimes are long. A typical household will keep a refrigerator for 10–15 years; a washing machine may not be upgraded until it breaks.

Home appliance manufacturers are beginning to realise that there is a lesson here to be learned from the computer industry. Think how many people have upgraded their 286-based machines to a Pentium. Innovation does not only win you market share from your competition, it also prevents market saturation. In effect, it can expand the size of a market.

Some appliance companies have explicitly tried to follow this model. Maytag, for example, has gone all out to sell itself as an innovative company. Even its advertising in the US has stood out for being quirky and unusual. Linda Eggress, manager of marketing and media relations, says the company wants to draw consumers into the appliance market, rather than have them waiting for appliances to wear out.

The strategy seems to have worked. Although Neptune is a top-end product (it sells in the US for $1,099, at quite a premium over other machines), Maytag has had to upgrade production three times since its launch to meet the demand.

Where are the ideas coming from? Jenne Westerberg, inventor of the Flashbake oven, was inspired in a pizza restaurant by the observation that pizzas have similar relative dimensions to computer chips. That led him to wonder whether the high-intensity light used to fuse computer circuits could be used to cook pizza.

None of the other household innovations mentioned have origins quite so picaresque. One curious thing that many of the designs *do* have in common, however, is cross-fertilisation from different cultures.

Many of the high-efficiency washers coming on to the market were inspired by the threat of regulation by the US Department of Energy. However, the technology employed frequently turns out to be a US adaptation of European engineering. Both the Neptune and the Precision Wash represent US improvements on what are essentially European designs. Tony Evans at Frigidaire says the Precision Wash drew on Electrolux technology. (Electrolux of Sweden has owned Frigidaire for the past decade.)

Even at the Media Lab, an interaction with a foreign culture proved beneficial.

Mr Kaye received his inspiration for the button-less microwave oven while living in Japan. There, unable to read Kanji, he came to the conclusion that 'if there's a lot of writing on something, it is probably a bad design'.

That, however, is not a philosophy that is universal among appliance designers. Toastmaster recently launched a toaster that prints 'I love you' or 'Good morning' on your toast. Perhaps the kitchen is not such an unusual subject of research for a Media Laboratory, after all.

Source: Financial Times, 12 December 1998

9.7 How does NPD benefit the organisation in terms of the overall market?

9.8 With regard to the consumer behaviour of the markets discussed, how could this be influenced and changed by such NPD?

9.9 Illustrate how NPD can serve to extend or refresh the PLC of existing products, and how such research may shorten the PLC in some cases by hastening the demise of existing products.

Article 9.D   FT

Nintendo's errors could well end up costing it the game

Mistakes and delays by the Japanese electronic games maker have left it way behind its rivals, writes Paul Abrahams

Last Christmas was not a season of good cheer for Nintendo. The unit of the Japanese electronic games group responsible for domestic sales of its flagship 64-bit games console, the N64, offered a case-study of how not to launch a new product.

Yoshi's Story was the business' hottest software title and supposed to become a blockbuster. Instead, mistakes in management, manufacturing and distribution resulted in what the company admits was a calamitous performance.

Critical delays are becoming an unfortunate habit at Nintendo. In August, the group postponed the launch of its new hardware platform, the N64DD, from December until June. In the meantime, Sony, with its 32-bit PlayStation, has cemented its market lead, while Sega is scheduled to launch its 128-bit Dreamcast console next month.

Christmas and new year will be critical to Nintendo, because the company generates about 40 per cent of all domestic N64 sales during this period.

Last year's cock-up was particularly disappointing since reviewers and games players loved *Yoshi's Story*. But the game was delivered late because software designers refused to let go of the product; manufacturing volumes were too small to meet demand; and the limited stocks that did reach distributors went to the wrong sales channels.

The result was a dismal sales performance, and within a month of launch *Yoshi's Story* was being discounted by more than 50 per cent. 'Last year was truly disastrous,' admits Hiroshi Imanishi, a general manager at Nintendo.

The company is determined not to shoot itself in the foot this year.

The most important launch this autumn will be *Legend of Zelda*, a reworking of a classic game. Japanese television has been bombarding consumers with advertisements for *Legend*, which was originally scheduled for release last year and is now due to be launched on November 14. Another important issue will be *Ogre Battle 3*, due for release in December.

However, these titles may not be enough. Critics argue that Nintendo's broader software strategy is flawed. The domestic licensing department seems obsessed by quality over quantity, preferring to decide what the public will like rather than leaving it to the market. That makes life difficult for software designers. By March this year, there were only 64 titles for the N64, against more than 500 for the Sony PlayStation.

The number of titles is vital because the games console market has changed from being hardware-driven to software-driven: Moody's, the US ratings agency, says software was key to the success of Sony's PlayStation.

Mr Imanishi admits that Sony invested a lot more than Nintendo in software development. The result was that some significant software developers – including Square, makers of *Final Fantasy VII*, and Enix, designers of *Dragon Quest* – defected to Sony.

The relationship with the developers has also been damaged by repeated delays to the N64DD, which was originally to have been released at the end of 1996.

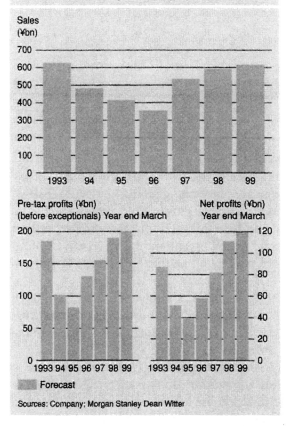

Will Yoshi's Story end happy ever after?

Sales (¥bn)

Pre-tax profits (¥bn)
(before exceptionals) Year end March

Net profits (¥bn)
Year end March

Forecast

Sources: Company; Morgan Stanley Dean Witter

Nintendo may be running out of time. The N64's product cycle is nearing its end, and in the short-term the company has no replacement. The biggest problem is next month's launch of Sega's 128-bit Dreamcast machine, which will use a double-density CD-Rom drive with more than one gigabit of memory – allowing much faster and more complicated graphics.

Although Mr Imanishi says he does not think Dreamcast will be 'a fatal blow', Nintendo is forecasting domestic sales of only 2m N64 console units this financial year and many analysts believe that could be optimistic.

As for international sales, these will be hit by the yen's recent appreciation. Last year, the group used Y132 to the dollar for its consolidated results, compared with Y115 yesterday. Brokers Morgan Stanley Dean Witter estimate Nintendo loses Y1.9bn ($16m) in revenue and profit for every Y1 appreciation against the dollar, and predict earnings before interest, tax, depreciation and amortisation this year will be Y190bn.

Nintendo is no longer a one-product company. Its Pocket Monster GameBoy has been a huge success, selling 9m units, a performance boosted by the *Pocket Monster* animated movie. Additions to the series – *Pocket Monster Gold and Silver* – are being launched soon. In addition, strong sales are expected from the autumn launch of Game Boy Colour, a hand-held product.

But despite its efforts to diversify, Nintendo remains dependent on its mainstream consoles and software business. The N64 is expected to generate 67 per cent of parent company sales this year. Nintendo is in no immediate danger – its balance sheet is strong – but it will live or die by its game consoles business and for the moment the outlook is bleak.

Source: Financial Times, 17 October 1998

9.10 You have been engaged by Nintendo to investigate their problems, and to suggest solutions to them. Using this article and some secondary research to establish comparisons with similar organisations, prepare a concise report for the board, showing clearly where mistakes and delays led to loss of market share, and what may be done to regain lost ground.

10 Price

For all its apparent simplicity and obviousness, price is one of the most exciting and dynamic tools available to the marketer. Price is the manifestation of much of the effort expended in researching the marketplace, developing product in its wider sense, the establishment of positioning in the target customer's mind, all coming together to match the requirements of the customer and the organisation. The 'proper' price is the one which returns the expected reward to the organisation and yet sits comfortably within the customer's willingness to pay, being neither too expensive nor too cheap.

Price, of course, has a relationship to the actual cost of production, but this is often of minor significance in the final pricing decisions, this acknowledging the fact that price is a leading indicator of the perceived value of the product itself, in the mind of both the supplying organisation and of the customer.

Remember also that price is not always money related, since there is an element of 'cost' incurred by the customer in finding the product and 'risking' the purchase or adoption itself. The marketer's job is to reduce these 'costs' as far as possible and to ensure at the same time that the end result in the customer's mind is agreement as to quality and fitness for promoted purpose with regard to the price asked in return. The end result must also be that the organisation is able to express satisfaction in terms of the desired profit as they see it.

So we see that price and its implications are subject to forces both within and without the organisation, has to be firmly rooted in a thorough understanding of internal and external factors and a detailed knowledge of customers' needs and perceptions with particular reference as to how these may be addressed and communicated.

Without being highfalutin about the process of establishing the right price, this is based in psychology and how the mind of the customer works in making a judgement between one product and another. Notwithstanding how excellent the product might be in all respects, if we pitch the price too high the customer may not be prepared to pay as a way of securing the benefits sought. Conversely, if we pitch the price too low the customer may consider it to be so cheap as to be not worth having, in spite of all we may say about the product in terms of high value for money. Throw into this equation the idea that some products are promoted as being of high price, not high intrinsic value, the price being justified by exclusivity. As if all this was not enough, consider how supply and demand affect price and are very often entirely outside our control and yet we have to try to navigate these stormy waters.

In order to successfully complete the tasks in this chapter you will need to be familiar with:

- demand curves;
- price elasticity;
- customer price assessment;
- price elasticity of demand;
- external and internal influences of pricing companies.

Article 10.A

FT

Travel companies hold duty-free prices

By Richard Tomkins

Airport and ferry operators say they will absorb most of the extra cost for travellers of the abolition, on Thursday, of duty-free sales within the European Union.

BAA, the airport group, and P&O Stena Lines, the ferry operator, said they would reduce profit margins, hoping to make up the difference by selling higher volumes of goods.

P&O pointed out that travellers are allowed to buy only limited quantities of duty-free goods but there are no limits on duty-paid goods bought for personal use.

'We will be moving from a low-volume, high-margin situation, in which people bought a litre of spirits and 200 cigarettes, to a high-volume, low-margin situation, based on people buying as much as they like,' said P&O.

BAA said it was so confident of big increases in sales that it planned to build a further 150,000 sq ft of retail space at its UK airports over the next 18 months – an increase of 15 per cent.

The two companies outlined their plans as travellers rushed to take advantage of the last weekend of duty-free shopping.

P&O, which operates the 'booze cruise' ferry route between Dover and Calais, said: 'We had a very busy weekend, with many of our sailings fully booked.'

About 80 per cent of P&O's passengers on the Dover-Calais route are British, partly because UK taxes on alcohol and tobacco are higher than in France. P&O said bookings were about 20 per cent higher than usual.

After midnight on Wednesday, goods bought by people travelling within the EU – except those bought for consumption on board – will be subject to the same duty and taxes as those applying on land.

P&O, however, said prices of spirits in its on-board shops would be unchanged from duty-free levels. A bottle of Famous Grouse scotch whisky would cost £12.25, about £6 less than the UK high street price.

The price of 200 Benson & Hedges cigarettes would rise from £16.95 to between £20 and £21 because the company could not absorb all the extra tax. But that would still be less than the high street price of £38.

P&O would keep prices down by selling only in French waters, where taxes were lower. 'In many ways, we're taking on the French high street and the French hypermarket,' the company said. 'We're bringing French hypermarket prices 12 miles nearer Dover.'

BAA said it had agreed with its retail partners to absorb all the $17^{1}/_2$ per cent value-added tax and most other duty that would become payable on goods bought in its UK airport stores.

'Ninety per cent of traditional duty and tax-free products will be available to EU passengers at the same prices,' it said. Exceptions would be cigarettes and certain brands of spirits.

The UK Customs & Excise says it will assume that up to 800 cigarettes and 10 litres of spirits are for personal use. Levels above that may be questioned.

Source: Financial Times, 28 June 1999

10.1 Using the external influences on a pricing decision, produce an analysis of the travel companies' pricing policy.

10.2 How might airport and ferry operators use demand curves to maximise their potential return?

10.3 The customers' perception/assessment of price needs to be understood. How and for what reasons?

10.4 Draw out the similarities between airlines and ferry operators with regard to their use of the 7P's of the marketing mix, and their ticketing arrangements.

Article 10.B   **FT**

Pressure grows on Dixons over its PC pricing policy

Criticism of high street retailer comes at a time of increased competition in the sector, write Paul Taylor and Peggy Hollinger

The Consumers Association yesterday called on the government to investigate 'Dixons' monopoly position in the high street PC market.'

The association claimed British consumers appeared to be getting a 'raw deal' and said the competition authorities should force Dixons, the electrical retailer, to explain its pricing policy.

'Dixons controls over half the high street distribution of PCs and they seem to be using this enormous market power to keep prices to consumers high.'

The call came after accusations by Intel, the world's largest semiconductor chipmaker, that high prices charged for home PCs by Dixons were holding back PC sales in the UK.

Intel's claims echoed those of leading home PC makers such as Compaq Computer and Fujitsu that PC buyers in Britain are paying too much for their machines.

Yesterday Dixons rejected the claims and accused Intel of abusing its dominant position in the market for microprocessors.

'If anybody is profiteering in this market place start by looking at Intel,' said John Clare, Dixon's chief executive. Mr Clare insisted Dixons made lower margins on its PC sales than on any other product category.

He also dismissed claims that PC prices in the UK were on average higher than in continental Europe.

However, Peter Day who runs the PC Home Tracking service for Woking-based Inteco, the market research company, says evidence shows British consumers are paying more for their PCs. Although UK consumers tend to buy more powerful and fully featured machines, overall specifications are 'not enough to justify the price difference compared to, say Germany,' he says.

He believes first-time buyers in the UK are less knowledgeable than on the continent and, 'the inexperienced are more likely to buy from high street retail'. This means they are more susceptible to a sales pitch for a higher-priced machine.

Analysts say British consumers are also less price conscious than in other European markets. For

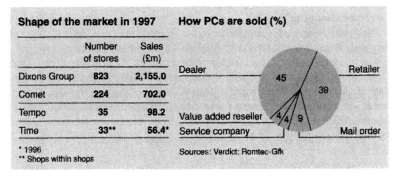

Shape of the market in 1997		
	Number of stores	Sales (£m)
Dixons Group	823	2,155.0
Comet	224	702.0
Tempo	35	98.2
Time	33**	56.4*

* 1996
** Shops within shops

How PCs are sold (%)

Dealer 45 / Retailer 39 / Value added reseller 4 / 4 / 9 / Service company / Mail order

Sources: Verdict; Romtec-Gfk

example, the German market is notoriously price-driven having been hit by price wars among big supermarkets selling PCs in bulk.

Aldi, a big German supermarket, last week reduced prices to DM1998 (£716) per computer, triggering huge queues at its stores. It sold 200,000 machines in one day.

In the UK Mr Day says the higher proportion of high-income households buying PCs creates a vicious circle. 'The consumers can afford it so the prices stay higher.'

According to Phil Burnham, senior research analyst at Romtec-GfK, the market research company, about 2.75m desktop PCs were sold in Britain last year. These include home PCs and corporate sales via all channels.

Consumers buy home PCs through three main channels in the UK. Direct from the manufacturer, for example from Dell Computer or Eversham Micros; through independent mail-order companies such as Action Computer and Software Warehouse; and through retailers, such as PC World, Dixons, Comet or Tempo.

Dixons, which owns PC World, Dixons and Currys and acquired the Byte chain of PC stores in April, claims it has only 14 to 15 per cent of the UK PC market excluding sales to big companies.

However, rivals say the Dixons Group controls about 45 per cent of home PC sales sold through high street stores. They also claim its hold on the high street has created opportunities for others to come in with lower-priced machines.

One distributor said: 'Because their prices are high, we can sell significantly below them.' But while small, independent PC resellers may be able to match or undercut Dixons, they lack the marketing muscle that gives Dixons a significant advantage.

Dixons now faces perhaps its biggest challenge in the PC market with the cash-rich British supermarkets entering the fray. Tesco and Asda have sold cut-price PCs in recent months.

And Time Computer Systems, a traditional mail-order supplier, has in the past six months increased its retail outlets from 40 to 120.

These moves forced Dixons to sell its own cut-priced machines. However, rivals suggest less-informed UK consumers remain susceptible to the sales pitch. 'Dixons is not making a massive margin on its entry level computer, they use that as a loss leader,' said one rival. 'They then rely on the salesman to "upsell" the customer into a higher-price machine with a higher profit margin.' *Additional reporting by Graham Bowley in Frankfurt.*

Source: Financial Times, 2 November 1998

10.5 Identify and discuss those factors which you think may influence price sensitivity in the PC market.

10.6 How do you think the customer views the pricing tactics of the Dixons group?

10.7 Are the customers influenced by these views and how?

10.8 Identify and discuss the price elasticity curve in the PC market.

Article 10.C **FT**

Drugs pricing shake-up proves to be a bitter pill

Industry warns that threat of government interference may lead to exodus of groups, writes David Pilling

Talks between the government and the pharmaceuticals industry over drug pricing are getting dirtier. Last month the Department of Health threw down the gauntlet by hinting that it might be prepared to scrap a 40-year-old voluntary agreement with the industry in favour of a mandatory scheme designed to rein in the NHS drugs bill of about £5bn.

Far from being cowed, the industry has responded with a report suggesting that taxes and government interference are driving drugs companies away in search of friendlier environments.

Pharmaceuticals sales

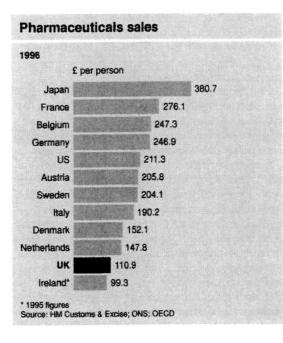

1996

£ per person

Japan	380.7
France	276.1
Belgium	247.3
Germany	246.9
US	211.3
Austria	205.8
Sweden	204.1
Italy	190.2
Denmark	152.1
Netherlands	147.8
UK	110.9
Ireland*	99.3

* 1995 figures
Source: HM Customs & Excise; ONS; OECD

UK pharmaceuticals trade*

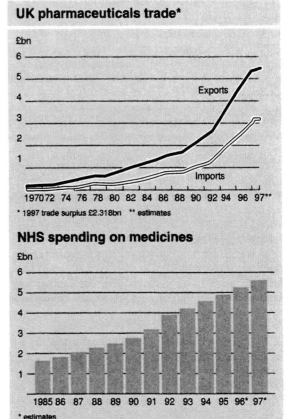

* 1997 trade surplus £2.318bn   ** estimates

NHS spending on medicines

* estimates
Source: HM Customs & Excise; ONS; OECD

The report by PricewaterhouseCoopers, the accountancy firm, was commissioned by the Association of the British Pharmaceutical Industry. It said 7,000 manufacturing jobs in the sector had been lost in the last six years, a decline of 20 per cent. Trevor Jones, director-general of the ABPI, said if the government kept 'using crude instruments to constantly whack the industry, then it will choose to go somewhere else'.

There were already signs of the exodus from Britain, particularly to Ireland, hitting the country's balance of trade, he said. Based on the first four months of 1998, the ABPI predicts the trade surplus in pharmaceuticals will slip to £2bn this year against £2.3bn in 1997, the first decline in a decade. Pharmaceuticals are the UK's third-biggest export.

Dr Jones said the reversal was not due to the strength of sterling but reflected a structural decline in manufacturing. This was due to high corporate taxes and unease at some aspects of the Pharmaceutical Price Regulation Scheme, whose terms are the subject of negotiations.

He said the PPRS, which caps profits according to capital employed, acted as a disincentive to companies using Britain as an export base. The more goods they exported, the less capital they were deemed to have spent in the UK, thereby reducing their allowable profits, he said.

In addition, 'a number of demand-side measures have crept in', said Dr Jones, including a mandatory price reduction forced through in the mid-1990s and the refusal to prescribe certain new (and expensive) drugs on the NHS. 'All of this is tantamount to increased levels of government interference.'

The PPRS is designed to pursue the seemingly conflicting aims of encouraging a strong and profitable UK-based pharmaceuticals industry while ensuring drugs are reasonably priced. The UK has shunned the free pricing of the US and the price-fixing of continental Europe in favour of a scheme that seeks to control overall profits. In effect, this allows drug companies to recoup research and development costs by charging high prices for new products and lower ones for drugs nearing patent expiration.

Insofar as the UK has the biggest drugs industry in the world after the US, the PPRS is seen to have served Britain well. But the scheme is regarded as favouring UK companies, notably Glaxo Wellcome, SmithKline Beecham and Zeneca, and companies with significant R&D investment in Britain, over their foreign counterparts. US companies, in particular, view the scheme as an anachronism from an era of state control.

A senior executive from a big US company described the PPRS 'as unacceptable meddling in our profit and loss account' and 'based on a premise that is about 20 years out of date'. The industry was organised globally and the UK, which only accounted for 4 per cent of world drug sales, could not expect to trap investment within the country, he said.

Drugs groups such as Warner Lambert of the US have been lured from Britain to Ireland where, the ABPI estimates, 9,000 manufacturing jobs have been created in the past few years. Warner Lambert shifted 2,000 jobs to Ireland, where corporation tax is 10 per cent.

The ABPI insists timing of the PwC report is 'fortuitous' and not designed as a bargaining chip. But the implied threat in the survey – *Driving out the golden goose?* – will not be lost on government negotiators.

Source: Financial Times, 20 October 1998

10.9 In a free market economy, why is it necessary for the government to control prices and profits in this way?

10.10 How do such control mechanisms distort the mechanism of market and strategic pricing?

10.11 Should the consumer be aware of the actual prices of drugs rather than have them filtered through the NHS prescription systems?

10.12 Using the STEP framework, construct an analysis of the UK pharmaceutical market.

11 Pricing Strategies

Having established that price is a dynamic part of the marketing discipline we now turn to the process of making decisions, and how price is part of a significant group of strategic tools available to decision makers. Price setting relates closely to matching the organisation's objectives, whether they are set by reference to financial targets or sales targets, turnover or volume. We may have financial targets which set out profit or turnover, volume or cash flow requirements. Sales targets express the organisation's desire to achieve a particular market share, the position within a specified market or aims in terms of volume.

We need also to consider the outside world with special regard to the actions and reactions of our competitors. After all, it is unlikely that the competition will sit quietly while we make decisions which can affect their own situation within the market. Price wars break out on occasions when one party makes a pre-emptive price reduction in an attempt to snatch market share, an action which is then matched by their competitors in order to maintain their own position. Examples may be cited such as the recent bread wars, and previous baked beans wars waged between the major supermarket groups in England. These situations may exist as a deliberate policy or they may be forced upon organisations as a result of difficult trading conditions and are witness to the use of price as a survival mechanism.

Under more orderly conditions the setting of price is as a result of careful consideration and decision making as part of a broader and longer-term strategy, but we should be aware that price can be used as a rapid and simple method of changing position or gaining market share, and thus demonstrates the versatility of price as a part of the overall strategy of an organisation in its longer-term aims. Yet at the same time it can be used at the other end of the spectrum as an emergency survival technique, and all points between.

In order to successfully complete the tasks in this chapter you will need to be familiar with:

- service sector pricing;
- market dominance;
- market niching;
- pricing methods;
- pricing strategies;
- pricing adjustments.

Low-cost, no-frills airlines tighten seat belts

Flying cut-price skies is good for consumers but overcrowding is beginning to drive profits down, reports Michael Skapinker

At the beginning of the year, Andrew Light, aviation analyst at Salomon Smith Barney, was enthusiastic about Virgin Express, the Brussels-based low-cost airline.

This week, he cut his annual pre-tax profits forecast by more than 90 per cent – from BFr743m to BFr65m (£13m to £1.2m).

Debonair, a low-cost carrier based at London's Luton airport, floated on Easdaq, the European stock exchange, last year.

Its shares were three times subscribed, raising £28.2m. Over the past two years, Debonair has lost a total of £32.3m.

Is Europe's fledgling low-cost airline industry about to crash barely a year after it first took off?

Probably not – although there might be some casualties.

Europe's no-frills carriers have demonstrated there is no shortage of people who are prepared to fly if the fares are low enough. When Ryanair, the Irish low-cost carrier, began flying from Dublin to London in 1985, about 1m people flew between the two cities every year. This year, about 4m are expected to travel between them.

The question is how many new carriers – most of which emerged to take advantage of last year's liberalisation of Europe's skies – can serve the demand for cut-price travel while still making a profit. The experience of the US, which deregulated its airline industry 20 years ago, suggests few of the European carriers will make it.

Only Southwest Airlines, the model for several of the European low-cost carriers, has thrived in the US. A report this year by the US Department of Transportation said others had been pushed out of business by the large carriers, which had reduced fares and increased capacity until the new-comers had disappeared.

Starting a new airline is not for the bashful, and all Europe's best-known independents – Virgin Express, Debonair, EasyJet and Ryanair – insist they will be among the survivors, in spite of competition from Go, British Airways' new low-cost offshoot.

Jim Swigart, chief executive of Virgin Express, which is 51 per cent owned by Richard Branson's Virgin group, says his problems have been caused by a shortage of pilots in Belgium, along with the country's high social costs. Virgin Express has now formed a new Irish subsidiary, based in Shannon, and hopes to register its pilots there. Mr Swigart says it will be easier to recruit pilots if they know they are going to pay Irish rather than Belgian taxes.

Virgin Express is not going to move its operating base from Brussels. It depends on its hub there for its most important contract – flying on behalf of Sabena, the Belgian carrier. Virgin Express operates flights from Brussels to London, Barcelona and Rome which were previously flown by Sabena. The Belgian airline sells tickets on Virgin Express flights and its passengers sit in a separate business class section.

Mr Light believes that if Virgin Express manages to move its pilots' contracts to Ireland, the airline could still succeed. 'The market is there and Virgin has a great brand name.'

So, who will be the first casualty? Analysts have expressed concern about Debonair, but Franco Mancassola, its chairman, says he will next month unveil the first quarterly profit.

Debonair's strategy is different from some of the other low-cost carriers. The airline offers a free snack and tea or coffee – for which the others charge. Next week, it is introducing a business class section. Mr Mancassola, who previously worked in the US airline industry, believes the Southwest no-frills model will not work in Europe. 'The European traveller is more sophisticated,' he says.

EasyJet and Ryanair disagree and follow the Southwest model closely. Ryanair is Europe's most successful low-cost carrier, with pre-tax profits last year of I£37.1m (£34.7m), an increase of 51 per cent.

Michael O'Leary, Ryanair's chief executive, rates EasyJet as Europe's next best cut-price airline. Mr O'Leary argues, however, that Ryanair's practice of flying to secondary airports in cities such as Paris and Brussels will be more successful than EasyJet's strategy. Although EasyJet operates from Luton, it flies to central airports in cities such as Amsterdam and Barcelona.

'Secondary airports are too remote for my liking,' says Stelios Haji-Ioannou, EasyJet's chairman. 'You can still convince some people to fly there, but you have to give them a bigger discount.'

EasyJet is privately-owned, with a holding company registered in Jersey and a UK-based operating company. The operating company lost £3.3m before tax last year, but Mr Haji-Ioannou says the entire operation will be profitable this time.

He argues that European low-cost carriers will have a higher survival rate than those in the US. New technology will help them to lower distribution costs; EasyJet takes 10 per cent of its bookings over the internet.

Mr Haji-Ioannou says European regulators also seem more prepared to protect new airlines than their US counterparts were. When the European Commission began investigating EasyJet's complaints against KLM, Mr Haji-Ioannou says the Dutch carrier behaved less aggressively towards him.

He has been given permission by the high court in London to challenge BA's support for Go. Next week, he is going to Brussels to complain about Go's cost-cutting on the London-Edinburgh route. 'The European authorities are much more on the ball,' he says.

Source: Financial Times, 22 October 1998

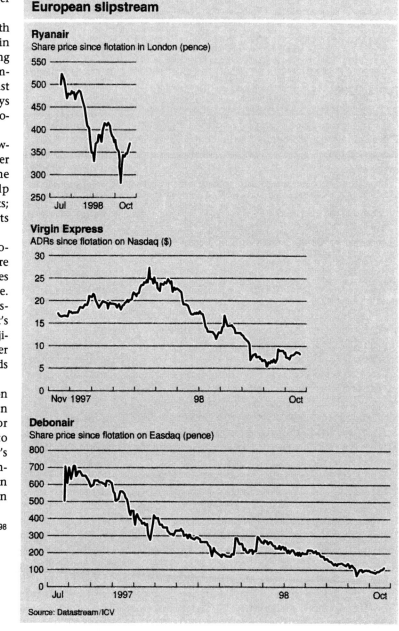

European slipstream

Ryanair
Share price since flotation in London (pence)

Virgin Express
ADRs since flotation on Nasdaq ($)

Debonair
Share price since flotation on Easdaq (pence)

Source: Datastream/ICV

11.1 Viewing the low-cost, no-frills airline market in the long term, do you think there is a future for a number of players in this market? Present your argument for entry into this particular segment.

11.2 The article illustrates some of the problems facing low-cost operators. How could such an operator differentiate itself from its competitors?

11.3 Established airlines have reacted in a number of ways to these new market entrants. Discuss these tactics, and describe how the much smaller airlines have countered these actions.

11.4 Describe the market segment which was identified and led to the establishment of low-cost airlines.

Article 11.B   FT

Increased fares buoy P&O Stena

By Charles Batchelor

Higher passenger fares helped P&O Stena Line to a profit of £3.5m in the first quarter of 1999, but this was before a one-off charge of £10.4m resulting from the closure of its Newhaven-Dieppe service.

The company, formed by the merger of the cross-Channel activities of P&O of the UK and Stena of Sweden, carried 2.2m passengers during the three-month period, accounting for 36 per cent of the total market. It also carried 289,000 trucks and containers, some 50 per cent of the market.

Comparable figures were not available because the merger did not take effect until March 10 of last year. The first quarter is normally the least busy of the year for tourist traffic. In the final quarter of 1998 P&O Stena made pre-tax profits of £22.3m, making a total of £54.5m over the 9½-month period when restructuring costs were £25.2m.

Yields from tourist and freight traffic increased significantly and freight volumes were particularly strong in the first quarter of 1999, the company said. A price rise for freight shipments was successfully introduced in January.

'The medium and longer term outlook is highly positive,' it added.

P&O Stena operates two routes, between Dover and Calais and a freight-only route between Dover and Zeebrugge. It shut its lossmaking Newhaven-Dieppe sailing in January. Operating profits during the quarter were £8.5m before interest and other charges of £5m.

Before the merger, brought about by the opening of the Channel tunnel in 1994, the two companies faced declining profits or losses, offset by duty-free and other sales, which are due to end on June 30.

Source: Financial Times, 27 April 1999

11.5 What factors influence the obvious price insensitivity of this market, and what limitations do you think there might be?

11.6 Might there be an opportunity for a low-cost operator in this market? What problems would they have to overcome, and how are the existing operators likely to react?

11.7 By reference to the fare structures of the competing organisations in this market, show what similarities may exist between them. What other sectors of the travel industry may they be compared with and in what ways?

Tesco prepares to defend pricing policies

Britain's biggest food retailer faces at least a year of uncertainty as competition officials investigate. Peggy Hollinger reports

It has not been a happy week for food retailers, with the Office of Fair Trading confirming plans to refer the industry to the Competition Commission. This means it will face at least a year of uncertainty – and possibly two if, as a result of the findings, any new restrictions have to be tested before being implemented.

Tesco, the market leader, will inevitably face questioning about the implications when it reports its annual results on Tuesday.

However, it is unlikely to have much to add to its statement this week when it declared: 'The Competition Commission will find what Tesco and our customers already know: we champion the consumers' cause.'

Like other food retailers, Tesco believes it operates in a highly competitive market. Margins throughout the industry have fallen over the past five years, costs have mounted and price increases have been virtually impossible to implement.

Yet the company continues to be accused of exploiting its market power at the expense of consumers and suppliers. No doubt Terry Leahy, the chief executive, will deny this robustly on Tuesday.

But while the inquiry is important for the industry, it will not be all that concerns shareholders as they read through the numbers next week. Tesco is expected to show a 6.5 per cent improvement in

profits, to about £870m, on a 6 per rise in sales, to an estimated £17.1bn.

The profitability of the growing overseas businesses will be a key focus. More specifically, analysts suggest that investors are becoming disillusioned over the group's progress in eastern Europe. 'Everyone was oversold into Tesco last year because they had a good story on eastern Europe and good cashflow to invest in developing markets,' says one analyst.

'But that story is beginning to look a little less attractive than people thought because they have only really cracked the nut in Hungary and the real gem is Poland, where they face greater competition.'

Even so, Tesco is the only UK supermarket group with any real international exposure; it operates in Thailand and South Korea as well as Europe. This is still considered an advantage, particularly in light of the clouds hanging over the UK industry.

At home, Tesco is expected to show continuing like-for-like sales growth. It will also be questioned on its plans for the Club Card loyalty scheme, which is to be relaunched later this year to improve rewards to its biggest spenders. But the scheme costs about £140m a year already, and investors will certainly want to know more about any extra outlay.

More encouragingly, analysts are expecting Leahy to signal somewhat better prospects for food retailers this year than they had in the past 12 months. 'This time last year, he said things would get tougher – and he was right,' said one, citing deflation, the slowdown in consumer spending and aggressive price campaigns by the biggest players as contributing to difficult trading conditions. 'I think he will agree that things are looking stable, or at least they are not deteriorating and they might even be getting a little better,' the analyst added.

Tesco will not, however, be commenting on current trading, the quarterly statement that previously has allowed investors to judge progress by the big four supermarket groups in the race for supremacy. Like others, it has decided just to report quarterly results.

This, in its view, negates the need for statements. But the omission could take the one bit of excitement out of what is expected to be a fairly straightforward set of results.

Source: Financial Times, 10 April 1999

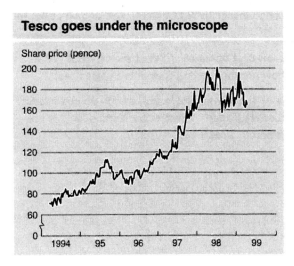

Tesco goes under the microscope

Share price (pence)

11.8   How truthful is Tesco when it says 'we champion the consumers' cause'? Justify your response.

11.9   What market position does Tesco hold in Britain, and how are their pricing decisions affected by this?

11.10 More competition produces a better deal for the customer, so it is said. Using your knowledge of pricing objectives, strategies and tactics, outline the benefits and drawbacks of increased competition with reference to pricing policies.

12 Marketing Channels

Selecting the right marketing channel for you and your customer is a significant area of strategic decision making which necessitates clear consideration and understanding of what we do, how we do it and how we want to be seen and understood by our end consumer.

Marketing channels come in many shapes and sizes and, on the whole, reflect the sophistication or otherwise of the particular market in which they exist. For example, economies with a high disposable per capita income will have a well-developed network of supermarkets and groupings of other major retail outlets, often in out-of-town settings. Less-developed economies will maintain a vast network of small local retail outlets, operated on a neighbourhood basis usually with a very restricted availability of goods and services. The difference? Motor cars. Personal transport enables the search for the right product at the right price in the right surroundings to be conducted much further from home than in situations where a lack of personal transport exists. There is even evidence of this in the poorer neighbourhoods within developed economies such as the UK and the USA.

The conclusion therefore is that we have to study the requirements of our intended consumers and then make decisions about how we might best serve that consumer base by selecting the form of channel which matches these revealed perceptions, needs and demands most nearly.

The options range from selling direct to the end consumer from the farm gate to logistics and distribution networks placing goods in front of consumers when and where they want them, and involving a number of intermediaries (agents, wholesalers, retailers) in an interlocking set of mutually satisfying relationships.

In order to successfully complete the tasks in this chapter you will need to be familiar with:

- the definition of a channel of distribution;
- how marketing channels contribute to the overall effectiveness of the effort;
- how channels behave;
- channel strategy and design;
- what types of intermediary exist;
- power-dependency considerations;
- intensity of distribution;
- the part that logistics plays in designing channels;
- what factors influence channel design.

Chemists take scientific approach to expansion

The UK high street chain has teamed up with logistics experts at MSAS to help navigate entry into the tricky Thai market. By Susanna Voyle

International expansion is not just about strategy – there is a lot of nitty gritty to sort out to make sure the vision is delivered.

When Boots, the UK-based high street chemist chain, decided to roll out its business in Thailand, the group knew that getting the logistics right was a key part of the equation.

Under its plan for overseas expansion, started two years ago, Boots is planning up to 100 shops in Bangkok, a forthcoming move into Japan via a joint venture, and the development of a 26-store chain in the Irish Republic.

The group knew all the pitfalls because it had ventured overseas before. It once had a sizeable chain in Canada, but this was sold in 1988, while a 17-year attempt to succeed in France with Sephora, a chain of perfume and cosmetics shops, ended in disposal in 1993.

The critical issue in any overseas expansion in retail is getting stocks on to the shelves accurately and reliably. Achieving this in combination with a rapid programme of store openings makes the task more complicated.

Boots first worked with one of its local suppliers, but congestion and the lack of expansion capacity had a severe impact on service levels.

In July last year the contract went to MSAS Global Logistics, a subsidiary of London-listed Ocean Group. Phil Beck, regional manager for MSAS in indo China, says supporting Boots in Thailand combined the group's existing air freight skills in south-east Asia with inventory and warehousing skills built up in the UK under another Ocean subsidiary, McGregor Cory Logistics.

The group took over the contract in July last year when Boots had six stores open and took its first products in August. Since then the number of stores has increased to 26, and the group will be delivering to 40 stores by March next year. The final target of 100 is due to be achieved over the next five years.

MSAS first sourced and designed a suitable warehouse and installed appropriate air conditioning, insulation, lighting, racking, IT systems and telecommunications.

A skilled warehousing manager joined the operation from the UK to set up and manage the facility.

To keep pace with the shop opening programme, the whole operation had to be completed in a very tight time period – six months from decision to first deliveries.

The transition from receipt of products in the warehouse to order preparation and store delivery was achieved in 10 days.

MSAS is also responsible for the management of shop fittings for new stores as well as the supply of products for new store openings. Due to the ambitious roll-out programme, huge demands will be put on the warehouse – and MSAS is carrying out very careful planning in conjunction with Boots.

MSAS employs about 85 people to support the Boots work – mainly Thai nationals, although at least three senior staff have come out from the UK.

'Thailand is an extremely difficult market to enter,' says Mr Beck. 'There are 66m people in the country and very few of them would ever have heard of Boots. That makes getting it right more important than ever.'

The stores – which have seen sales consistently beat expectations – display Boots' own-branded products prominently. About 40 per cent of the products sold are sourced from the UK and MSAS provides air and sea freight – as well as handling the complex Thai customs and licensing procedures.

The warehouse processes between three and four 40 foot containers each week for Boots. Each container requires 30,000 separate labels under the strict Thai customs laws – and the job is highly labour intensive.

MSAS hopes the success of the operation to date could lead to other work in south-east Asia. Mr Beck believes European retailers will be increasingly attracted to the area now that the worst of its economic uncertainties seem to be behind it.

And Boots is continuing to grow. At the start of this year the group announced a £49m plan to expand in the Netherlands – a move which might provide a blueprint for a European roll-out.

Source: Financial Times, 17 June 1999

12.1 Describe the type of channel Boots presently uses in its UK-based operations, what intermediaries may be involved, and what part logistics plays in their offering.

12.2 Boots have taken a radical step to change their approach to the Thai market by contracting out their logistics. What went wrong previously and why should the new system be better?

12.3 What alternative strategies might Boots have adopted, and why do you think they chose this particular one?

Article 12.B   FT

Shoppers weigh up costs and convenience

Supermarkets continue to squeeze out local rivals. By Juliette Jowit

Auchinleck Square in Birmingham is everything a shopping centre should not be. The butcher's, fruit shop, newsagent and post office, are among the 12 empty units, and Mister Minit, the shoe repairers, is up for lease.

As with many run-down shopping centres, locals blame the nearby supermarket. But within the Auchinleck complex a Select & Save minimarket is thriving and a handful of others surviving.

Yesterday the Competition Commission visited the UK's second city to see how local shops were affected by competition from supermarkets as part of their inquiry for the Department of Trade and Industry into supermarket pricing.

Mr Derek Morris, Competition Commission chairman, said: 'Supermarkets are great for the large weekly shop . . . the question is to what extent are local stores able to compete by their location, by holding products to fill niches and by serving other customer needs.'

The shoppers at Tesco were all attracted by the range and prices. They were also drawn by the large car park and well-served bus stops outside both entrances.

'Tesco is very competitive on price, the products they sell are great and there's good variety,' said Carol Egan, a 38-year-old senior care assistant.

None of the three local shopping centres appealed to Jane Stanley, a 24-year-old mother of two. 'They are fairly expensive and there's not really the variety.'

Ishtaq Rehman's Select & Save mini-market illustrates Mr Morris's comments – of 13 items, the Dolmio sauce, Roses chocolates and cheap tea bags were cheaper than in Tesco; a Bounty bar and Hobnobs biscuits were the same price. Items that were more expensive ranged from a pint of milk at 3p more to a Bird's Eye microwave meal at 50p extra.

'We take sometimes a 3 or 4 per cent margin, possibly we have to lose 5p or 10p; if we have to lose it, we lose it,' said Mr Rehman.

Variety is limited by space – 3,500 sq ft against Tesco's 40,000 sq ft – but within its range there was a good choice and the food was fresh. And as demand for weekly shops at the mini-market has been replaced by *ad hoc* buying, Mr Rehman has added a post office, off-licence and video rentals.

Customers testified that convenience, not cost, was the issue. 'I just go to the closest one, I very rarely look at the prices,' said Peter Hoffman, a 31-year-old civil engineer.

Other local shops have suffered from competition from two other nearby shopping centres. And Tesco has added more hours and more services, including a pharmacy, clothes, gifts and electrical goods.

The 'aesthetic' of Auchinleck was a disadvantage said Bharat Mehta, owner of the Everymood card and gift shop.

'It's just not inviting for customers, it's very windy. Prince Charles would have called it a concrete jungle, and there's quite a lot of insecurity, we have had lots of muggings and so on.'

Source: Financial Times, 26 November 1999

12.4 What special benefits might a corner shop possess as part of a marketing channel, and by what segmentational characteristics could we define its role?

12.5 What techniques are Tesco using to reinforce their attractiveness to shoppers, and why would this be attractive to their suppliers as well?

12.6 How does the corner shop relate to the manufacturer of, for example, Hobnobs or Roses chocolates and how far might such an outlet play a part in such a manufacturer's marketing channel strategy?

Article 12.C   **FT**

Route to big delivery savings mapped out

It was a tortuous journey, but Rhône-Poulenc's chemicals arm discovered a way of sharply reducing transport costs with the help of consultants, Jenny Luesby writes

There are few areas left within the world's largest companies where one close look can deliver instant savings of 1 per cent of sales. For Rhodia, the chemicals arm of French conglomerate Rhône-Poulenc, scrutiny of the company's transport costs in the UK led to just such savings.

It was the arrival of Chris Andrews in 1995 as chairman and chief executive of the group's UK operation that triggered a review by management consultants A.T. Kearney.

They scoured order books, invoices and transport logs at the group's 14 UK sites. Some transport they could not account for at all: there were simply no records.

Overall, transport accounted for 10 per cent of the company's traceable spending in the UK. There were 70 main suppliers but many occasional providers. During a 12-month period, 235 different hauliers had moved products for the group. The company was also running a 30-strong fleet of its own.

Michael Clow, the UK purchasing director, who worked with consultants on the project, put it bluntly: 'The results of A.T. Kearney's initial survey horrified us. The results were worse than we had ever imagined. But the opportunity to improve was huge.'

Transport buying was being dictated by the backgrounds of the buyers, rather than rational criteria, says Charles Davis, the A.T. Kearney principal responsible for the Rhodia review.

None had come into logistics as part of a management career. Typically, they were former drivers or site workers who bought transport from a 'network of buddies' built up over many years.

'They would just pick up the phone, and say: "Bob, when could you get 10 cartons to Sheffield", and the deal would be done,' says Mr Davis.

This purchasing hotch-potch was made no easier by the fragmented nature of the haulage industry. According to A.T. Kearney, there are 86,000 hauliers in the UK and no standard rates.

Even where buyers were seeking the cheapest transport, their task was complicated by numerous different tariffs for different measures. For A.T. Kearney, the solution lay in a comprehensive, standardised tendering process. During the following weeks, tenders were invited from all the company's existing suppliers, its own fleet, and others.

Most fell at the first hurdle. Across four types of freight – packaged goods, liquid products, domestic deliveries and exports – the consultants sought quotes for 8,000 different rates. For each starting point and destination, the rates were broken down into 10 weight bands.

In all, the tender document ran to 150 pages. 'The majority simply threw their hands up in horror,' says Mr Davis. But more than 60 did tender and four-fifths returned their quotes on disc. Even so, two graduates worked for three months standardising their responses and inputting the quotes that arrived on paper.

The quotes were then analysed using A.T. Kearney software that cut the data 20 different ways. Modelling began: what if this part of the business was given to X, and this part to Y – what does it do to costs?

Finally, the company went back to the most promising applicants offering deals for packages of business. It also wrote in requirements for improvements in costs, flexibility and reliability.

Inevitably, this process favoured large suppliers. But small hauliers were not automatically excluded. In one case, a driver with his own lorry, who had been hauling for the group for years, submitted a tender. A sub-contracting arrangement was made for him with one of the final suppliers.

Similarly, drivers working for the group's own fleet transferred to the haulier that won their business as an outsourcing contract.

Today, Rhodia has five main hauliers: Suttons, Swift, Bulkhaul, Bernard and LEP. They account for 90 per cent of the group's transport spending. All rates are standardised: the whole system is a 'very simple' one, says Mr Davis.

But perhaps the most extraordinary outcome from this monumental number-crunching exercise was the bottom line impact.

Before the review, transport was eating up 3 per cent of Rhône-Poulenc's UK sales revenue. The new set-up has delivered savings of more than 25 per cent.

And there is more to come, says Mr Clow. The group is 'rethinking earlier deals to win even more savings', he says.

Source: Financial Times, 1 October 1998

12.7   As chemical producers Rhône-Poulenc have little or no contact with the final consumer and yet they are paying great attention to their logistic considerations. Why should this be and is cost the only consideration?

12.8   What similarities does this article demonstrate as between organisational markets and consumer markets? What dissimilarities might you find?

12.9   Efficiency in distribution can aid strategic marketing channel considerations. How and why?

Article 12.D

FT

Campbell Soup plans kiosk sales

Campbell Soup, the US food company, yesterday said it was thinking of setting up soup kiosks in shopping malls and airports for Americans eating on the hoof, **writes Richard Tomkins in New York**.

It said it was responding to the trend in the US and other countries for people to spend more on restaurant and take-away meals and less time cooking at home.

The company said it was setting up a new division called 'Campbell away from home' to increase sales of Campbell's Soup and its other brands through non-traditional channels.

'Consumers now spend more than 50 per cent of their food dollars on food prepared and consumed away from home,' the company said.

Campbell Soup already has a food service business which supplies its products to restaurants, hospitals and schools. However, consumers are rarely aware they are Campbell's.

The company wants to change this by getting its name on the products at the point of sale, in the hope that people will be more inclined to buy them if they know they are Campbell's.

It has experimented by putting its name on soups sold at help-yourself bars in US colleges, and plans to extend this to convenience stores and other locations.

It is also trying to get its soups on to the menus of fast-food restaurant chains. They are already being sold by the Long John Silver's chain in the US.

But Craig Rydin, who will head the 'away from home' division from October 1, said the biggest departure from existing practice was the idea of setting up free-standing Campbell's soup kiosks in railway stations, airports, shopping malls and other busy areas, overseas as well as the US.

Source: Financial Times, 17 September 1998

Moneybox plans to put ATMs in nightclubs

By Clay Harris

A cash machine could be coming to your local convenience store, nightclub or betting shop, but it will cost £1 per transaction to use it.

Moneybox, a new subsidiary of Ambient Media, an AIM-listed publishing and marketing company, will announce plans today to install at least 1,000 automatic teller machines in 'convenient' locations throughout Britain in the next 12 months, adding to the 26,000 cash machines already in operation.

The ATMs will be serviced by Woolwich and be part of the former building society's Link network – the UK's largest cash machine network. As well as cash, the machines will dispense products such as airtime cards for pre-paid mobile phones and stamps. Eventually they will be able to handle e-commerce.

Moneybox's £1 fee will be monitored by other ATM operators, which so far have not charged card users, although some UK banks levy non-customers who use their machines. Most ATMs in the US already charge, a trend that has been criticised by consumer groups and politicians.

Paul Stanley, Moneybox managing director, said: 'Customers are getting used to paying for convenience.'

The ATMs will be installed in locations that other operators do not consider to have enough traffic to support a traditional machine.

Moneybox will sweeten the pill by dispensing money-off vouchers with each transaction. Another Ambient business, Electronic Media Promotions, pioneered advertising on the back of ATM receipts.

Apax Partners, the private equity group, is paying £3.5m for a 25 per cent stake in Moneybox. It will also have the right to subscribe up to £5m in Ambient shares.

Appleton Group, a South African financial services company, has agreed to invest £4.88m in Ambient in return for a 20.11 per cent stake. The shares will be issued at 75p, compared with yesterday's market price of 107$\frac{1}{2}$p.

Source: Financial Times, 11 June 1999

12.10 How might other channel members react to Campbell Soup's move and how can Campbell maintain their existing relationships?

12.11 The two articles illustrate a major change in marketing channel strategies. How does this reflect changes in the power-dependency structure of these markets and would such outlets be available or practical for all types of marketing distribution?

12.12 The rapid growth of electronic facilities for data gathering, and communication with customers influences channel strategy and design considerations. Show how the ideas illustrated by the articles might be further developed in both the fast-moving consumer goods sector and the luxury goods sector.

12.13 How could such developments be applied to other parts of the service sector?

13 Retailers and Wholesalers

Since in the majority of cases a product needs to have a way of being exposed to the greater public to achieve the sale, then we have to discuss the systems and methods by which such a transfer can be achieved. Clearly we exclude in this consideration direct sales to the public by the manufacturer, where the distribution is undertaken from the factory. Many organisations claim to offer goods at factory prices, but in most cases they are acting as wholesale or retail distributors, using price and the apparent factory connection to comprise their unique selling proposition (USP). Retailers and wholesalers do not manufacture, instead they perform other functions in the chain of distribution.

As a rule of thumb retailers expose products for sale direct to the final consumer, and may indeed consider the atmosphere, display skills and reputation they have as a product in its own right, a service product. Retailers can act as independent operators, buying in their own right or they might be part of a group which still operates independently, but using their combined strength to gain economies in bulk purchasing. Chain stores are wholly owned groups of shops which operate under a common policy, strategy and image. But in all cases they have direct contact with the public and sell single products to individual consumers, who take the goods away and consume or use them for their own benefit. The costs to the retailer are considerable in terms of staff, premises and stockholding and require a considerable mark-up in sale price over purchase price.

Wholesalers, on the other hand, rarely have direct contact with the general public, buying goods from manufacturers in bulk which they stock and sell to resellers (retailers) in smaller quantities. They carry a number of responsibilities, for which they expect a return, most particularly the expense of paying for the bulk quantities, stocking and warehousing them and very often extending credit to the retailer. They may also be engaged in product training with the retailer.

In a number of circumstances the buyer–seller relationship may be complicated by high demand by manufacturers for distribution, which leads, for instance, to the supermarket groups 'listing' products for display and sale. Not to be listed or, even worse, to be de-listed is the dread of every marketing manager, especially in the fast-moving consumer goods (FMCG) sector.

It is important that a manufacturer is clear about the sort of distribution they wish to pursue and to establish a good working relationship with the distribution channel members.

Within these broad definitions there are subdivisions, describing the specialist functions which are performed by wholesalers and retailers, some wholesalers, for instance, accepting members of the public under certain circumstances. Retailers may provide high levels of personal attention and service, or may operate a help-yourself system with low levels of attention and service. Indeed the experience among the supermarket chains is that the level of service can be the main differentiator available to them in a highly competitive marketplace.

There is also a growing acceptance of a 'partnership' between manufacturers and the chain of distribution, since in many ways the channel members are interdependent. The best evidence for this is that many supermarkets are now enabling their suppliers to go on-line with their internal computer systems so that the suppliers can be immediately aware of stock fluctuations and take steps to remedy over- or especially undersupply in specific stores. The advent of major players, particularly Wal-Mart, is causing much reorganisation and regrouping in the European retail industry in an attempt to gain economies of scale and reductions in operating costs.

In order to successfully complete the tasks in this chapter you will need to be familiar with:

- types of retail stores;
- supply chain relationships;
- breadth and depth of range;
- store image, atmosphere and positioning;
- level of service;
- discounting and channel competition;
- forms of distributed ownership.

Article 13.A   **FT**

The benefits of service with a smile

Contented, committed employees can influence sales, write Stephen Bevan and Linda Barber

A familiar tale: a large retailer, held in esteem by consumers for decades and a national institution. Suddenly, through over-expansion or slack management, profitability plummets and alarm bells ring in the stock market.

Shaken out of complacency, the company appoints a new chief executive, overhauls senior management and begins the slow process of rebuilding its reputation, profits and market share.

No need to look up Baker Street for the identity of this business. It is not Marks and Spencer. Rather, cast your gaze back to Chicago, 1992. The company is Sears, which was in serious trouble with net losses of almost $3.9bn (£2.4bn).

The key to its subsequent turnround, led by Arthur Martinez, the new chief executive, was what Sears called the 'service-profit chain'. This states that happy and committed employees lead to happy and loyal customers; which in turn increases revenue, raises profits and improves shareholder value.

Mr Martinez aimed to make Sears 'a compelling place to work, to shop and to invest' and made the explicit links between these three facets of business central to re-building the company.

Through simple measures of employee and customer satisfaction, and using the first to predict the second, Sears was able to harness the talent and enthusiasm of its staff.

But isn't the service-profit chain only a complicated way of stating the obvious importance of keeping customers happy? An empirical test at a leading UK retail business by the Institute for Employment Studies presents objective evidence why companies should not wait until rescue remedies are the only available option for survival.

Based on data from 65,000 staff and 25,000 customers in almost 100 of the group's stores, the study carried out a robust statistical survey of employee commitment and customer satisfaction, to establish a direct and strong link to sales increases at store level.

The resulting model can be used to predict which aspects of employee and customer satisfaction need to be improved to increase sales. Indeed, a one-point increase in employee commitment led, through the chain, to a monthly increase of £200,000 per store.

One finding is worth emphasising. Measuring customer satisfaction by itself is not enough. Recent work by Bain & Co, the management consultants, has shown that up to 80 per cent of customers who report being 'satisfied' subsequently defect.

Customer loyalty, and an intention to spend again, were far better predictors of sales growth than customer satisfaction, the IES model found. Yet when looking at customer data from other businesses, we discovered reliable loyalty measures were thin on the ground.

This work has some important messages for service sector businesses in the UK. The first is that customer satisfaction, without loyalty, is not enough to improve business performance.

Second, despite their stated desire for customer satisfaction and loyalty, many retail businesses use woefully inadequate methods to measure them.

Third, human resource management in the retail sector has a significant part to play in making the service-profit chain work. Keys to success include a positive organisation culture, good quality line management, committed employees and low rates of sickness.

Data of the kind used in the IES study can readily be used to develop the right performance indicators. However, most UK retail sector businesses do not collect or analyse the necessary data. Few collect adequate information on employee satisfaction and commitment. Most rely on 'mystery shopper' surveys or face-to-face questionnaires to measure customer satisfaction.

Products, prices and loyalty bonuses are easy to copy; companies should take employee satisfaction measurement more seriously. Relying on financial information alone to monitor business performance is like driving a car while looking in the rear view mirror. Employee satisfaction measures help predict hazards ahead.

The message is clear: good people management policies and practices can result in tangible business benefits.

From People to Profits, £19.95, tel 01476 541061. Stephen Bevan is associate director and Linda Barber is research fellow at the Institute for Employment Studies at Sussex University

Source: Financial Times, 22 June 1999

13.1 Identify the elements which lead to the conclusion that a retail outlet is as much a product or offering as the good contained within it. Compare and contrast two high street stores which, although offering a largely similar range of products to each other, differentiate their offering through variation in their 'product'.

13.2 What are the specific advantages that flow from increased employee satisfaction? How might these be positioned to counter competition?

13.3 Marks & Spencer has always had an enviable reputation for attention to the generation of loyalty and satisfaction among their employees. They have experienced a severe downturn in sales and profits. How may they take advantage of their good relations and communications with staff to help them through this period? Does this situation in fact reflect some changes in management/staff relationships? You may need to conduct some research to establish the link, if any.

Supreme storeman with a sharp eye for detail

The head of the world's largest retailer tells Richard Tomkins about the formula for sales success and his plans for further growth

Frugality is almost a religion at Wal-Mart Stores, the world's biggest retailer, and David Glass, chairman and chief executive, is loathe to squander precious minutes giving newspaper interviews.

Still, in a rare lapse, he allows himself to be cornered at the launch of Wal-Mart's newest retailing experiment: a food store called Neighborhood Market that has just opened in the company's home town of Bentonville, Arkansas.

He leads the way into the manager's office – a bare, cramped cubicle – and frowns with mock disapproval at its 'opulence'. 'I'll have to have a word with him about this,' he growls.

Then, the concession to small-talk over, it's straight down to the matter at hand: Wal-Mart, and its remorseless growth.

The cornerstone of its empire is the chain of 2,400 discount stores – big, out-of-town retail sheds selling a mix of clothes, household goods, electronics and toys at irresistibly low prices.

A few years ago, Wal-Mart started adding groceries to these stores, renaming them Supercenters. Now comes Neighborhood Market, a much smaller format that will extend Wal-Mart's reach – and low prices – further into the fabric of American life.

Is this a declaration of war on the supermarket chains? 'That's just a coincidence,' Mr Glass answers obliquely. 'What we are really trying to do is complement our Supercenters with a convenience offering,' catching customers who do not have time to go to the big out-of-town stores.

He says people in the grocery business have been telling him the 40,000 sq ft stores are too small to work, because others are building supermarkets measuring 60,000 sq ft to 80,000 sq ft.

'But they are trying to build destination stores, and we are not. This is a convenience store, and will be designed to serve a particular neighbourhood. If we put it in a Hispanic area, it will look like a Hispanic store. If we put it in a low-income neighbourhood, it will have a different assortment from a store in a high-income neighbourhood. Each of them may very well have totally different merchandise and characteristics.'

Closely watched as the new venture may be, Mr Glass describes it as 'minuscule' compared with the core business. Only a handful of Neighborhood Markets are opening in the first phase, while Wal-Mart plans to open 150–200 stores in the US and up to 80 in other countries next year.

Indeed, the company appears to have little need for new avenues of growth. The existing stores are roaring ahead: year-on-year sales rose 9.5 per cent last month and including the contribution from new stores, sales rose 15.5 per cent.

Much of this is due to Wal-Mart's technological edge. Mr Glass describes how it shares computer sales data with big suppliers such as Procter & Gamble, allowing both to monitor movement of products by item, colour or size in every store.

This produces highly effective inventory management: Wal-Mart rarely runs out of popular items, nor does it have piles of unneeded stock sitting in warehouses. But now, Mr Glass says, the company has gone a step further, using point-of-sale information to analyse the contents of shoppers' baskets – and thus, their shopping habits.

Wal-Mart can tell from this information which route shoppers are taking through its stores, and change the traffic pattern by putting goods in different places. Or it can stimulate sales by putting items close to other products often bought on the same visit – for example, putting Kleenex next to the cold remedies.

'There is an unbelievable amount of information available – not just to us, but to the people who sell us merchandise, who can trace sales of their products all over the world,' Mr Glass says.

Technology has a role in resolving internal disputes, too. In retailing, he says, there is a natural conflict between the people who operate the stores and those who choose which goods go on the shelves.

'The operator will come in and say: "Who in the world bought this doggy item, and why?". And the buyers will say: "Well, if you knew how to display it better or handled it better at the store level, it would sell".'

At Wal-Mart, the facts are almost indisputable because one store's sales of a product can instantly be compared with those of the others, revealing whether the product or store is to blame. 'Before we had all this detailed item movement information, you could look at numbers in the aggregate, but they would mask all the things you really needed to know.'

The other big factor behind Wal-Mart's growth is its culture. One aspect of this is a near-fanatical obsession with keeping costs low, but it also means putting a heavy emphasis on employee involvement.

An hourly-paid employee in charge of the infants' department, for example, would not only be paid a share of the store's profits, but would also be encouraged to run the department as if it were his or her own business.

'You are encouraged to be an entrepreneur. You are given financial information: you know what your sales are, what your inventory is, what your expenses are, and what your profit is on a monthly basis.

'You are also getting this information from other stores that are the same size as yours, so you can compare how you are doing with them. And you get a lot of recognition for any achievements or suggestions or ideas you have that enable us to improve our company.'

Presumably, it creates a competitive atmosphere, too? 'That's for a fact,' Mr Glass says.

In the US, Wal-Mart is already more than three times the size of the next biggest retailer, Sears Roebuck. Now it is growing in other countries, too – although more rapidly in South America and Asia than in Europe, where its only in-road has been last December's purchase of the Wertkauf chain in Germany.

Mr Glass says the main obstacle to European expansion is building stores quickly enough to get critical mass. 'It's the regulatory problems. In some of the countries in Europe, it would take you my lifetime to get regulatory approval to do something.' But he says more acquisitions could come, if opportunities arise.

If regulation does not stifle Wal-Mart's growth, could the internet? Some hold that electronic shopping will eventually spell doom for retailers of basic commodities such as packaged foods.

It is already possible to shop from Wal-Mart on the internet in the US. But Mr Glass does not believe electronic retailing will ever account for more than a small percentage of sales.

'Shopping is a social experience for many people in the world,' he says. 'People enjoy going to shop, and you are never going to lose that. I don't think non-store retailing will ever grow to the extent that it threatens retail stores.'

Source: Financial Times, 22 October 1998

13.4 From the article and your outside reading what are the key features which differentiate Wal-Mart from other retailers? Do you think these features are transferable to the European setting? What particular differences might be noted when contrasting Europe and the USA?

13.5 How do other retailers view the takeover by Wal-Mart of the Asda chain, and how might they counter any perceived threat?

13.6 Evaluate the importance of the relationships retailers have with their suppliers and show how various elements of the marketing mix might be employed to further these relationships.

Japanese wholesalers announce merger plan

Move to create country's biggest supplier follows similar consolidation among drugs groups. By Paul Abrahams in Tokyo

Three Japanese pharmaceutical wholesalers yester-day announced they would merge, creating the biggest supplier in the Japanese market with sales of Y831bn ($7.04bn).

The move by Kuraya, the country's second biggest wholesaler, Sanseido, the fourth largest, and Tokyo Pharmaceutical, follows similar consolidation among Japanese drugs wholesalers whose margins have been hit by healthcare reforms. Similar consolidation has taken place in Europe and the US where wholesalers have been squeezed between purchasers and drugs manufacturers.

Takashi Yamada, president of Sanseido, will become chief executive of the new group, which will have a market capitalisation of about Y1,400bn. Sanseido's shares will continue to be quoted and the new entity will be called Kuraya Sanseido. The deal is expected to be concluded by April next year.

Mr Yamada said: 'The pie is getting smaller and profits will not grow in this environment. It is becoming necessary to seek greater volume and reduce costs.' The deal should give the new group greater geographical reach – though not a true national network – and about 16 per cent market share. All 6,500 staff would continue to be employed at the merged entity.

Last April Suzuken, the country's leading whole-saler, merged with Akiyama, the biggest supplier in Hokkaido, northern Japan. In October, Nippon Shoji Kaisha merged with Showa Pharmaceutical to create the country's third largest group, called Azwell. Shionogi, a drugs company, plans to merge its 11 wholesale subsidiaries.

'The consolidation of this still fragmented industry is inevitable,' said Martin Reeves, a vice-president at Boston Consulting Group in Tokyo. 'No companies have the economies of scale that a truly national network would create, manufacturers are squeezing wholesale margins, and few can afford to invest adequately in information technology,' he said.

All three groups have strong links with Takeda, the country's biggest drugs maker, which owns 22.5 per cent of Sanseido, 2.9 per cent of Kuraya and 71.9 per cent of Tokyo Pharmaceutical.

Source: Financial Times, 21 April 1999

13.7 Describe other industries which use the wholesaler as an important part of the supply chain, and identify the reasons why they do so. Is the growth and development in communications, transport and computer based or Internet marketing and retailing likely to affect these decisions?

13.8 Imagine yourself a textile wholesaler. Make use of environmental scanning to evaluate your future position and make recommendations as to how you might address the SWOT implications.

13.9 The pharmaceutical industry has particular characteristics which are best served with a healthy wholesale activity. If this is so, what are these characteristics and might there be an alternative?

A grab for impulse shoppers

How do you get online shoppers to buy what they didn't know they needed?
Alison Smith finds out

Begin a search on the internet for any subject – from aardvarks to Zwingli, a sixteenth century religious reformer – and you are likely to see an onscreen advertisement from Amazon.com. The ad means that you are only one move away from browsing through the books the online store carries on your chosen topic.

Amazon reached the agreement to show these ads with five of the six most used web aggregators or portals, including Alta Vista and Yahoo!, slightly more than a year ago. The almost seamless shift from searching to buying is one of the most striking examples of how the internet can be used to draw people into making impulse purchases.

'You can go from an information-seeking experience to a shopping experience with one click,' says Brian Cauley, president of APL Digital, part of advertising network Ammirati Puris Lintas.

Encouraging people to buy items they had not intended to buy is an art that high street retailers have honed during many years.

Eye-catching displays, juxtaposition of complementary items, and tempting shows of treats such as chocolates and magazines near supermarket checkouts are common practice in conventional stores. Online retailers, however, are only just beginning to think of ways of stimulating unplanned demand.

'If I go round a supermarket my trolley includes special offers but if I do my shopping on the web I stick pretty much to the same list of items,' says Keith Wills, European retail analyst at Goldman Sachs.

'One of the dangers for retailers is that people end up with a utilitarian set of purchases online, and visit a real-world supermarket for fresh and added value produce.

'If the online shopping basket goes back to basics then retailers lose margin gains.'

Ease of purchase is perhaps the most important way for both internet and conventional stores to encourage impulse buying, says Mr Wills.

'After buying a football shirt, does the customer have to scroll through a dozen screens to get the matching shorts and socks? What about quick access to the checkout? Just as in a store, the customer will not want to search through countless options but

rather be guided to a handful of products that suit their taste and budget.'

Online purchasing clearly has its drawbacks: shopping on the screen cannot replicate the sight, smell and feel of being surrounded by potential purchases. Grocery shopping may also be affected by the absence of pester power: there may not, for instance, be any children around trying to influence your choice.

The sense of having performed a chore that deserves a treat will be less marked when shopping is more convenient. 'The web is never going to be able to satisfy the urge for that kind of immediate, low price indulgence,' says Mr Cauley.

But in other respects, online retailing may be better suited to encouraging unplanned buying than high street stores are. One advantage is flexibility, says Eric Salama, director of strategy at marketing services group WPP, a group involved in Peapod, a US online grocery service.

'You can design the store you want without being constrained by the physical surroundings. By creating, say, an aisle of Christmas purchases or Easter eggs and related goods, you can use events to stimulate buying.' It is also possible to address consumers online in a more sophisticated way. David Risher, Amazon's senior vice-president of marketing product development, says the company is still refining the linkages that it is possible to make.

Someone considering a new novel, for example, can readily be shown not only reviews of the book but also other books purchased by people who have already bought that particular book. And someone buying a book for a baby can be informed about CDs of lullabies.

Being able to build up a detailed picture of each customer means that online retailers can accurately target their offers. 'Instead of a kid tugging your sleeve to buy ice cream or breakfast cereal, the website can tug your sleeve and say "Are you sure you don't want one of these? You usually buy them",' says Mr Salama.

'The internet retailer can track you over a longer period of time and come back to you with an offer targeted at your known preferences at some later date,' says Mr Wills. 'The high street retailer can't come back to you in the same way.'

At present, however, many retailing websites may be failing to capitalise on their potential advantages, producing a functional environment rather than an enjoyable experience. But this seems likely to change as technology improves and the size of the market grows.

'It is early days at the moment, but the internet allows you to adapt what you're doing in response to your audience,' says Mark Wilson of marketing consultancy Bamber Forsyth. 'Provided retailers are listening to their customers, they can learn and change their sites in just a few months.'

Source: Financial Times, 18 September 1998

13.10 What features may be described as 'part of the shopping experience'? How important are these to retailers trying to compete with on-line shopping? Using these features, how might a retailer vary the offering to successfully differentiate themselves from on-line retailers, and should they join the process?

13.11 What disadvantages does the article discuss in relation to on-line shopping (and any others you adduce yourself) and how should these be best addressed?

14 Communication and the Promotional Mix

Wonderful products, efficient manufacturing processes, well-motivated staff and accurate segmentation analysis are all of no value if the intended customer is not aware of the offering you are making. Therefore careful attention has to be paid to the generation and distribution of 'the message'. But generating and sending the message is only half the task, since it is essential that we build into our system the facility to monitor the results of our efforts. We have to know accurately, on a continuous basis, how effective our message is and whether any adjustment or modification is necessary.

In other chapters there is discussion of the specific functions carried out by the various components available to us such as advertising, sales promotion, personal selling and public relations, but it is important to understand why all these activities must be integrated and considered together in order to arrive at a well-developed, balanced and costed way of creating and promulgating the message.

The essential core requirement is that the organisation should send a series of messages through one or a number of media which reach the intended customer in as clear and comprehensible form as possible. As well as transmitting the message in the above manner we have to acknowledge that there are different reasons for using each particular medium, and that each medium has its own advantages and drawbacks. Also the message will rarely reach the intended receiver in exactly the way you would wish because of many possibilities for interference with the message either in the process of transmission or within the understanding of the receiver.

Having considered all the possibilities for failure and selected the most likely way to succeed in getting our message over we have also to consider alongside these debates the cost of using these services and whether they match the budgetary constraints placed on us. On top of all these considerations we have to consider how our communications match the organisation's requirements strategically and how they are related to the overall corporate image.

Remember that none of the decisions taken in planning such campaigns are cast in stone and therefore we can and should change and adjust to more nearly create the best possible exposure for our organisation and its products. Mistakes abound in promotional campaigns and only by being able to monitor can we correct these errors. As ever, customers will always have a few surprises up their sleeves, so beware!

In order to successfully complete the tasks in this chapter you will need to be familiar with:

- the theory of communication models;
- source credibilty;
- the VisCAP model of presenter characteristics;
- personal/impersonal communication methods;
- judgemental/data-based budget setting;
- response hierarchy models;
- alternative media;
- push/pull strategies.

Article 14.A   FT

A spillage of goodwill

Richard Tomkins examines the flaws in Coca-Cola's approach to product contamination, and the lessons it might have learned from history

In 1982, the US healthcare products group Johnson & Johnson wrote the book on crisis management with its deft handling of the poisoned Tylenol affair. This week, Coca-Cola appeared to be tearing the book up in its response to an unfolding fiasco in Europe over sales of tainted Coke.

The partial withdrawal of Coca-Cola products from four European countries is likely to set the record for the biggest product recall yet by a packaged goods manufacturer. But a much greater cost could arise from the damage done to Coca-Cola's brand, meticulously managed over the past 113 years.

On Tuesday, the world's biggest soft drinks maker acknowledged that Coca-Cola products going mainly into the Belgian market had been tainted in two separate incidents. One involved the accidental injection of 'defective' carbon dioxide gas into some cola. In the other, the outside of soft drink cans was contaminated by a fungicide used to treat wooden shipping pallets.

But the admission came only after Coca-Cola had spent most of the preceeding week assuring consumers that its products were safe. It made that claim as dozens of Belgian children were being taken to hospital, complaining of stomach cramps, vomiting and dizziness after drinking Coca-Cola products.

So far there have been no confirmed reports of any serious illnesses directly attributable to Coca-Cola's products, and Coca-Cola says no health or safety issues have been identified. But its proposed solution to the problem fell far short of what the authorities demanded.

Coca-Cola's plan was for a targeted withdrawal of the affected products. Instead, by yesterday, sales of nearly all Coca-Cola's canned and bottled products had been banned by the governments of Belgium and Luxembourg. And in France, where only the affected products were banned, some retail chains such as Carrefour removed all Coca-Cola products from their shelves rather than risk confusion.

Coca-Cola also earned hostile headlines in much of northern Europe. In the countries affected, it became the butt of cartoon jokes – such as one showing its trade-mark polar bear writhing in pain, and another changing its name to 'Coca-Colic'.

In terms of the textbook method of dealing with crises such as these, Coca-Cola seems to have broken nearly all the basic rules. One is to act quickly to recall the affected products. Another is to be open with consumers about what went wrong, and a third is to show contrition.

The textbook was devised by Johnson & Johnson 17 years ago. It acted after an extortionist tried to wring money out of the company by lacing capsules of its Tylenol painkiller with cyanide, and seven people died.

While the government was still considering what to do, and before the media had time to put the company on the defensive, Johnson & Johnson recalled all Tylenol products. That cost about $100m and it lost short-term sales. But it emerged from the episode with consumer confidence at a higher level than ever, and quickly regained its leadership of the painkiller market.

Another large product recall conducted according to the textbook was a bizarre case in 1995 involving Philip Morris. The US company recalled its entire stocks of Marlboro cigarettes from the US market, fearing they could harm smokers' health. It turned out that a batch of filters had become contaminated with a chemical that could cause slight coughing and sneezing. As in the Johnson & Johnson case, Philip Morris went to great lengths to explain the reasons for its actions. It took full-page advertisements in newspapers, set up a free inquiry service for wholesalers, retailers and customers, and kept media and stock market analysts briefed. The recall cost $200m, and may have contributed to Marlboro's subsequent rise in market share.

But Coca-Cola's approach has been more reminiscent of Perrier, the French manufacturer of sparkling water. Perrier was seen as acting tardily and grudgingly when traces of benzene were found in its bottled water in 1990. Initially reluctant to act, it was forced to recall every bottle at a cost of about $200m, and its reputation suffered.

In fairness to Coca-Cola, the soft drinks scare has come at a time when European sensitivities about food safety have been increased by food scandals, including the recent discovery in Belgium of cancer-causing dioxin in animal feed.

Prof Ulrich Steger of the International Institute for Management Development in Lausanne also points out that consumer goods companies are frequently targeted by extortionists threatening to taint their products. 'In these cases, it's difficult to decide when you are going to inform the public and when you are going to be silent. Maybe this biased their view,' he says.

In 1993, Coca-Cola's nearest rival, Pepsi-Cola, became the victim of widespread allegations that its cans had been found to contain syringes. Pepsi decided the allegations were false and executives appeared on US television to say so. They showed footage of canning operations to demonstrate how hard it would be to tamper with them.

Within a few days, it became clear that the incident was a hoax, and Pepsi was able to run full-page advertisements in national newspapers saying so. The company came across as sensitive to public concerns without being arrogant, and probably emerged with additional goodwill from the public.

The Coca-Cola case, however, is neither a hoax nor an extortion attempt. Ian Wright, vice president of Britain's Institute of Public Relations, says the company's speed of reaction to the events may have been constrained by a lack of internal communications. Messages had to pass among its global headquarters in Atlanta, Georgia, its national base in Belgium, and the bottling plants in Antwerp and Dunkirk.

'It's pretty typical of big international companies now, that they will base their production in one country and have operational management in another country. That sometimes leads to a communications break,' he says.

'The interesting question now is what the impact will be in other countries. These things have a tendency to burn out of control over wide areas. Coke has a big job to do to restore confidence not just in Belgium but across northern Europe.

'I think that's something they will be very good at, but it's going to be a very tough job.'

Source: Financial Times, 17 June 1999

14.1 Coca-Cola's predicament was principally communication based. How should they have reacted to this situation? What could they do to reduce the negative impact of this unexpected situation?

14.2 As a competitor of Coca-Cola, how would you make use of this occurrence, and how would you learn the lessons exposed by this?

14.3 How could an integrated communication campaign turn such a disaster into a benefit for the company?

14.4 Explain the crucial significances of effective communication to successful product management.

The case of the misleading coffin

It's no joking matter. Alison Maitland looks at some embarrassing mistakes in translating business documents and how to avoid them

Translating business documents correctly can be a matter of life and death. Take Golden Wonder, the snack manufacturer, which nearly exported crisps to Greece in boxes marked 'coffin' after a non-Greek translator picked the wrong word for 'case'.

The mistake was picked up when the UK company checked the wording with its local distributors, says Deborah Thompson, export sales and marketing manager. At first they expressed disbelief, 'but then they laughed about it'.

Not that it would have been a joking matter if the company had had no safety net. Businesses can damage their image by conveying the wrong message through poor translation. A sign in a Copenhagen airline ticket office confirmed every traveller's fear by promising to 'take your bags and send them in all directions'.

A sales brochure from a Swedish property agent described an office block as 'built in very venture-some architecture, with daylight coming through the roof'.

Misuse of a foreign language in corporate documents 'looks as if you haven't considered the customers' interests', says Rick Johns, who oversees translation projects as a manager in Visa International's commercial products department.

Having seen mistranslations into German of English banking terms such as 'credit' and 'closing balance', he was determined to avoid errors by involving translators from the start in Visa's new Info-Span software, designed for companies in Europe to monitor and control purchasing expenditure.

'If you're developing software, you have to build it with translation in mind,' he says. 'You must make sure the translation company understands not only what it is they've got to do, but what the business objectives are. You can mess up your product strategy if you make a half-hearted attempt to get it translated at the last minute.'

Yet a slapdash approach to translation is common, says Chris Durban, a Paris-based specialist in financial translation who reports on corporate *faux pas* in a regular column for the Institute of Translation and Interpreting in London.

French delegates to a World Energy Council congress in Houston last year were shocked to be greeted by a sign saying 'Bienvenu' (Welcom). Other horrors were an emergency exit sign reading 'Urgence sort seul' (literally 'Emergency leaves alone') and a photo booth described as 'baraque de la photographie' (photo shanty or dive). French was an official conference language.

Many problems can be put down to a 'black hole' in communication between the client and the translator, says Janet Fraser, senior lecturer in translation at the University of Westminster. Her research found that only 8 per cent of UK translators were always told the intended readership and use of a document. One translator said he had been given a list of machine parts to translate but not told what the machine was.

'A lot of clients don't make it clear how the text is going to be used and who it's for, and a lot of translators don't ask,' she says. 'It's not a satisfactory situation.'

This appears to have been the case with a full-page advertisement carried in European business newspapers earlier this year by Electricité de France, the French state-owned utility that sees itself expanding further across Europe. The English version of the advert said the company offered 'competitive energetic solutions' and was 'willing to accompany your development by following you on all of your sites in Europe and beyond'.

Ms Durban contacted EdF and its advertising agency to investigate what had gone wrong. 'I was passed on to the translation company who had no idea they were handling copy for an international advertising campaign,' she says. It told her it had approached the job as if it were an in-house memo.

EdF says this was its first international publicity campaign and future translations will be checked with its offices in target countries. In spite of the stylistic problems, it says the advertisement generated business inquiries.

Standards could be raised if companies gave better briefings and translators, or their agencies, stood by their work by putting their names on it, says Ms Durban.

Translators say clients often have little idea of what the job involves, notably in handling specialised text or rendering software programmes intelligible in another culture.

The quality of translation depends on the quality of the source material, says Geoffrey Samuelsson-

Brown, managing director of Aardvark, a Bracknell-based translation company whose clients include Visa International and Coca-Cola. 'This is known as the GiGo factor – Garbage In, Garbage Out.'

There are many reasons why translators need to be told the context of the work, he says. A text can expand by up to 30 per cent in translation. Without careful planning, it might not fit a page, or might run alongside unrelated illustrations.

An advertisement for a European antacid tablet gave quite the wrong message in Arabic when the wording ran from right to left but the pictures, showing an indigestion sufferer recovering, ran from left to right.

Absolute precision is required, particularly in legal documents, where the position of a comma can change a verdict, says Mr Samuelsson-Brown. In Swedish, 'benadas, ej avrättas' means 'reprieved, not executed', whereas 'benadas ej, avrättas' means 'not reprieved, executed'.

Despite the demands of the job, many translators complain they are undervalued. A UK translator has been asked to quote for 'photocopying into French'.

Some specialisms, such as translating software or advertising copy, command higher status and remuneration, says Jane Hibbert, secretary of the Institute of Translation and Interpreting.

But companies are often reluctant to hire experts because the costs are considerable while potential losses from bad translation are hard to measure.

Are there limits to the use of translation? Witty advertising that works well in a specific culture can become anodyne when converted into a multinational campaign. Ms Hibbert believes experts can be found for every translation job, though their skills may be rare. 'It depends on whether the client is prepared to look for the right person and to foot the bill when the advice comes through.'

Coca-Cola's Middle East and North Africa division uses outside translators to turn English training manuals, newsletters and advertising into French and Arabic. 'The price of translating advertising materials can be costly,' says Tim Wilkinson, external affairs manager. 'It's not just the cost of translating the English, you also have to take into consideration design and layouts that often have to change, especially with Arabic.'

But he has no doubt it is worth it. Coca-Cola claimed last year to have established market leadership in the region after only a few years' presence – although this was disputed by PepsiCo. 'You cannot put a price on communication,' says Mr Wilkinson.

Source: Financial Times, 17 June 1999

14.5 The offering is only as good as the communication and promotional mix employed to inform the target market. Enlarge this statement, and illustrate by the use of examples.

14.6 Do the problems as discussed in the article only exist where translation into another language is called for? What other factors contribute to potential 'noise' during the generation of the communication?

14.7 What differences in the type of communication are evident in the different stages of the response hierarchy models? Are these likely to be varied by cultural/national characteristics?

FT

Celebrity endorsement proves recipe for success

Delia Smith's praise for a frying-pan sent sales soaring but Clark Gable did the opposite for vests, says Cathy Newman

When the celebrity chef Delia Smith sent sales of an aluminium frying-pan soaring after she recommended it on television, she was hailed by the popular press as the most powerful woman in Britain.

But the extraordinary influence broadcast media has over consumers and their wallets is not new, and Delia Smith is not the only personality to wield such power.

True, Delia Smith has in her time been held responsible for dramatic increases in the sales of products such as cranberries, eggs and yeast. But back in the 1930s, the actor Clark Gable exerted as strong an influence, although with the opposite effect. He appeared without a vest in the film *It Happened One Night*. A slump in vest sales was said to have ensued.

Television programmes regularly boost retail sales. 'It's an old phenomenon,' says Peter Bazalgette, of Bazal, the independent producer that makes the *Food and Drink* show for the BBC. 'In 1985 we demonstrated an apple-corer on the *Food and Drink* programme, and two factories were set up in the Far East [to meet orders from the English market]'. The following year, Mr Bazalgette adds, ingredients for an Oxtail soup recipe used on the programme 'had to be imported frozen from Holland in a special consignment' to satisfy demand whipped up by the TV show.

A product does not even need to be mentioned favourably to guarantee an increase in sales. Bookings at the Adelphi Hotel in Liverpool, subject of a somewhat unflattering BBC fly-on-the-wall documentary, reportedly went up by 20 per cent in the five weeks following the programme.

Why do viewers feel the urge to spend money on products endorsed – or simply shown – on television? Helga Dittmar, a senior lecturer in psychology at Sussex University, who has conducted research into impulsive shopping habits, says Delia Smith and others pander to people's aspirations. 'Products are associated with particular types of images or famous personalities. You're somehow moving closer to that image if you buy the product, almost by a magical means.'

Television has incredible power because it is a mass medium. Peter York, management consultant and social trend-spotter, says television provokes a different response to that of newspapers and magazines because it 'creates at speed mass enthusiasms which didn't quite exist before. It puts a whole area of activity on the agenda.'

New media – such as the internet and hundreds of channels on offer from digital television – will increasingly fragment mass audiences. But although Delia Smith and others may not be watched by millions simultaneously for much longer, they will still be trusted because they are seen as impartial and authoritative. She's a 'pretty good all-round person', says Mr York. That is especially important when consumers are bombarded with advertising messages, and need to turn to someone neutral for guidance.

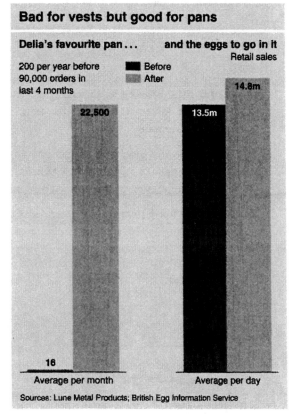

Bad for vests but good for pans

Delia's favourite pan . . .   and the eggs to go in it

200 per year before
90,000 orders in
last 4 months

■ Before
▨ After

Retail sales

22,500

16

Average per month

13.5m

14.8m

Average per day

Sources: Lune Metal Products; British Egg Information Service

John Billett, chairman of the Billett Consultancy, which measures media effectiveness, suggests people have turned to programmes such as *Food and Drink*, or the BBC's DIY series, *Changing Rooms*, because they are becoming wary of advertisers' claims. 'More people are getting more informed. Advertisers aren't any longer writing on a blank blackboard as their pupils are coming forward with more knowledge,' he says.

If an advert may be less effective at selling a product than a good word from Delia Smith, isn't there a danger the distinction between editorial and promotion may become blurred? The BBC is keen to point out that Delia Smith did not specifically mention the brand-name of the frying-pan, and that a reader offer in the Radio Times featuring the pan she used was 'totally separate'. The Radio Times is controlled by BBC Worldwide, the BBC's commercial arm.

Mr Bazalgette says 'power has to be used carefully', with Delia Smith and other presenters giving advice 'without fear or favour'. She and her husband are involved in publishing a magazine for J Sainsbury, the supermarket group, and she is no doubt keen to guard her editorial independence jealously, so as not to lay herself open to accusations of favouring that supermarket over others.

If Clark Gable had kept his vest on, perhaps he would have had to have watched his relationship with underwear manufacturers just as carefully.

Source: Financial Times, 23 November 1998

14.8 The use of celebrity endorsement is a long-established promotional tool. Discuss the benefits and potential drawbacks of the use of such endorsements as part of a communication strategy.

14.9 The article illustrates how effective a push strategy can be. Describe how such a strategy works and contrast this with the other generic strategy available. Can we mix the two?

14.10 Why should such endorsements be so effective and how might they be affected as the move to electronic-based communications gathers pace?

14.11 This article illustrates which model very clearly? Show the linkage between model and article and explain to which other model this might be related.

Article 14.D   **FT**

Liverpool seeks to polish up tarnished image

By Sheila Jones

Think of Liverpool, and what springs to mind? The Beatles? Football? A trading port? Or perhaps the Militant era of the 1980s when Liverpool became synonymous with loony leftism.

Whatever the reality, the city feels it has an image problem and it is one it wants to nail.

In January Liverpool launches a new brand. Trains, airports and even the London Underground will be blitzed with billboard posters in a campaign aimed at London and the south-east of England. Holiday packages will spotlight cities with which Liverpool has historical links, such as New York.

Liverpool is not the first city to bring in the brand consultants, and it is conscious that 'slogan fatigue' could torpedo its efforts. Alex Batchelor, of Interbrand Newell & Sorrell, the brand consultant, said Liverpool faced an uphill challenge, but the dividends could be high.

Market research indicated Liverpool, and the wider Merseyside region, had to 'reposition its corporate marketing and give a constant, clear and focused' message, according to Neil Rami, marketing director of Mersey Partnership, the regeneration agency.

'We're not going for a slogan,' he said. 'People are fed up with them. We are creating a new brand that is contemporary, flexible and simple.' Posters focus on heritage, culture, music and sport. The brand, created by McCann Erickson, picks out the 'Me' in Merseyside and the 'Live' in Liverpool. Leaflets will go to homes across Merseyside to try to ensure the people of the city 'are equipped to promote the place'.

Liverpool has moved on from the bad old days of industrial strife, according to Mr Rami. Industrial relations are no better or worse than anywhere in the UK and productivity is above average. Investment is rising. This week EasyJet, the cut-price airline, announced four new routes to continental Europe from Liverpool Airport, creating 300 jobs.

But the region is still failing to win over some investors. 'We are now on the shopping list, but we realised that while we were being shortlisted for investments we were not closing enough and getting the deals,' said Mr Rami. Businesses say the region has the right infrastructure, workforce and attitude, but they are less sure about persuading managers to relocate to Merseyside. 'There is clearly still an image issue but much less so. Now, it is about environment, quality of life and business confidence. People don't know what Liverpool and Merseyside have to offer,' he said.

Local employers are backing the new brand. 'Merseyside has a wealth of strengths and it is better placed to promote these if it presents a united front,' said James Ross, chairman of the Littlewoods Organisation.

Robert Wade-Smith, who created Liverpool's Wade Smith retailer, now part of the Arcadia group, is one of Merseyside's millionaires. An import from Yorkshire, he says the reality of Merseyside is 'far more impressive' than the reputation. 'The people here spend more and save less. It's a live for today attitude the economy needs.'

Source: Financial Times, 24 November 1998

14.12 A change of brand may be an important communication tool in that it sends out a set of images to the potential consumer, but what other aspects of communication will need to be considered in this situation?

14.13 The article considers alternative media. What are these and how can they be used to best effect? Can you think of any other forms which could be utilised or developed for this campaign?

14.14 Should Liverpool look to other examples to help them and should they use judgemental or data-based budgeting to arrive at a monetary cost to the authority? Explain the difference and justify your choice.

Article 14.E   FT

Exit geek, enter salesman

Paul Maidment sees a significant change in the standard of entries as an increasing number of companies and customers embrace the web

This was the year big companies took their web sites away from their IT departments and gave them to sales and marketing. And, boy, does it show.

As a judge for the FT Business Web Site of the Year Awards this year and last, I can testify there has been a radical improvement in the standard of design among big companies' web sites over the intervening 12 months.

Any one of the eight finalists in the large organisations category this year would have walked away with last year's competition. Those finalists included companies such as BP, British Airways, Eastman Kodak and PepsiCo, experienced in evoking their brands and communicating with customers. These were sites on which money and attention had been well spent.

It was not just a succession of elegant 'looks and feel' that impressed the judges. Nor whizzy features. There were barely any new technology-driven features to be seen.

It was the execution of the sites that struck us. This year's best sites really work as ways of doing business. None did anything just because it could be done. All the sites did something that customers needed.

The reason is no secret. Where once web pages were designed by geeks for geeks who would see something cool and peer into the source code to see how it was done, now they have to be designed to make buyers peer into their wallets for a credit card.

Online shopping – e-commerce in web jargon – is growing like Topsy. US shoppers alone are expected to spend $2.3bn (£1.4bn) online during the 1998 holiday season, up from $1.1bn last year, according to Jupiter Communications, a market research company. Only 16 per cent of those purchases are expected to be gift-related.

Online retailing is but the tip of the e-commerce iceberg. Out of sight is a mass of business-to-business transactions, for which it is difficult to get firm sales volumes because many are conducted through semi-private internets and extranets linking companies with their suppliers.

Over the past year a critical mass has built up of consumers and purchasing managers who need the net to make busy lives quick and easy.

Simple, intuitive navigation and good looks are the two attributes of web sites most valued by consumers, according to a survey of financial services sites by NFO Worldwide, a market research group. Our winning site in the large organisations category, Dell Europe, (*www.dell.co.uk*) is selling more than $5m worth of personal computers online a week to individuals and businesses. Worldwide, Dell Computer is a $2bn online business.

Dell tackles the retail and business-to-business markets with one site, the design of which aims to make buying and owning a computer as simple as possible. As a consequence, Dell is not only changing the computer buying market by selling direct, it is also restructuring the sales chain.

The site is catalogue, sales clerk, after sales assistant, complaints department, technical manual and repair technician rolled in to one. With a few keyboard clicks, Dell's customers can review, configure and price any computer system the company sells, place an order and track its progress from manufacturing to shipping.

Once they receive the PC, customers can get online support and download software upgrades. Corporate customers receive the invoices, tax receipts and other records that businesses require.

The golden rule of good site design is 'architecture precedes aesthetics'. The navigation of Dell's site leads the customer intuitively and speedily in the one direction the company wants, from information to purchase to support, providing a customised route for each customer, be they individual or company.

Many sites still demand too many clicks to purchase, too many keystrokes to enter credit card and shipping information, too much extraneous marketing data to fill out before the customer is allowed to get away. E-commerce does not allow for the instant gratification of taking away goods just bought. The substitute online has to be the experience of the purchase itself.

In conventional shops, successful retailers know how to create an environment which makes shopping a pleasurable experience beyond the mere transaction. Pure online companies like Amazon.com, a books retailer, and CDNow, which sells music, were the pioneers in e-commerce, but established retailers like The Gap, Levi Strauss and Sears are belatedly taking to the net, bringing with them customer-focused know-how.

Financial markets are putting a price on the value of good design. Recent announcements of site revamps by Egghead, a seller of computer software, and Books-A-Million, a chain of bookstores, both prompted investors to run up the companies' share price. The logic is that a better designed site will generate more sales and thus earnings.

It is not only design that is spurring internet commerce. The net now has millions of consumers who have been online for more than a year. They are daily becoming more comfortable and confident about shopping electronically. The cost savings and convenience of online systems is driving business-to-business sales. In the US, the Clinton administration's promise that internet commerce will not be taxed for at least three years, and its efforts to extend that policy worldwide, is also a boost.

But it will be mainly by design not accident if a forecast by George Colony, president of Forrester Research, the market researchers, is to come true. He expects that 5 per cent of the world's commerce – more than $3,500bn of business – will be conducted on the net by 2003.

Source: Financial Times, 4 December 1998

14.15 What part of the promotional mix does the web comprise, and does it replace advertising? Explain your answer and illustrate with examples.

14.16 What particular characteristics of the web are especially important to any integrated marketing effort, and what do these contribute to the effectiveness of database marketing?

14.17 How could we use the web as part of our situational analysis efforts? Are there particular advantages and disadvantages in the use of the web for this purpose?

15 Advertising

Advertising is the single most obvious part of the whole marketing process, the one thing that most outsiders immediately think of when asked what they know of marketing. This, of course, is perfectly natural since advertising is all round us and is present whenever we turn on the television, open a newspaper or magazine, drive along a road, go shopping or to the cinema. All these occasions and activities are viewed by marketers as opportunities to impress a message upon us. The essence of advertising is that the advertiser, who is clearly identified with the advertisement, pays for it, and that the message is aimed at a mass audience.

There are many ways of using advertising, and many reasons for doing so. We may wish to advertise our products, enhance our company image, change the target audience's attitudes or activities (e.g. public service advertising concerning drink/driving) or reinforce previous messages. However we use advertising, it is only one component of the whole promotion exercise, albeit the most obvious.

The selection of the channels through which we expose our message is crucial, and will depend very largely on the type and size of target audience. The less specific the target customer, the greater the audience we will attempt to approach. Thus mass marketing campaigns for, say, washing powder will commonly use television advertising as the principal message-transmission medium, backed up by in-store promotions, coupons in magazines and perhaps free samples. Producers of more specialised products such as expensive watches will prefer quality glossy magazines as their principal transmission medium, together with promotions by selected outlets.

With the advent of electronic advertising via the Internet many of the old definitions are being stretched and blurred, since it is becoming increasingly possible to approach well-understood customer groups with more and more personally directed and tailored messages. This combined with the increasing ability of organisations to capture information on customers' buying habits (e.g. through loyalty cards) makes it possible for an organisation to approach customers, knowing their preferences beforehand and thereby creating a much greater chance of the message being responded to positively. This development is generating enormous change in the advertising world, causing advertisers to examine much more closely the effectiveness of their advertising activities. This in turn is demanding greater creativity on the part of the advertising agencies, the fruitfulness of whose activities is being examined much more critically both by the organisations paying for their services and other organisations whose brief may be political, environmental or moral judgement.

In order to successfully complete the tasks in this chapter you will need to be familiar with:

- integrated marketing;
- formulating an advertising message;
- the role of the creative department;
- planning advertising campaigns;
- TV advertising;
- radio advertising;
- competitive/comparative advertising;
- environmental scanning.

Tuned in to advertisers and seeking freedom of the airwaves

Cathy Newman on the concerns facing commercial radio over regulation and digital broadcasting

A quarter of a century ago next week an advertisement for Birds Eye fish fingers marked the start of UK commercial radio.

'This is London Broadcasting, the news and information service of independent radio' was LBC's rather austere introduction on October 8 1973.

Today commercial radio – with celebrity disc jockeys such as Chris Evans – is more likely to get ticked off for bad language than for austerity. There are now more than 200 commercial radio stations, three of them national. Another 100 are expected by 2002.

There is an appetite for new radio services, but onerous regulations in the 1970s made it difficult to attract listeners. John Perriss, chairman of Zenith Media Worldwide, a media buying agency, recalls tuning in to a crackly LBC at dawn in 1973.

'You had to promise ridiculously high-quality BBC-like programming, which got zero audiences, and people applying for licences had to stuff their board with the great and the good – a trade union leader, a playwright, or a priest,' he says.

A gradual loosening of regulation helped commercial radio to overtake the BBC's share of listeners in 1994. As the number of listeners rose, radio became more attractive to advertisers, particularly as it was cheaper than advertising on television.

The Radio Advertising Bureau has also helped convince advertisers of the benefits of the medium: commercial radio's share of display advertising revenue is now more than 5 per cent.

There are some bullish forecasts about how much more of the advertising cake radio can grab. Paul Brown, chief executive of the Commercial Radio Companies Association, the trade body, believes radio should be able to take between 8 and 9 per cent, as it does in Europe and the US.

Analysts are more pessimistic. Lorna Tilbian, media analyst at Panmure Gordon, says: 'The big test is the advertising downturn. Has radio gone from a 2 per cent advertising share to just under 6 per cent because it's been in a bull market?'

Commercial radio groups say they are now better placed than in the 1970s to withstand recession. For a start, Mr Brown estimates the five top groups represent 70 per cent of commercial radio revenues. Consolidation of ownership has helped radio take off as larger groups have invested in programming, and are headed by professional management, some of them drawn from a commercial or advertising background.

Changes to ownership regulation have eased consolidation. Ralph Bernard, chief executive of GWR

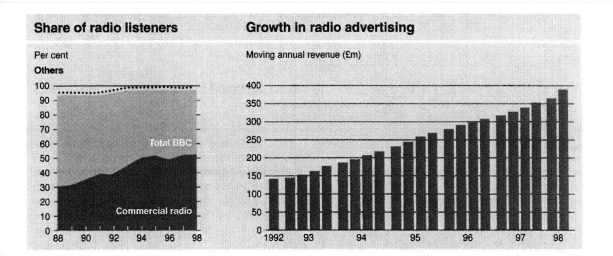

Share of radio listeners

Per cent
Others

(chart showing Total BBC and Commercial radio shares, years 88 to 98)

Growth in radio advertising

Moving annual revenue (£m)

(bar chart showing revenue growth from 1992 to 98)

Group, says commercial radio in the 1970s was 'an infant virtually strangled at birth by regulation'. The 1990 and 1996 Broadcasting Acts in particular freed the larger groups to acquire licences.

The regulations prevent one group owning more than 15 per cent of total points, based on population covered by each operator. Tony Stoller, chief executive of the Radio Authority, the regulator, says that would enable seven groups to own the industry. But many in the industry, Mr Bernard included, insist the regulations need further relaxing.

Tim Schoonmaker, chief executive of Emap Radio, says: 'The regulator is unwilling to let go. The ownership regulations are far more restrictive than for television, so perhaps a single regulator for radio is a bad idea.'

Operators' regulation concerns are linked to another worry: the advent of digital radio. There was only one application for a national digital radio licence, as many companies said the benefits of the new technology were uncertain.

David Mansfield, chief executive of Capital Radio, says regulators must allow more ownership consolidation to enable the industry to fund digital broadcasting.

Capital marks its 25th anniversary on October 19. Like LBC, it struggled in the early years because of regulation and recession. A quarter of a century on, it is keen to ensure regulation does not threaten to strangle another infant at birth.

Source: Financial Times, 2 October 1998

15.1 Considering the regional nature of commercial radio, how can this be of value to an advertiser?

15.2 Does local commercial radio contribute to the growth of advertising as a method of communication, or does it reflect a move away from the traditional forms of advertising? A consideration of the rise in Internet promotion and shopping will assist your argument.

15.3 Commercial radio is seen as a cheaper alternative to television advertising. How might the commercial radio companies improve their image in the minds of potential and existing advertisers to reduce or eliminate this perception, and yet maintain their regional characteristics?

Go big with the message

A new printing system allows advertisers to attract attention by means of sheer scale as well as by unusual surfaces, says David Murphy

Every day consumers are bombarded by advertising, much of which misses its intended target.

To get their message noticed amid all this competition, an increasing number of companies are coming to the conclusion that size is important.

They are turning to Very Large Format Digital (VLFD) printers, which can produce prints up to 5m wide on virtually any rolled material, including PVC, mesh (perforated) PVC, front and backlit vinyl, silk, paper and even carpet. This allows an alternative to screenprinting, which is more messy and labour intensive.

Screenprinting can still be cost-effective for print runs of up to 2,000 smaller prints. VLFD printing is ideal where a larger image with more impact is required, or where the client wishes to use a non-standard substrate (printing surface). The process is also suitable for short runs or 'one-off' prints, or for customising a poster to tie in with a local marketing campaign.

'The image goes direct from the PC to the printer in one pass with no printing plates,' says Louise Cole, marketing manager for NUR, the Israeli VLFD printer manufacturer. 'If you need to incorporate slight differences between posters, such as a local phone number or a branch address, you simply create a new file and make the necessary changes. In this respect, it's just like printing a document from your PC.'

Size, though, is without doubt an important factor in the emerging popularity of VLFD printers, says Michael Ayerst, managing director of Reading-based Vinyl Graphics, which recently installed its first NUR Blueboard VLFD printer. 'More and more companies are starting to produce large outdoor images that can be seen by a lot of people. The simple fact is that the bigger the image, the more people will see it and the more impact it will have.'

One of the first orders VGL received after installing its Blueboard printer was from Reading Football Club, which commissioned an 18m-diameter print including the sponsor's name and logo on mesh PVC for the centre circle.

'That print will sit on the pitch for an hour before kick-off and have 10 times the impact of a hoarding around the side of the ground,' says Mr Ayerst.

VLFD prints are being used as scenic backdrops in theatres and on television, and as decorative covers for scaffolding around buildings. In Paris this year, the Arc de Triomphe was covered for six months by three 15-metre square images, each in three 'tiles' printed on mesh, showing how the monument would look after the restoration had been completed.

Ms Cole says the ability to print on a wide variety of substrates is another important selling point. 'When we first developed the Outboard VLFD printer six years ago, we thought our customers would primarily be printing on to paper and self-adhesive vinyl,' she says. 'But they started experimenting with different materials and now their customers will routinely ask them to try new substrates to see what's possible.'

NUR's VLFD printers incorporate a dual Pentium Windows NT computer, and use continuous inkjet (CIJ) technology to transfer the image on to the substrate. In CIJ printing, electrically conductive ink flows continuously within a closed loop. The ink for the four-colour printing process (cyan, magenta, yellow and black) is stored in four cabinets. Solvent, used to fix the ink to the substrate, is stored in another, and water, to regulate the humidity, in another.

The ink is formed into a steady continuous stream of uniform microdrops by a piezoelectric resonator, which passes an electric charge through a special crystal, causing it to change shape.

These drops are directed on to a selected area or recovered and returned to the correct ink store. Each of the eight print nozzles can dispense up to 62,000 drops a second, ensuring high precision at greater distances from the substrate. Print speeds can exceed 60 sq m an hour.

While popular, CIJ technology does not have the VLFD printing field to itself. US company Vutek, based in Meredith, New Hampshire, can also offer 5m-wide prints on its 5,300 printer. It uses 'drop-on-demand' inkjet technology, similar to the system used in desktop computer printers. Ink is fired intermittently on to the substrate as required.

Drop-on-demand VLFD printers cost less initially than their CIJ counterparts, but CIJ supporters argue that drop-on-demand machines require more cleaning and maintenance because the heads can clog. Print heads built into a CIJ printer are permanent fixtures but drop-on-demand heads must be replaced if too many nozzles become clogged. While drop-on-demand printers work on a wide variety of substrates, they cannot as yet handle carpet, which NUR says is popular among corporate clients for exhibition displays.

Ms Cole believes that as more companies use VLFD printing and the results are seen by more people, there will be a snowball effect and the company's clients, already finding a ready market, will be busier than ever.

Source: Financial Times, 15 September 1998

FT

In a jam? Read the back of a bus

Motorists at city crawl speeds are advertisers' targets, says Thomas Barlow

To most people, it is not immediately apparent how a bus might be run through a printing press. But Londoners may have been pondering that very question after seeing a series of large advertisements on the backs of double-decker buses.

The images – of near-magazine quality – are printed, it seems, directly on to the body and rear windows of each bus. They are produced by a technology called Mega Rear, developed by Israeli-based NUR and used by Vinyl Graphics of Reading to print the images on many of the London buses.

The secret is in the vinyl. Four large panels of very thin vinyl are printed digitally with the desired image. These panels are then fixed like wallpaper on to the back of the bus. Because the vinyl constituting each panel is only one tenth of a millimetre thick, the image appears to be painted directly on to the surface of the bus.

Over the windows, a mesh of perforations in the vinyl allow passengers to see out. The effect from the inside is similar to that created by tinted glass.

Two hundred and fifty London buses have their backs covered using the Mega Rear technology, with advertisers including London Zoo, Wolford, VW Golf, London Dungeon, and the fashion house DKNY. A Yardley promotion last year saw one bus fully wrapped in Linda Evangelista – giving every London commuter the chance to travel inside a supermodel.

Robert Thurner, marketing manager of Transport Displays Incorporated (TDI), which deals with the advertising for London Transport, says most high density urban areas can expect to see more Mega Rears. London Transport recently authorised TDI to double the number of such buses to 500. This month TDI sold its first Mega Rear package to Peugeot, for 62 buses across the UK.

Another advertising format London commuters will soon be seeing more of is the illuminated billboard. These have been developed by TDI in conjunction with Altered States Images, a company that manufactures 'electric paper' for outdoor advertising and illuminated drinks' dispensers in pubs.

Employing the same technology used to back-light watches, clocks and Psion organisers, 10 trial buses carried back-lit billboards in London last January. The technology won a Millennium Products Award, and has since been launched in New York. TDI is planning to expand its fleet of illuminated London buses in the autumn.

With traffic speeds in most large cities down to a trickle, sides and backs of buses must be attractive sites to advertisers. But what do consumers think?

Source: Financial Times, 15 September 1998

15.4 How might an advertiser take maximum advantage from these new developments in display advertising? What must they pay particular attention to, and how could such displays complement other parts of the marketing mix?

15.5 In an integrated marketing communication programme, what special place could such dramatic presentations occupy? What particular areas of the consumer buying-decision process could they be most effectively used to reinforce?

Global events prove exception to no-adverts rule

Tobacco manufacturers are fuming over the move to end sponsorship, write Nicholas Timmins and David Blackwell

The government yesterday moved to bring a swift end to tobacco advertising, but promised an extension to July 2006 for sponsorship of 'exceptional global events' that will include Formula One motor racing and probably the Embassy world snooker championship.

Billboard and press advertising will be halted from December 10 – the anniversary of the government's white paper on the proposed ban – while in-store advertising will be limited to price lists and stock display units.

Ministers promised tough action against any attempts at 'brand-stretching' – using tobacco brand names on other goods or services such as clothing and footwear, and reserved the right to introduce further legislation if that occurs.

Much sponsorship will cease in July 2003. But Formula One, with sponsorship worth £35m a year, and probably the snooker world championship, will be allowed to continue for three more years. However, the sponsorship will have to be cut by a fifth in each of the extra years.

The Tobacco Manufacturers' Association reacted furiously, accusing the government of 'blatant disregard for the legal position', given a European Court hearing next year in which the big four UK manufacturers and the German government are arguing that the European Union directive on which the government's legislation is based is illegal.

They maintain it should have been introduced under a health, not a single market directive, and that it breaches principles of subsidiarity, proportionality and human rights.

David Swann, the association's chief executive, hinted at further legal action, arguing that the prohibition of direct mail was 'a clear violation of individuals' rights to information about a legally available product'.

UK tobacco shares closed only marginally down, despite a warning from Mr Swann that tens of thousands of jobs would be put at risk.

The government's impact assessment of the draft regulations, however, says the ban is likely to reduce consumption by about only 2.5 per cent, costing the tobacco manufacturers about £300m of their £13bn turnover, and £20m a year in profits. Those figures could rise if price competition intensifies.

In the short-term the ban will save 1,500 lives a year, rising to 3,000 or more, the assessment says, with the costs to the National Health Service of treating smoking-related disease falling by £20m to £40m a year.

The government, however is likely to lose around £250m in value added tax and excise duty, a figure that could more than double if the lack of advertising produces stronger price competition.

Small retailers may suffer disproportionately, according to the study, although the National Confederation of Retail Newsagents said it expected 'no impact on sales' in the short-term. Longer-term it predicted an increase in smuggling.

Effects of UK tobacco ban

Tobacco manufacturing
- £300m+ in lost turnover
- £20m a year in lost profits

Advertising industry
- May gain from the £300m reduction in tobacco expenditure going on other products and services

Government
- £250m to £500m+ in lost tax revenues

Sport
- Formula One to lose £35m in sponsorship
- Non-F1 sports lose £8m

NHS
- Annual savings of £20m to £40m in treating smoking-related disease
- 1,500 lives saved annually, rising to 3,000 (assuming 2.5 per cent reduction in tobacco consumption)

The assessment quotes a study commissioned by the Tobacco Manufacturers' Association suggesting the move could cost 1,700 jobs, but argues that the £300m reduction in tobacco expenditure 'will be matched by savings to consumers and increases in business to other parts of the economy'.

Prices and profitability in the advertising industry will be reduced by the disappearance of £50m in press and poster advertising, it adds, but lower prices may help other companies advertise. Breaches of the draft regulations will involve fines of between £1,000 and £5,000.

A further £50m in sports and arts sponsorship will go, at least £15m of it by 2003. But global events will qualify for the extension to 2006 where they involve at least three countries on two continents with sponsorship of more than £2.5m a year. Outside Formula One only the snooker world championship is expected to qualify.

Ministers defended that as a level of sponsorship genuinely more difficult to replace than lower sums. After Bernie Ecclestone's £1m donation to the Labour party – since returned – the chosen criteria also have the political advantage that not only Formula One will receive an extension to the sponsorship ban.

Medical organisations welcomed the speed of the government's action – it had until July 2001 to implement the EU directive.

But Ian Birks, head of corporate affairs at Gallaher, said a December timetable was unrealistic to wind down coupon gift schemes.

He accused the government of posturing when smoking was rising for the first time in living memory and tobacco revenues were collapsing from smuggling.

Source: Financial Times, 18 June 1999

15.7 Government regulatory control is necessary to curb the excesses of advertisers, and reflect the wishes of the general public on environmental and other issues. How do you think that the advertising industry should counter this suggestion, and what effect might such extension of regulation have on the use of advertising?

15.8 How should the advertising industry replace the lost revenues from such a ban?

15.9 Explain the link between environmental scanning and the creative departments of advertising agencies and their clients.

Article 15.E   FT

Split-screen BMW makes the break

The carmaker's image has taken a knock so the challenge was to generate new ideas. The result is a ground-breaking TV ad, says Haig Simonian

Viewers of SAT.1, the German broadcaster, had every reason to believe their television sets were faulty.

The commercial break began with a spot for BMW's new 3 Series coupe which was, as usual, followed by a string of other adverts. Strangely, however, the other commercials did not fill the entire screen. Above or below, the new BMW raced across a horizontal strip.

And between each spot, the car no longer went horizontally, but snaked its way to the top or the bottom of the screen in a tight curve. Gremlins? Interference? Or just time to buy a new TV?

The answer came the following day after blanket coverage for the German carmaker's 'world premiere' split-screen commercial.

Even rival advertisers and broadcasters admit BMW's extraordinary six-minute advertisement broke new ground. The unusually long break – possible under German rules limiting advertising during films broadcast on television but allowing much longer commercial breaks at the beginning and end – provided the opportunity. 'The response has been fantastic,' says Christine Krepold, a BMW official. 'It created huge awareness.'

SAT.1 declines to provide viewing figures, amid suggestions that the advert, aired at prime-time on only three consecutive evenings, failed to generate significant additional audiences.

But the free publicity and awareness generated were more than satisfactory, argues Sabine Tennyson, head of public relations at Jung von Matt, the Hamburg advertising agency which took over the BMW account in January. 'BMW is a big challenge for us,' says Stefan Zschaler, a creative partner at the agency and one of the two people behind the campaign.

The situation was very different for the Bavarian carmaker a few years back. Innovative engineering and quality production gave BMW a blue-chip image that sold itself. Classy advertising drove home the cars' sporty, driver-oriented image, and prestige sponsorship linking the brand with top notch sporting and cultural events did the rest.

Few at BMW's Munich headquarters are prepared to admit those days are over. While the brand remains a badge of success for young professionals, BMW's image has taken a knock. The group's inability to master Rover, its lossmaking UK subsidiary, more than five years since its takeover, has tarnished BMW's reputation for invincibility among shareholders and analysts.

Even BMW's cars no longer command the respect they once did. Stronger rivalry from Volkswagen's upmarket Audi subsidiary and the revitalisation of Mercedes-Benz have posed big challenges. Even Alfa Romeo has become a serious rival.

BMW, meanwhile, has appeared to rest on its laurels. Its 'evolutionary' approach to exterior styling has prompted criticism that its cars all look alike.

Hence the need for fresh ideas – of which the TV ad was just a start, says Mr Zschaler. Jung von Matt's plans for BMW eschew conventional broadcast or print campaigns in favour of what Mr Zschaler calls 'event' advertising. That means fewer, but much more striking, adverts spread over significantly fewer publications and broadcasters.

The fact that necessity may have been the mother of invention in view of tighter budgets because of Rover's massive losses is implicit, but unstated.

The first print 'event' came last month, with a lavish spread in auto motor + sport, the respected German car magazine. Rather than the familiar two-page BMW colour spread of a car with a short strap along the bottom, Jung von Matt went for a six-page special. Colour gave way to black and white, while a folded pull-out map of a return driving route from BMW's Munich headquarters to Florence was intended to emphasise the new coupé's

performance and touring qualities on winding roads.

More of the same will follow. Recent advertisements for the revised version of BMW's US-built Z3 roadster focus on its six cylinder engines, compared with less powerful four-cylinder units in many competing models.

BMW and the agency are understandably coy about how their 'events' will develop, beyond revealing that the next will feature new diesel motors. Unconventional TV advertising will continue to play an important part: the latest spot for the 3 Series saloon involves two black and white adverts, broadcast at either end of a normal two to three-minute commercial break.

The first – a teaser – involves a skid in an unidentified rental car and its consequences. The second is almost identical, frame for frame, except that the vehicle is obviously a 3 Series and the outcome – of both the road incident and subsequent events – very different.

Such suggestive advertising is rare in Germany, and uncommon even wider afield. But both the agency and SAT.1 agree the split-screen commercial was probably a one-off.

Organising the six-minute spot was a mammoth task, says Klaus-Peter Schulz, SAT.1's director of sales and service. The company, a leading private-sector broadcaster, admits it was chosen by BMW and the agency as much because it could create the necessary space for such a long commercial within the tight deadline for the car's launch as for any special audience or demographic factors.

Mr Schulz identifies two main problems: creating the necessary space, given the long lead times in booking TV advertising; and persuading the eight other advertisers involved to forsake the top or bottom slice of the screen – comprising 20 per cent of the picture – to allow the 3 Series coupe to appear simultaneously. 'They all reacted negatively to begin with. It took a lot of convincing.'

To complicate matters, the BMW advert could only run alongside particular products. Rival vehicles were obviously out. BMW also rejected products deemed inappropriate to its image. 'Pampers [nappies] would not have been acceptable,' notes Ms Krepold.

SAT.1 sweetened the pill for other advertisers by cutting the price for their commercials by 20 per cent – reflecting the compressed space.

And it convinced advertisers such as McDonald's, Viag Interkom, the mobile phones group, and Schöller, the ice cream company, that sharing the screen with BMW could be in their interest.

'We told them there would be a much better audience flow and far greater awareness,' says Mr Schulz. SAT.1 also emphasised its own marketing efforts to draw attention to the commercial breaks.

Some advertisers welcomed the opportunity. 'Our appearance in the BMW advertising block suited the launch of the campaign for Mövenpick La Crema excellently,' says Karin Gebhardt, Schöller's managing director of marketing.

Now the dust has settled, broadcaster, agency and client all appear delighted with their screen splitting 'event'. None, however, intends to repeat the experiment. First, because the impact of the commercial lay in its uniqueness. And, second, having already been done by BMW, it is unlikely another carmaker will rush to have a go.

Source: Financial Times, 18 June 1999

15.10 What was the principal purpose of this original approach and how can it be related to the buyer's decision-making process?

15.11 What other advanced techniques have you observed recently and do they potentially replace 'traditional' forms of TV advertising, supplement them or are they a 'flash in the pan' with no future?

15.12 Since advertising is only one part of the whole promotional mix, explain how an advertising campaign should be part of a much wider approach to exposing the organisation's message, and what other components are available to the marketer.

16 Sales Promotion

Another weapon in the armoury available to the marketer is sales promotion, a weapon which has perhaps less glamour than the creation and distribution of advertising, but nevertheless a valuable contributor to the whole marketing effort. Sales promotion is generally thought of and used as a short-term tactical exercise to impress the idea of personalisation and added value to a product, accelerating the buyers' movement towards purchase and use of the product.

This activity may take many forms, for example the simple money-off coupon, the voucher collection scheme, rebates against a purchase, two for one introductory offers, prize draws, competitions, and free or very cheap promotional items available on proof of purchase. These activities can also be conducted throughout the supply chain. Staff in shops or wholesalers may be offered cash bonuses, prize draws, etc. for achieving specified sales targets. For instance, the friendly enquiry at the petrol filling station 'and have you checked your oil?' may not display an interest in the wellbeing of your engine but could indicate that the oil company is offering an incentive to the staff or the site to generate increased sales of oil.

It is the golden rule, however and wherever the promotions are carried out, that they should be part of an integrated communications mix, that the message and impression should conform to the overall objectives, and that the use and timing of such activities should complement the other communication activities in both their style and content and their timing.

Beyond all this it can now be seen that sales promotion is assuming an even more important role than before, as the ideas growing from Internet marketing enable the use of sales promotional techniques on a much wider scale, directed at a client base that is better understood as we make more use of the Internet itself, together with computer data capture capability and we become more familiar with the interpretation of the flow of data and how to use it more effectively.

Where sales promotion activities excel is in the rapid and clear results that can be obtained, giving the marketer an almost instant record of how effective the message is, and providing detailed feedback as to customer response. More than this, it can provide a very useful source of customer data, in terms of their reaction to the offering and to the provision of extra information such as mailing addresses, preferences, buying habits and so on. Although sales promotion has been regarded as a junior member of the promotional mix in the past, it is assuming a greater importance as technology and data handling are refined.

In order to successfully complete the tasks in this chapter you will need to be familiar with:

- manufacturer/customer sales promotion objectives and techniques;
- customer-loyalty schemes;
- sales promotion evaluation;
- the importance of monitoring;
- joint promotions;
- 11P's of loyalty marketing;
- European sales promotion regulations;
- good sales promotion practice – and bad!

Article 16.A

FT

After the dust has settled

Roland Adburgham and Diane Summers look at the impact of Hoover's ill-fated free-flights promotion.

For well over half a century Hoover has been the generic term for a vacuum cleaner. However, after more than 18 months of being linked constantly to the phrase 'free-flights fiasco', the name may now be as readily associated in some minds with a disastrous sales promotion.

Last week Maytag, Hoover's US parent company, disclosed that the ill-fated promotion had cost the company more than £48m – more than double the sum originally feared when Maytag took stock of the damage early last year.

The promotion which caused all the trouble closes this week. In reality, Hoover will feel the reverberations of its free-flights offer for some time to come. There are also signs that consumer attitudes have hardened towards 'free offers' in general, with companies more cautious in their approach to sales promotions of every kind.

The problem for Hoover started in autumn 1992 when it promised customers who spent at least £100 on a Hoover product two free air tickets to continental Europe or the US. From the customers' point of view, it seemed the bargain of the decade. Demand was such that Hoover, which employs 3,500 people in the UK, had to step up production of vacuum cleaners which were just over the £100 threshold.

It rapidly became clear that Hoover had grotesquely underestimated the take-up of the offer. Thousands of customers were infuriated by delays in obtaining flights. Maytag intervened. Three senior executives lost their jobs and a taskforce, at its peak employing 250 people, was set up.

Peter le Conte, chairman of the Institute of Sales Promotion (ISP), says that Hoover could have done 'a lot more a lot earlier' when it became clear the promotion was going awry.

'Perhaps instead of wriggling, it would have been better to have come clean and try and do something else,' he says. Le Conte suggests, for example, that the company might have been able to fulfil its obligations on flights over a period of years.

The offer itself was flawed from the first, he adds: 'In my book it doesn't stack up to be able to buy a product for £100–£200 and fly to America for significantly more than the cost of the product you purchased.' The sheer scale of the take-up of the promotion has been breathtaking: Hoover says 220,000 people have now flown or are booked on flights up to June. The taskforce is now winding down.

'By the end of this month, or by the end of June, Hoover will have fulfilled its commitments and obligations,' says Hoover spokeswoman, Caroline Knight. Not so, claims a group of dissatisfied consumers which has organised itself as the Hoover Holiday Pressure Group. Last week three leaders of the group flew to Maytag's headquarters in Iowa accompanied by boxes containing what the group said were 7,000 letters of complaint, and on Tuesday the group's representatives spoke at the company's annual general meeting.

The group has yet to decide whether it will pursue legal action in the High Court in London. Hoover has already faced about 70 cases in small claims courts, all of which it has defended, and about one in five of which it has lost.

The Advertising Standards Authority (ASA), the advertising watchdog, is currently investigating seven consumer complaints and the ISP has also asked the ASA to examine whether the promotions industry's voluntary code of practice has been breached.

The code sets out, in general terms, promoters' responsibilities not to disappoint consumers and to make realistic calculations of the likely response to a promotion. However, according to Keith Richards, a barrister at the Consumers' Association, the code lacks teeth. The association, which is still dealing with complaints from dissatisfied Hoover customers, would like to see the ASA, or a similar body, having the power to fine companies which breach the code.

'I'm sure consumers are now shaken and will not be so readily willing to be taken in by sales promotions,' says Richards.

Le Conte agrees that the Hoover case has 'caused people to be more cynical, which is extremely unfortunate'. But he says the ISP has seen a big upturn in companies seeking legal and copy advice before they go ahead with promotions. 'Everybody is super-aware that promotions that go wrong can seriously damage your health,' he says.

Hoover denies that any long-term damage has been done either to sales or to the company's image. Says Knight: 'Customers are able to differentiate between a quality product and, regrettably, a flawed promotion. Our sales figures indicate that the brand has not suffered and we have maintained market share.'

There does not appear to be any evidence that Hoover sales have been damaged. Scottish Power, one of Scotland's largest electrical retailers, says there was a temporary dip in Hoover sales after the offer, which was promoted particularly hard in its territory and provoked a great deal of adverse publicity.

It may be, though, that this dip was caused by a glut of second-hand vacuum cleaners on the market, as people disposed of machines purchased only to fulfill the conditions of the promotion. Whatever the reason, sales soon recovered, says the retailer.

Hoover even had enough confidence last year to offer a new travel promotion and could do so again in the future. Says Knight: 'Travel remains a very key motivator in sales promotions.'

Although the company must be assuming the worst is over, it looks likely that the consequences of the offer will drag on for months, if not years. In the longer term it can only hope the 'free-flights fiasco' will be a relatively short-lived association and that Hoover will mean vacuum cleaners for at least another 50 years.

Source: Financial Times, 28 April 1994

16.1 In many ways the Hoover offer achieved its goal, and yet was an unmitigated disaster and drove Hoover UK to the brink of bankruptcy. In the light of the above, define the role of promotional activities, and how they play a part in the overall communications mix.

16.2 What alternative sales promotion techniques were available to Hoover?

16.3 By conducting reading outside this article, show how Hoover repaired the damage done to their image. What other activities might they have used?

16.4 This disaster marked a turning point in the use of promotional techniques. What lessons can be learned, and what steps should we take to avoid such a disaster in the future?

Return of 'instant redemption'

Virginia Matthews finds that shoppers are being persuaded to develop a taste for in-store coupons, once considered to be downmarket, thanks to in-store dispensers

Money-off coupons, long dismissed as tacky and downmarket, are to be given a new lease of life. J. Sainsbury's, Budgens and Iceland are testing an in-store coupon dispenser at 400 supermarkets in the UK.

Food and drink manufacturers believe shoppers can be persuaded to adopt the habit with as much enthusiasm as in the US, where even affluent consumers can be seen with special coupon organiser wallets on shopping trips.

Initial results suggest that this new form of 'instant redemption' is attractive to shoppers of all socio-economic backgrounds.

The Instant Coupon Machine is placed at eye level next to the brand being discounted, with a flashing red light to attract attention. Once the customer has withdrawn a paper coupon – the discounts range from 10p to £1 – a timer delay system prevents a shopper from taking too many coupons.

The introduction of an ICM – either on a single brand or on a collection of grocery and household lines – can have a remarkable effect on sales. Kelloggs, Cadbury's, Unilever's Van den Bergh Foods and Danone, all taking part in the trials, report sales increases of more than 60 per cent.

Sales of Bic razors have increased by 257 per cent, while the sales boost for Shredded Wheat has been 207 per cent.

Sole UK distribution and marketing rights to the ICM, invented in the US by News America Marketing, are held by Aspen, a London specialist media company whose interests include in-flight entertainment as well as traditional sales promotion.

Aspen's own research, conducted this year among 1000 shoppers, suggests that up to 50 per cent of non-coupon users will use coupon machines if they find them in-store. Among those who had used an ICM, 76 per cent said they would use it again.

'People hate cutting coupons out of newspapers because it takes time and because they invariably get screwed up and torn long before they reach the cashier's hand,' says Jeremy Williams, Aspen's client services director.

'But to position them on-shelf, while people are actually doing their shopping, is quite another matter. We believe that the coupon habit will catch on among all sections of society.'

While consumers say they enjoy buying top brands for a bargain price, Mr Williams believes the benefits to manufacturers are twofold: 'First, it's an incentive to try out a new brand that the manufacturer might be rolling out; and second, it's a way of building loyalty to the company. Having been offered 30p or 50p off a particular brand last week, a consumer is likely to head straight for the same brand next time.

'Coupons create awareness of, and interest in, particular brands even if the coupon campaign has been replaced by something else such as extra free product or two for the price of three.'

For retailers such as Budgens, who pay nothing to have the machine in their stores but who reap the rewards of extra sales, the return of couponing comes at a time when shopper loyalty has never been so highly prized.

'We are finding that men, in particular, are keen to get instant discounts as they go around our stores. Most shoppers appear happy to try new brands if there is sufficient incentive for them to do so,' says Joanne Nixey, marketing manager.

Source: Financial Times, 30 April 1999

16.5   **How does such a system contribute to sales promotion evaluation and the building of customer loyalty?**

16.6   **How would such a technique assist in retailers' promotion objectives? What are these and how does it satisfy them?**

16.7   What special role might these activities play in the introduction of a new product?

16.8   How might such a technique be employed in, for example, France and Germany? How does it stand with regard to European legislation and national regulation?

Article 16.C   FT

When beenz means virtual Green Shield stamps

A small interactive agency has invented an internet currency that can be earned and spent at various web sites. By Tim Jackson

Does anyone remember Green Shield stamps? A loyalty device in which shops give consumers paper stamps that they stick into books and exchange for products may not seem like much of a model for a web business.

But to Charles Cohen, owner of a small interactive agency in London, the Green Shield model had a big advantage over the other loyalty schemes to which he belonged. His credit card points, frequent-flyer miles and video-store bonuses were all proprietary to a single company or a few companies. The Green Shield model, however, built multiple companies into a single network with powerful customer loyalty.

In Beenz.com, the company Mr Cohen founded in March 1998, he has updated the Green Shield model for the web age. Dispensing with physical stamps and books, it has created a virtual currency, the 'beenz', which can be earned and spent at web sites without any delay.

As the 'bank' issuing this currency, the Beenz company sells beenz to merchants at one US cent each, encouraging site owners to give them out as promotional rewards for providing an e-mail address, opening an account, or even viewing a single web page. The beenz can be spent at the same or other web sites. Beenz.com buys them back for half a cent each.

The system relies on a clever combination of client and server software. Users can download a 476K 'beenz counter' from *www.beenz.com*, a Java package that sits on their desktop and shows their points balance. To give away beenz or accept them in payment, merchants simply paste a few lines of code into the HTML (hypertext mark-up language) of their web sites. In the back office, an Oracle database keeps track of everyone's balances.

Lack of paper is not the only advantage over loyalty stamps. The Beenz system is instantaneous;

it allows users to spend their beenz with many merchants; and the client-server model allows beenz to be personal to each merchant and user, so Beenz.com can prevent a secondary market emerging.

The problem with the idea, as with many network-economics businesses, was how to get it going. Mr Cohen recruited Philip Letts as chief executive. Mr Letts – a software manager who had previously carried out a management buy-out of a British IT information company – executed a fine guerrilla marketing campaign to launch the business. He sent bogus beenz statements to UK journalists, styled to look like American Express bills. A team from his PR agency stuck Beenz logos to cashpoint machines all over London, to make it look as though the machines accepted beenz as well as plastic cards. And he parked a security van painted in the company's livery outside newspaper offices.

Over the past two months, the company has recruited 125 web sites to give away beenz on a trial basis, and has persuaded 25,000 consumers to open beenz accounts. Mr Cohen says about 12,000 are regular users, and the number is growing at 15 per cent a week.

Mr Letts has recruited a number of experienced managers in Europe and the US. He has also brought in 45 seed investors, including the head of Oracle's UK business, the chairman of a leading UK direct reseller of computer goods, and a Luxembourg-based investment bank.

Initially, Beenz.com was a British company, but recognising that America could prove the biggest market, it is now a Delaware corporation with offices in New York and San Francisco. Mr Letts plans to spend $8m (£4.9m) on consumer marketing this year, split equally between the UK and US, and hopes to recruit 750 merchants by the end of 1999 and 1,500 by mid-2000.

He also hopes to turn beenz into a marketing tool for businesses that sell to businesses, just as frequent-flyer miles are a powerful incentive in corporate travel.

The risk facing the company is that its currency's value as a promotional tool could diminish sharply if everyone started offering it. But by then Mr Cohen and Mr Letts hope they are billionaires, and Beenz.com a public company.

Tim Jackson is founder of QXL.com, an online auction business. e-mail tim.jackson@ft.com

Source: Financial Times, 8 June 1999

16.9 How does this new approach relate to the 11P's of loyalty marketing? Does it display any particular weaknesses?

16.10 How could such a service be extended to organisational markets?

16.11 Given that, as stated in the article, the 'beenz' are non-proprietary in the sense that they do not have their brand or logo attached, what is the attraction of such an approach to manufacturers and distributors?

16.12 Could such a scheme work throughout Europe and how might it be affected by currency variations and European regulations?

17 Personal Selling and Sales Management

Here is the communication tool which has the most direct contact with the customer. Personal selling is the point at which a sales person actually talks directly to the customer and replays the corporate message and image on a one-to-one basis. Clearly we are not going to attempt to sell tins of beans or boxes of soap powder to a domestic shopper in a supermarket or on the doorstep, since it would be a highly unproductive and uneconomic way of distributing such basic products to a mass market. On the other hand, we would personally sell tins of beans or boxes of soap powder to a supermarket itself, as their purchase would be many thousands of units, therefore being both economic and effective.

Many sales forces are built and exist to serve a client base which is well known and understood by the organisation, and serve the multiple purposes of establishing a good personal rapport with the customer, servicing the customer well, and ensuring their satisfaction by dealing with problems as they arise, as well as reporting information obtained from their customer contacts. This information can relate to market conditions, market trends, competitor activity and new customer leads. All this information is reported to the sales manager.

The management of sales is a crucial task in that the sales force has to be made familiar with the products they are expected to sell, with the sales territory they have to cover and the message and image they are expected to transmit about their employer. At the same time the information flow returning via the sales force must be monitored, collated and the inferences drawn and reported. All these activities are undertaken with reference to the organisational mission statement, the marketing plan, budgets for both sales and cost of sales and staff management and motivation.

Remember that selling does not just happen, it has to be organised, the sales force instructed, the information from the field processed and passed on to other departments and levels of management. All of this happens while keeping an eye on how the effort is matching sales predictions and demands of the production and other functions of the organisation. The sales manager's task is to match sales effort with organisational expectations.

In order to successfully complete the tasks in this chapter you will need to be familiar with:

- training/motivation/compensation considerations and balances;
- telesales;
- managing relationships internally and externally;
- personal selling ethical practice;
- monitoring competitors;
- the personal selling process;
- the difference between order takers and order makers;
- monitoring performance.

Article 17.A   FT

Eastern axes staff as doorstep selling costs bite

By Andrew Taylor

Eastern Group, Britain's biggest power supplier, yesterday became the first electricity company to axe sales staff employed to take advantage of competition in the electricity and gas market.

It is particularly disenchanted with the high cost of doorstep selling.

The group, owned by Texas Utilities of the US, is cutting 500 jobs from offices in north London and Peterborough.

A further 200 will be transferred elsewhere. The cuts represent 15 per cent of Eastern Energy's permanent staff in the UK and will save about £15m this year.

The company will look to increase electricity and gas customers either through acquisitions and joint ventures or by stepping up sales through telephone marketing and the internet.

Eastern is considered a potential bidder for the electricity supply businesses of SWEB, the south west of England electricity company owned by Southern Energy of the US, and Swalec, the south Wales electricity company owned by Hyder.

The company is also considering joint ventures with retail groups in other sectors, which would enable it to sell a broader range of products from a single marketing and software system.

Phil Turberville, chief executive, said electricity supply margins were too thin to justify the expenditure being made by the industry on winning customers.

A substantial reshaping of the sector was required to allow fewer, larger suppliers to sell an increased product range to more customers.

Competition for all 24m UK domestic electricity customers was introduced last month. All 18m domestic gas customers have been able to choose a rival supplier since May last year.

Electricity and gas companies have found that door-to-door selling has been most effective in winning customers, but expensive.

Marketing techniques of sales staff, most of whom have been sub-contracted, have also prompted complaints from consumer groups. The electricity and gas industry regulator recently introduced rules to halt mis-selling.

Eastern estimated that it cost the company at least £30 to win each new electricity or gas customer. It would take up to two years before a new contract moved into profit based on current charges.

There was also the possibility that customers would decide to move again before the two years elapsed. One in three customers agreeing to change suppliers subsequently changed their minds, said Mr Turberville.

The group, which supplies 3.3m electricity and 700,000 gas customers, said it was still committed to reaching 5m–10m customers but would be looking at less-expensive ways of achieving this target.

Source: Financial Times, 11 June 1999

17.1 By reference to this article describe the process of gaining customers by the use of telesales.

17.2 How might you derive a compensation and motivation package for (a) a telesales operator and (b) a sales representative?

17.3 How would you monitor the efforts of a doorstep sales force particularly in the light of potential accusations of mis-selling?

17.4 In what ways can a sales force be used to gain information? What information may be obtained, and how would a sales manager make use of such information?

17.5 In terms of personal selling what attributes would be most appreciated by (a) an organisational buyer and (b) a member of the public in their own home? What are the crucial differences and how might we provide the correct motivation in each case?

Article 17.B   **FT**

Farepak goes online to clean up

By David Blackwell

The Super Wonder Mop is not only going on the internet but is poised to invade continental Europe.

The two moves are part of Farepak's plans to continue the profits growth being generated from Kleeneze, the door-to-door household goods business acquired four years ago.

Last year's rise in group pre-tax profits from £10.4m to £11.5m was thanks to a 33 per cent rise at Kleeneze to operating profits of £4.07m.

The group expects profits from Kleeneze to overtake those from its traditional Christmas hamper business next year, and is planning to adopt the Kleeneze name to reflect the changing nature of the group.

Bob Johnson, the chairman who controls just over half the shares, said his army of 14,000 distributors would be able to order direct through the internet from July 18, and use of the internet would be spread throughout the operation.

'We will be totally pro-active: we will be able to show each distributor how to structure his agency and maximise his sales,' he said.

Last year Kleeneze sales in Ireland – which the group regards as the first move into continental Europe – rose by 90 per cent.

Mr Johnson said the Irish success over the past three years should allay any fears about the group's

ability to expand profitably into Europe, and it would be looking at moving into the northern part of the Continent in the next 18 months.

Group sales in the 12 months to April 30 rose from £128.1m to £145.7m.

The proposed final dividend of 5p lifts the total from 6p to 6.75p, payable from earnings per share up from 15.27p to 16.9p.

Comment

● Farepak is cleaning up with Kleeneze, which has turned out to be an astute acquisition. The old cash-based mail order business is fading, as a preference for vouchers over the traditional Christmas hamper eats into margins and interest rates on the cash holdings decline. It is also important to keep Kleeneze's internet move in perspective – although 50 per cent of distributors' orders already arrive by fax, moving the salesforce to computers will be a leap for many. Further, there have to be question marks over the group's ability to move the formula into continental Europe. Profits this year of £12.8m give a multiple of 17. The shares have had a good run over the past 12 months, and yesterday's $11\frac{1}{2}$p fall to $323\frac{1}{2}$p speaks for itself.

Source: Financial Times, 30 June 1999

17.6 How does such a move to use the Internet benefit Kleeneze's customers?

17.7 What advantages does the innovation as described in the article have for the sales management team, and how would you use the method to improve your relationship with the customer and the sales force?

17.8 Show the stages in the personal selling process and how each might benefit (or otherwise) from the use of the Internet in this way.

17.9 Construct a typical management structure chart, showing how a sales force might be constructed, and the specific line responsibilities of each component together with the most efficient communication and decision routes.

18 Direct and Internet Marketing

The growth in the respectability of direct marketing as an activity is a notable development of recent years. It is true that many still think of direct marketing as being the delivery of 'junk mail', but this is only a small part of the whole exercise, and even this is becoming increasingly accurate in its targeting of the customer most likely to react in the preferred manner.

The direct marketing route is becoming a communication tool of increasing capability and effectiveness, especially with the advent of the Internet. As the penetration of personal contact with the World Wide Web becomes increasingly universal, the ability to target and approach more perfectly segmented markets is now possible.

Associated with this is the ability to process vast amounts of information effectively and the growth of interactive instant response use of television and printed matter advertising, asking for a customer response, which can be processed and followed up rapidly, generating a high level of success.

The argument for the use of direct marketing hinges around two principal positions. First, the use of techniques available increases the speed at which a customer may be moved through the process of creating awareness and on to adoption. Second, such use enables the marketer to generate a dialogue with the customer and thereby grow a relationship which will aim to reinforce the customer's conviction that they made the right choice in the first place, and that other offerings from the same source are likely to provide the same level of satisfaction.

Concerning satisfaction, it should also become clear that if we open up these channels of communication with the customer, they will feel much more free to express not just their satisfaction with the product but also their dissatisfactions in general and in detail. This information becomes a significant part of the monitoring process. It is good to talk, as they say!

In order to successfully complete the tasks in this chapter you will need to be familiar with:

- the Internet;
- techniques of direct marketing;
- mailing list/subscriber information;
- databases;
- mail order;
- telemarketing.

Interview: Peter Williams, Daily Mail and General Trust finance director

Cathy Newman finds newspaper executives relying on their brands to fight off new online rivals for revenue

Several newspapers can be found free of charge on the internet: a growing number of people have taken to reading their favourite papers online, at home or in the office, instead of venturing out to a newsagent and opening their wallets.

The implications are worrying for national newspaper owners such as the UK's Daily Mail and General Trust. Peter Williams, finance director, agrees the plethora of free news and information on the internet is a challenge for titles like the Daily Mail.

However, he says, DMGT has avoided cannibalising sales of its print newspaper by offering themed internet sites related to the Daily Mail rather than reproducing the title wholesale online.

One of DMGT's main consumer web sites is Soccernet, a football themed site. The group is also considering developing an internet version of the Daily Mail's Femail women's section.

Although Mr Williams does not feel too threatened by free editorial online, he does have concerns about classified advertising on the internet.

'That is the big area where we will be affected because the internet search engine is suited to someone finding the right sort of car and making the transaction,' he says.

New media ventures like The Monster Board, the US-backed online recruitment company founded in 1994, are trespassing on the territory of traditional media groups. DMGT's regional newspaper group – Northcliffe Newspapers – is more threatened by digital business than its national titles, Mr Williams believes. Classified advertising represents between 30–40 per cent of Northcliffe's total revenues, compared with between 10–15 per cent of the national titles' turnover.

In response to this threat Northcliffe and other regional groups formed AdHunter, an online classified advertising database. The consortium has one big advantage over newer competitors – its well-known local brands. 'You go into AdHunter through your local newspaper,' Mr Williams explains. 'On the internet, the brands and quality of the product will win out.'

David Landau, chairman and co-founder of Loot, a UK-based classified advertising publication, agrees. 'There are now more than 1,000 small, new classified web sites in the US. They are not making it because they do not have brand recognition.'

The company now feels confident enough about its appeal over other, less well established online rivals, to have started charging for its internet edition. For £1.30, you can browse 14 regional editions from 6am the day they are published.

If you bought them all in their print format, it would cost nearly £20. In the first two days after it started charging, 3,500 people paid to view Loot over the internet. The company sells 300,000 print editions each week.

Mr Landau is positive about the impact digital business has already had. It has helped Loot expand into different fields. The decision to introduce its own loans service to finance readers' purchases, for example, was partly inspired by the ease with which the new venture could be publicised over the internet. The company did not need to go to the expense of advertising Loot Loans with flyers or other printed matter.

DMGT, although it does not charge for access to its consumer web sites, also benefits from a fee for entry to parts of the site owned by Euromoney Publications, the financial publisher in which DMGT has a 71 per cent stake. People are prepared to pay for specialised, detailed information delivered in an easily searchable online format, Mr Williams says.

He also believes the internet has helped DMGT broaden into other areas. Soccernet has set up a shop selling football merchandise, and even though access to the site is free it breaks even because the group gets a commission on the sale of goods.

But as DMGT begins to enter new fields it has also left old ones. The group once printed all its newspapers on its own presses but it now uses 10 plants owned by other companies. The unpicking of that particular part of the value chain allowed DMGT to make cost savings. 'We outsourced printing because it's extremely expensive to build print plants,' Mr Williams says.

He maintains there are other ways in which digital business, far from undermining the group's traditional economic basis, may help it by driving newsprint prices down. 'There have been suggestions in the States there hasn't been the same increase in demand for newsprint because more classified advertising is going online,' he says.

Mr Landau is perhaps more willing than Mr Williams to embrace digital business, because Loot, launched in 1985, has less of a heritage in print media. He is confident that, perhaps as soon as a decade hence, Loot will do most of its business online. 'If we managed to sell all our copies via the internet we'd be immensely rich,' he says. 'We wouldn't have to pay commission to newsagents, wholesalers, distributors; and we wouldn't have to pay for paper.'

Source: Financial Times, 15 October 1998

18.1 As a newspaper publisher DMGT is exploiting the possibilities of the Internet. How do they do this and how are they preserving their traditional newspaper publishing activities?

18.2 What other services might *Loot* develop using their on-line expertise?

18.3 What effect is DMGT's move having on their traditional suppliers/distributors? How might they try to maintain a commercial presence?

Article 18.B

FT

A question of trust for site visitors

An US software entrepreneur has come up with a scheme to encourage online data protection. By Tim Jackson

Threats of trade war between Europe and the US are usually to be taken with a pinch of salt. But John Borking, number two in the office of the Netherlands data protection ombudsman, issued a warning last week that should scare the pants off any US or European company that has a web site.

Starting on October 25, Mr Borking threatened, his organisation's enforcement officials would prosecute any company in the Netherlands that they found sending electronic data to the US for processing.

'My police will try to stop data streams when they can,' Mr Borking said at a technology conference in Copenhagen last Tuesday.

The story behind this extraordinary threat stretches back to 1991, when the European Union passed a directive guaranteeing minimum levels of protection of personal data across the EU. The 15 member states have until October 25 to enshrine the directive in their national legislation.

At first sight, the directive is anodyne stuff. It lays down four uncontroversial principles governing the electronic processing of people's personal data.

One is transparency: people have a right to see, and if necessary correct, information held on them. Another is informed consent: customers must be asked before their data are stored and used. A third is that data should be used only for the reason they were originally collected, unless the customer agrees otherwise. The last is proportionality: organisations should not collect more data on individuals than is strictly necessary for their declared purpose.

The threat of trade war comes from a minor wrinkle in the directive – a stipulation that data may not be processed abroad in countries that do not require standards equivalent to those of the EU.

The US is such a country. The country that matters most to the internet has few effective national laws protecting the privacy of personal data, and no independent government ombudsman equivalent to the data protection registrars of the EU's 15 countries.

In theory, then, any US company that exchanges customer data with its European subsidiaries could be at risk. So could any EU company with a US office and an intranet. Even small European businesses whose web sites are hosted on the other side of the Atlantic could be affected.

European data protection officials do not seriously expect the US Congress to pass a new data protection law between today and next Sunday. Yet officials on both sides are working behind the scenes in an attempt to defuse the stand-off.

The issue was high on the agenda at a two-day ministerial meeting on e-commerce, held by the Organisation for Economic Co-operation and Development in Ottawa earlier this month.

According to one account of the informal negotiations, the most likely way in which the two sides could both claim victory would be for the EU data protection officials to accept an independent, non-governmental body in the US as an equivalent ombudsman. One strong candidate for this title could be a not-for-profit organisation called TRUSTe.

TRUSTe – the web site is *www.truste.org* and the unwieldy acronym stands for TRusted Universal STandards in Electronic transactions – is the brainchild of Charles Jennings, a software entrepreneur from Portland, Oregon.

Its aim is to encourage web businesses to treat the personal data of their customers and site visitors with more respect, and to encourage customers to trust companies that meet high standards.

Paradoxically, TRUSTe does not set any standards itself. Instead, it merely asks web businesses to publish a privacy statement, explaining clearly what they will and will not do with customers' e-mails, postal addresses, phone numbers, social security numbers and so on – and then to stick to the policies enshrined in the statement.

TRUSTe's web site includes a 'wizard' that takes webmasters through a simple questionnaire about what kind of data they collect, what they do with it, and how customers can contact them to correct or remove their data. Once this is complete, the wizard spits out a ready-drafted privacy statement.

To become accredited to TRUSTe, the webmaster simply has to publish the statement, print out and sign two copies of a 13-page agreement governing the use of the TRUSTe trademark, and send a cheque to the organisation's offices in Palo Alto, California.

The fees start at $399 for web sites whose sales are less than $1m a year, and tops out at $5,000 for sites whose sales are more than $75m a year, such as Amazon, Dell, Cisco and E-Trade.

The purpose of this exercise – which took me 25 minutes, short of writing the cheque – is to become an approved TRUSTe web site, with the right to show a little icon that gives site visitors a strong degree of comfort that their data will be handled responsibly.

Click on the icon, and visitors will be transferred to a confirmation page at www.truste.org, confirming that the site really is as trustworthy as it seems.

The money is used to finance a number of enforcement activities. One is that TRUSTe officials will quietly 'seed' member web sites, so illicit attempts to sell mailing lists or send junk e-mail contrary to promises can be easily detected.

Another is that TRUSTe keeps tabs on the privacy statement, to ensure no unreasonable changes are made to it. Finally, TRUSTe can audit members' records either randomly or to follow up a complaint.

Breaching any of the promises made as part of the sign-up process carries no penalties – other than losing the right to use the trademark, and paying the 'reasonable costs' of an audit. But the programme is probably no less valuable for that.

My guess is that most companies on the web treat their users' data with reasonable care and respect, and most complaints from customers arise as a result of misunderstandings rather than because of deliberate malpractice.

So although TRUSTe will do nothing to curb the excesses of spammers and rip-off artists, it does a valuable job in getting data protection taken more seriously in the US. With luck, it may prove to be the independent ombudsman that averts a trade war between Europe and America.

Source: Financial Times, 19 October 1998

18.4 Similar problems have arisen in the past with the collection of consumer data. How have the authorities legislated to secure customer privacy?

18.5 Will on-line marketing replace direct marketing or is it a complementary promotional activity?

Tesco to expand home shopping

Supermarket chain to use loyalty cards in joint venture with catalogue specialist.
By Jonathan Ford

Tesco yesterday signalled a big expansion of its home shopping interests through a joint venture with Grattan, the catalogue retailer. It will offer clothes and household goods to Tesco's 10m loyalty card holders.

The supermarket chain has built a modest presence in the home shopping market since starting the service three-and-a-half years ago. It said the joint venture would allow it to expand the business more rapidly through access to Grattan's expertise in systems and distribution.

Analysts said the move would preserve Tesco's head start in home shopping. It remains the only UK supermarket chain with such a service, although the market is threatening to become more crowded. Asda is thought to be considering a similar venture, while Marks and Spencer's home shopping business is undergoing trials.

The direct home shopping market in the UK has doubled to £3bn in the last four years. 'Home shopping is becoming increasingly popular with all consumer sectors,' Tesco said.

The venture, owned equally by Tesco and Grattan, will sell products under the Tesco Direct brand name. They plan to launch four catalogues from March next year. The first will market baby clothes and toys.

By using Tesco's loyalty card database, Tesco Direct will be able to target the catalogue at purchasers of baby food products in the supermarkets.

Tesco said the venture would initially concentrate on selling clothes and household goods. In the longer term it aimed to expand into other areas, which could include soft furnishings and garden equipment.

Tesco Direct will be based near Grattan's headquarters in Bradford, West Yorkshire and will initially create about 350 jobs. Grattan will provide call-centre, warehouse and delivery facilities. Tesco will provide the products and access to its loyalty card database. The partners would not say how much they planned to invest in the venture.

Grattan, part of the German group, Otto Versand, is the third-largest catalogue retailer in the UK. It had sales last year of £570m. 'This is a rare opportunity to build an exceptional direct catalogue, rapidly, drawing on existing expertise and resources,' said Steve Bullas, chief executive of Grattan.

● Kim Howells, the competition and consumer affairs minister, has accepted undertakings from Littlewoods not to acquire control of Freemans, a rival catalogue retailer. The undertakings follow Littlewoods' proposed bid for Freemans, which was blocked last November following an inquiry by the Monopolies and Mergers Commission. Littlewoods has agreed not to acquire more than 10 per cent of Freemans, or any assets of its agency mail order business.

Source: Financial Times, 27 September 1998

18.6 Tesco is aiming to diversify sales from simply store-based activities. What particular advantages do Tesco and Grattan bring to this partnership?

18.7 In your work group, identify existing and potential competitors, and how the new joint venture might differentiate itself from these.

18.8 Since this grouping has strategic as well as promotional characteristics, how far could the alliance go, and could other partners be introduced? Who would you suggest?

FT

Shopping made simple with virtual warehouses

An internet start-up is bridging the gap between the click of the mouse and home delivery, writes Carlos Grande

Sometimes 300,000 square feet is just not enough. The 'pickers' at Total Home Entertainment, the distribution division of John Menzies, can find one of up to 250,000 products at the company warehouse in Newcastle-under-Lyme, Staffordshire.

The team in a small alcove of the same building can do even better, locating up to 1.2m items without getting sore fingers.

For where THE packs books, CDs, videos and computer games on to two floors of wooden shelves, its tenant, GlobalFulfillment.com, only searches stock via the internet.

GlobalFulfillment.com is a start-up created for the space between the click of the online shopper's mouse and the doorbell ring of the home delivery company.

Its role is to ensure consumer online purchases, which Jupiter Communications, the research company, estimates will total $6bn (£3.7bn) worldwide in the run-up to Christmas, arrive on time and as advertised.

Yet it does not own a single warehouse or courier van. Instead, it partners both web sites and warehouses to exploit 'bricks and mortar' infrastructure for e-commerce.

This contrasts with internet retailers, such as Amazon.com, which ships goods directly from its own warehouses. Charlie Gilreath, chief executive of GlobalFulfillment.com, said: 'Our goal is not to anticipate demand – the huge selection offered by the internet makes that a gamble – but to respond faster once a request is made.

'You can only do that by bringing the merchandise closer to the buyer. But why incur the expense of creating that infrastructure when it already exists?'

The company uses a central internet database sourcing goods worldwide and tied to a network of dispatch depots – or smart hubs – in different countries. Each smart hub is based in the premises of a 'bricks and mortar' partner company, usually a wholesaler.

In return for occupancy, GlobalFulfillment.com uses its landlord as a supplier for e-commerce orders. It then takes a share of revenues from its web site clients for dispatching orders directly to consumers.

When, for example, requests arrive from UK web site clients such as Tower Records, the music retailer, or Jungle.com, the online computer games seller, GlobalFulfillment.com sources many from THE stock.

If this fails, it will try its other UK suppliers before moving on to international outlets. All products are sourced electronically and delivered to the consumer from the nearest smart hub using a nationally based third party courier or mail service.

The hub, occasionally located in retail partners' stores, also provides the single point of return for unwanted goods. This structure is replicated across 12 countries including the US, Australia, Japan and western Europe where clients include Trans World Entertainment, the US music retailer, Sanity, the Australian entertainment retailer, and World Online, the Dutch ISP serving 15 countries.

Building the network has cost the company several million pounds in start-up costs. Since the total amount of online commerce is still small, its commission revenues are tiny. Annual turnover is not expected to reach £1.5m until 2004.

However Mr Gilreath argues that it gives e-commerce partners two key advantages: shorter delivery times and speed of implementation. Jungle.com, owned by Software Warehouse, is able to offer its customers next-day delivery and its fulfilment operation was set up from scratch in seven days.

Experienced online shoppers in the US, questioned for a new survey by Andersen Consulting, identified delivery and service as more important than price when choosing which web sites to buy from.

For wholesalers, the arrangement also means new business. Norman Smith, managing director of THE Group, predicts that 10 per cent of THE's total annual turnover of around £170m will come from e-commerce by April.

Source: Financial Times, 26 November 1999

18.9 It is increasingly apparent that rapid delivery is a problem for Internet retailers. How does this enterprise address this and what other solutions may be available?

18.10 Shopping is regarded by many as an enjoyable and sociable activity. Does the Internet threaten this, and how might traditional retailers fight the threat?

18.11 Have you and your friends had experience of the Internet in a buying situation? Discuss between you the strengths and weaknesses of the process. Construct a report to critically evaluate these experiences and how (a) an Internet provider and (b) a traditional retailer might perceive advantage.

Article 18.E   FT

BT internet marketing ploy broke fair competition rules

By Alan Cane

British Telecommunications' sales staff have been breaking rules over the use of information about customers in their efforts to sell the company's new pay-as-you-go internet service Click.

The practice has been abandoned after an urgent investigation by the Office of Telecommunications. David Edmonds, Oftel director-general, said yesterday that he might issue an order against BT if the offending behaviour was repeated.

Click, which connects customers to the internet at low cost and with minimum administration, has already antagonised competing service providers who see it as an example of BT abusing its market strength.

In the latest incident, telesales staff used customer calling information to identify regular internet users. The customers were then offered the new BT service.

The first complaints were received by Oftel about 10 days ago. Both Oftel and BT agreed the marketing ploy was a serious breach of the fair trading condition in BT's licence. Competing internet service providers would not have the same access to BT's calling information.

Mr Edmonds also announced changes to directory services which will allow more companies to offer phone books, electronic directories and inquiry services. The changes might result in fewer subscribers electing to go ex-directory.

Under the new provisions, consumers will have the right to paper or electronic directories and the right to have their number listed in these directories. These rights, Oftel says, will apply to all telephone customers and will have to be offered by any supplier of phone services, including mobile operators and pager services.

Mr Edmonds is also taking action against unwanted telemarketing calls and faxes, the chief cause of many subscribers asking for ex-directory numbers. Consumers could have, for example, only the name of their street and not the number of their house listed.

Source: Financial Times, 25 September 1998

18.12 A number of issues are raised in this article. Comment on how telephone sales, mailing list and other techniques could make use of access to this information.

18.13 By conducting some outside research, report on European rules relating to telemarketing, and how special aspects of this activity are being restricted.

18.14 What particular advantage did BT derive from this ploy and why did they risk investigation by OFTEL?

19 Public Relations, Sponsorship and Exhibitions

Organisations need to have ways of promoting their activities and image other than through the hard-sell techniques of advertising. They must reach all those publics who might not be direct customers of theirs but who consider themselves as having an interest in their affairs, directly or indirectly. In order to establish a relationship with these groups, and to enter into any public debate which might have a bearing on its activities, an organisation should develop a system of contact less direct than through a paid advertising format, in which the interested groups can approach the organisation and engage in a dialogue over which the organisation retains some element of control. The control, of course, is less direct than in paid-for advertising, since our message may be picked up and interpreted in a more or less critical manner. But consistency in the message together with monitoring of the effects of such messages enables the organisation to adjust and modify its response in the most appropriate and beneficial manner.

Sponsorship and exhibitions are extensions of this process enabling the organisation to associate itself with activities, personalities and causes which reflect well upon the organisation, as well as being able to promote the corporate image and message through personal contact with potential or actual purchasers. The judgement of when, where, and how to use such techniques must be part of the whole integrated communications decision process and should take place in areas which most nearly represent the more aspirational qualities inherent in the properties of the products/services offered, and the mission and corporate goals of the organisation.

In terms of the costs involved, it is less possible to judge the actual value achieved except to say that the more it costs, the more likely it is to be effective.

In order to successfully complete the tasks in this chapter you will need to be familiar with:

- the definition of PR;
- techniques in PR;
- evaluating PR and sponsorship;
- types of sponsorship;
- corporate hospitality;
- PR as a strategic and emergency tool;
- the role of PR and sponsorship;
- ethical PR.

The following articles illustrate how a major international corporation can be driven by public relations matters over which it has no direct control, and that even a company with the marketing sophistication of Coca-Cola can be caught unawares and have to use its public relations capacity to its maximum effect.

Coke's blunt number-cruncher

The company's chief executive has had a baptism of fire, say Betty Liu and Richard Tomkins

Douglas Ivester, chairman and chief executive of Coca-Cola, has come a long way to a difficult spot. The son of a factory foreman in Georgia, he trained as an accountant before rising to head the state's best-known company.

Mr Ivester has had little time to enjoy his success. Almost since the since the day he took over in 1997, the company has been bombarded by problems. First came a fall in Coke sales in emerging markets in Latin America and Asia amid a financial crisis.

The latest difficulty, a health scare in Europe after 200 people complained of sickness from drinking Coke, could prove his biggest challenge yet. The way in which Mr Ivester handles the crisis will speak volumes about his leadership, and ability to take the world's biggest soft drinks company into the next century.

So far, the signs are unpromising. The crisis started in Belgium after poor quality carbon monoxide was used at one bottling plant, and fungicide on pallets attached to cans at another. After sweeping through France, the crisis yesterday reached Spain. Coca-Cola has been widely attacked for responding too slowly. 'It's a bit disturbing that a big firm with worldwide fame did not take far-reaching measures more spontaneously and more promptly,' said Luc Van den Bossche, the Belgian health minister.

A short statement and apology by Mr Ivester on Wednesday only increased public agitation, since it came eight days after the first reports of illness from drinking Coke were reported in Belgium. The reports eventually led Belgium and several other European countries to ban or suspend shipping of Coke products despite the company's assurance that there was no health or safety problem.

All this prompted a rapid damage-limitation exercise yesterday. Mr Ivester flew to Europe to deal with the issue, and talk to the media. Handling such a public relations nightmare is unfamiliar territory for Mr Ivester, who for many years was the senior analytical figure at the company.

Under his predecessor, Roberto Goizueta, Mr Ivester engineered the successful spin-off of Coke's bottling business. This produced good returns for the parent company, and helped to secure his place as Mr Goizueta's second-in-command. His way with numbers had prompted Mr Goizueta to hire him away from the accounting firm, Ernst and Whinney, in the 1970s.

The two created a partnership that steered Coke through some of its best years. During Mr Goizueta's tenure, the company's shares rose by 3,500 per cent. Its worldwide sales volume increased at a brisk 7 to 8 per cent, and the brand became ubiquitous around the world. Mr Goizueta, a Cuban-born engineer, concentrated on branding and marketing while Mr Ivester worked behind the scenes to improve the company's bottom line.

That success has become something of a burden for Mr Ivester. Since taking up the reins after Mr Goizueta died two years ago, Mr Ivester has had to prove he can continue to create shareholder value – a hallmark of Mr Goizueta's leadership. But he is also under pressure to put his own stamp on the company that for nearly 16 years appeared to be Mr Goizueta's fiefdom.

His efforts to do so have hit obstacles. Coke's plans to purchase overseas European competitors perturbed regulators, who feared the already-dominant soft drinks player would wipe out competition in their local markets. Last month, Coke had to scale down its $1.85bn acquisition of Cadbury Schweppes' non-US business to exclude most European markets because of concerns about competition.

Regulators are becoming concerned that Coke is growing too big – and perhaps too confident – in its ability to dominate any market it wishes. In April, Karel Van Miert, the European Union's competition commissioner, rebuked Coke for what he regarded as bending the rules. He complained that it had not submitted its proposal to buy the Cadbury

Schweppes business to Brussels, and threatened the company with fines.

How much of Coke's new image problem can be attributed directly to Mr Ivester is debatable. However, analysts have noted that the company's push to buy up competitors reflects Mr Ivester's forceful business style. Some wonder whether his determination to expand Coca-Cola's empire has come to mean more than increasing the value of the company's 113-year-old brand.

Mr Ivester denied this yesterday, saying he monitored perceptions of the Coca-Cola brand in hundreds of countries around the world each month. 'Our brand health is as strong as ever, and growing,' he said, 'Nothing has been done on the distribution front that would in any way take away from our efforts with regard to our brand or our image.'

That does not convince all his rivals. 'Government regulators and perhaps politicians feel run over by Coke,' said one executive at a rival soft drinks company. 'There was not such a desperate attempt to buy up share and volume [in the past] as the one you see right now.'

Industry executives who know Mr Ivester say the chairman is a meticulous businessman. In contrast to Mr Goizueta, who was considered gentle and soft-spoken, Mr Ivester is regarded as blunt, and at times merciless, with his employees. He is known for tackling small problems personally, even travelling to remote parts of the world to hear Coke bottlers' complaints.

While analysts say Mr Ivester can stay the course at Coke, there are yet more troubles ahead. Global sales volumes are still declining as emerging economies continue to languish. A reinvigorated PepsiCo is experiencing great success with the launch of its one-calorie soda, PepsiOne. And in the background, two lawsuits are pending. One alleges racism at the company, and the other – filed by PepsiCo – accuses Coke of monopolising the market by pressuring independent distributors to buy its products.

Yesterday, Mr Ivester was putting a brave face on his time as chief executive. 'In a way, I'm probably fortunate to go through all of this in the first 18 months. You certainly wouldn't want to go through all of this in your last 18 months.

'The key thing for me is that we have a sort of internal compass of where this company is headed and where it can be. It's my job to ensure that, whether it's economic turmoil or something like this that's occurred in Belgium, it doesn't take our company off course.'

Source: Financial Times, 20 June 1999

Scare may not hit Coke profits

Group must exercise damage control. By Betty W. Liu in Atlanta

As Coca-Cola struggles to repair its image in Europe, first estimates from analysts suggest the health scare it suffered this month may barely hurt profits at the soft drinks group or at its anchor bottler, Coca-Cola Enterprises.

Their optimism comes with one caveat – that the scare is prevented from causing wider, longer-term harm to consumer confidence in Coke products.

But if it can quickly contain damage to its public image, the recall of millions of cases of Coke in northern Europe is expected to take only 1p per share off Coke's second-quarter earnings, according to Goldman Sachs.

Merrill Lynch says the 12 per cent or so decline in CCE's stock over the past two weeks may be a chance for investors to buy at bargain levels. Coke owns 42 per cent of CCE – the main bottler in Europe.

Analysts say the regions where most of the products are banned – Belgium, France and the Netherlands – make up less than 4 per cent of Coke's global volume.

CCE has indicated that some of the costs incurred from the recall will be covered by insurance.

Although Coke and CCE will face huge marketing expenses in convincing consumers that products are safe, both companies have enough cash to offset the costs.

'What this may cost [Coke] in the near term in lost sales and earnings is quite honestly small,' said Marc Cohen, beverage analyst at Goldman Sachs, who cut the group's second-quarter estimate by one cent to 40 cents per share. He also trimmed CCE's second-quarter earnings by 2 cents to 27 cents per share.

'If Coke is effective in getting the product back into distribution and in mending the consumer relationship, then this will be a minor event for the company.'

But Mr Cohen warned: 'The health scare itself is mostly limited to Belgium and parts of France. The brand image around the European continent is the wider issue.'

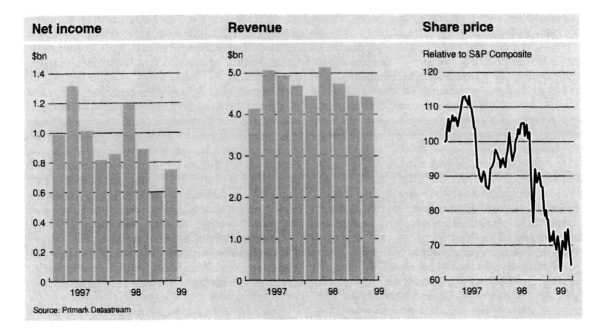

Net income

$bn

Source: Primark Datastream

Revenue

$bn

Share price

Relative to S&P Composite

Coke has launched an extensive advertising campaign in Europe apologising for the health scare that erupted two weeks ago after several children in Belgium fell ill after drinking Coke.

The company's first advertisements, appearing in France on Monday, said the quality of its products was beyond reproach, a statement some observers viewed as more pompous than apologetic.

'People like to see companies admit "We're human, we can make mistakes and we're doing the best we can,"' says Paul Holmes, editor of Reputation Management, a publication that specialises in managing corporate brands.

'That's a much more consumer friendly message than "Our products are perfect and we can do no wrong."'

Mr Holmes added: 'The reality is nobody died and the illnesses reported were fairly minor. This is the kind of crisis that a company like Coke should expect to go through every five or 10 years.'

Nevertheless, Coke seemed to change tactic with its second campaign, broadcast in Belgium yesterday, where Douglas Ivester, chairman, apologised for any discomfort or inconvenience brought on by its products.

However, health officials say more tests must be conducted before Coke products are allowed to return to the shelves – despite the company saying it had isolated the problems to defective carbon dioxide at one plant and foul-smelling fungicide that leaked on to Coke cans at another facility.

Source: Financial Times, 23 June 1999

Article 19.C

FT

Rat poison probe under way at French Coca-Cola plant

By Neil Buckley and Robert Graham

Coca-Cola's agony over a European health scare was prolonged last night when the French authorities opened an investigation into whether rat poison could have contaminated its cans.

The news of the probe at Coca-Cola's Dunkirk plant overshadowed the lifting of a 10-day-old ban

on the company's products in Belgium, which resulted in the biggest product recall in Coca-Cola's 113-year history.

Doug Ivester, chairman of Coca-Cola, said in Brussels he was 'very doubtful' rat poison had caused problems at Dunkirk, adding: 'We will work with the appropriate agencies and processes, just as we have done in Belgium, to ensure that they have complete confidence in our plants.'

He said he planned to 'buy everyone in Belgium a Coke' to reassure consumers about his product's safety. Executives were working on plans to get a free sample to the country's 10m inhabitants.

Belgium's health ministry banned Coca-Cola products from sale last week when more than 100 people complained of nausea and stomach upsets after drinking Coca-Cola.

The move resulted in some or all Coca-Cola products being withdrawn in three neighbouring countries – France, Luxembourg and the Netherlands – and as far afield as Kenya.

Luc Van den Bossche, health minister, lifted the ban on sales and on production at the Belgian factories in Antwerp and Ghent because there was 'only a remote chance' problems could recur.

But imports from the Dunkirk factory remained banned pending a decision by the French authorities to allow production to resume. Mr Ivester reiterated Coca-Cola's explanation that quality problems were caused when substandard carbon dioxide was used in bottled drinks at its Antwerp factory. Separately, the outside of cans from Dunkirk was contaminated with fungicide used to treat pallets in which they were transported to Belgium.

In both cases, an 'off' taste or smell could have provoked nausea, but there was no danger to health, Mr Ivester said.

Coca-Cola France said tests, including that of rat poison, by the French authorities had shown its products to be safe. 'All of those tests came back negative.'

Amboile, the company that put down the rat poison, said last night it could in no way be a contaminant and was benign to humans.

Source: Financial Times, 24 June 1999

Article 19.D   FT

France lifts ban on Coca-Cola

Laboratory checks find no contamination in soft drink. By Robert Graham in Paris

France yesterday lifted the damaging nine-day ban on the sale of Coca-Cola cans from the company's big soft drinks plant at Dunkirk after its products were given a clean bill of health.

Although public health laboratories at Bordeaux said they had found no contaminants in the products of the Atlanta-based drinks company, the cause of the mild poisoning that affected more than 100 people in Belgium and France remained a mystery. There had been complaints of severe stomach cramps followed by nausea.

'All risk has been excluded,' said Marylise Lebranchu, French consumer affairs minister, yesterday. She added: 'We haven't been able to establish any link between the illnesses in France and the drink itself.'

The all-clear came after AFSSA, a newly established food safety council, ruled out any health risk after considering the dossier for three days.

AFSSA also rejected any suggestion the illnesses could have been caused by rat poison. It had emerged on Wednesday that the public prosecutor's office had opened a judicial inquiry into the possibility

that rat poison sprayed by a Coca-Cola sub-contractor could have contaminated the outsides of cans.

The only caution offered by health and food safety experts at AFSSA was a recommendation that the collection of health data continue in order to study whether there is any relationship between the health problems observed and the consumption of the drinks.

Coca-Cola has suggested the scare might have been caused by fungicide sprayed on palettes transporting cans for the Belgian market, but French laboratories found no evidence for this.

French health officials said the difficulty in finding a rational explanation for the sudden outbreak of food poisoning had prevented a quick resumption of sales from the Dunkirk plant. This led to 50m cans being removed from supermarket shelves in France.

They also said it had taken longer than expected to trace the suspect cans of Coca-Cola, Coca Light, Fanta and Sprite because of the complex chain of distribution in the frontier area between Belgium and France.

However, the French health authorities refused to admit they had overreacted even though the AFSSA yesterday described the illnesses as 'benign and rapidly reversible'.

The Dunkirk plant supplies two-thirds of the French market as well as Belgium.

Source: Financial Times, 25 June 1999

FT

Coke recall cost is put at $60m

By Betty Liu in Atlanta

Coca-Cola Enterprises, Coca-Cola's anchor bottler, gave the first clear picture yesterday of damage from the health scare in Europe, saying the recall of Coke products in the past two weeks would cost $60m, or 8 cents per diluted common share, in the second quarter.

CCE, 40 per cent owned by Coca-Cola, recalled about 14m unit cases, more than the 10m or so cases analysts predicted. Nevertheless, it represents less than 1 per cent of the company's total annual volume which is expected to be about 3.9bn cases this year.

The products were pulled mostly in Belgium, France, the Netherlands and Luxembourg where the first reports of illness from drinking Coke products erupted. CCE is the exclusive bottler for Coke in northern Europe.

Though the initial estimates help in gauging the impact, questions remain over lost sales and profit.

CCE said there would be a 'negative impact on sales, cash operating profit and earnings per share in the second quarter', but the extent was 'difficult to determine'.

'The more consequential issue is the stuff that's not being quantified,' such as the loss in sales, said Marc Cohen, beverage analyst at Goldman Sachs who recently cut CCE's second-quarter earnings estimate by 2 cents to 27 cents per share. He also trimmed Coca-Cola's earnings by more than one cent to 40 cents.

The picture may be clearer in July when Coca-Cola and CCE release second-quarter earnings. Next week, Coca-Cola will publish second-quarter sales volumes, though they are not broken down country by country.

Other costs remain. Both companies are expected to spend heavily on marketing in Europe to regain consumer confidence. Coca-Cola has launched advertisements in France and Belgium to calm fears over its products. It plans to give free samples of products to Belgium's 10m citizens.

In mid-morning trading, CCE shares fell $\frac{9}{16}$ to $31\frac{13}{16}$. Coca-Cola shares rose $\frac{3}{8}$ to $62\frac{1}{8}$.

Source: Financial Times, 25 June 1999

19.1 Identify the role that public relations played in the handling of this event from the points of view of Coca-Cola and the French government.

19.2 What benefits could each side claim to have derived for themselves from this?

19.3 What message and impression do you think has been left with European (especially French) consumers after this affair?

19.4 In what ways, if any, could Coca-Cola have handled this matter better?

19.5 Success in handling such a situation leads to potential opportunities. How do we measure 'success' in this respect and what opportunities might show themselves?

19.6 The activities carried out by the company during this crisis are best described as corporate or marketing PR. What are the significant differences?

FT

Corporate sector pares down support

By Antony Thorncroft

As arts organisations have hunted for matching funding to justify grants from the lottery to create their new theatres and concert halls, one of the big surprises has been how comparatively mean companies have been and how generous individuals and trusts. Perhaps wary of shareholders, the corporate sector has not provided nearly as much cash for lottery projects as the private sector, and in particular, the charitable foundations.

Indeed, foundations are assuming an ever more vital role in funding the arts. Last week the Jerwood Foundation opened the Jerwood Space in Southwark, south London; and this week the Hamlyn Foundation announces its generous support for artists.

John Jerwood left the fortune he made from pearls and property mainly to the arts, with a bias towards young people. Last year the chairman of the foundation, Alan Grieve, conducted an overhaul of its activities which has led to a raft of new initiatives. With more than £1m to distribute a year, the Jerwood is a big sponsor. It can also co-operate on lottery projects.

The £3m Jerwood Space, an abandoned school which has been converted into studios for artists and rehearsal spaces for drama and dance companies at cut-price rates, was split between the arts lottery fund and the Jerwood. It could be the first of many capital developments sponsored by Jerwood.

The foundation is keen on the visual arts, which is obvious from its painting prize. At £30,000 for the winner – this year Madeleine Strindberg – it exceeds the Turner's £20,000 and NatWest's £25,000.

The Jerwood has also tested two new projects this year: an award for young film writers, and a fashion award. In both cases it got others involved: Working Title and Warner Bros for the film prize; the magazine Marie Claire, and department store Liberty for the fashion prize. But there is no guarantee that the prizes will be continued. Their impact on young people and how they improved their well-being is the main factor, rather than the amount of publicity.

The Jerwood's backing of music, in particular the work of the National Youth Orchestra and the Britten Pears Orchestra, is also being examined. But the arts will remain the main beneficiary of Jerwood's generosity.

Another leading cultural foundation which has changed its approach is the Paul Hamlyn. In the past it helped artists of all kinds, from poets to dramatists, sculptors to photographers. Now it is concentrating £150,000 a year on visual artists for the next three years. Five have been chosen to receive £30,000 each, which should enable them to concentrate on nothing but their art for a year or so. The fortunate five for 1998 are Brighid Lowe, Yinka Shonibare, Ross Sinclair, Gary Stevens and Richard Wright.

It may not be the end of the world when a sponsor suddenly withdraws. The Notting Hill Carnival seemed to be left in the lurch when Nestlé pulled out at the last minute, with the excuse that its new cold coffee drink, which was to have featured freely during the August Bank Holiday carnival, was not yet in the shops.

Always with an eye for media coverage, Richard Branson stepped in as the last-minute saviour with his Virgin Atlantic Airways. As a first-time sponsor the airline received a matching £17,000 under the government-financed Pairing Scheme. It also won much goodwill among the Caribbean community just when Virgin had started flights to that part of the world. So pleased is Virgin with the sponsorship that it is planning to continue the link.

Source: Financial Times, 2 October 1999

19.7 What do you see as the main differences between corporate sponsorship and funding from charity or private individuals?

19.8 What value could a commercial firm derive from the sponsorship of an orchestra, and what other activities could complement this? How could the firm evaluate the effectiveness of such sponsorship?

19.9 Increased sales are a clear measure of the success or otherwise of a PR campaign. What other measures may be of importance and how would you assess them?

Article 19.G ... FT

Article 19.G   **FT**

Fila to change sponsorship focus

By Patrick Harverson and Matthew Garrahan

The high cost of endorsement contracts and the growing risk of being associated with drugs rows and other scandals involving sports stars has persuaded Fila, the Italian sportswear group, to join the trend toward sponsoring more events and grassroots sport than individuals.

Yesterday, the company, which is based in Italy but is listed in New York, signed a £12m contract to sponsor the Super 9 tournaments of the ATP men's tennis tour for the next three years. Fila is following a trend set by several other top sportswear companies, among them Reebok and Nike of the US.

Although Fila is well known in tennis for sponsoring individual players – it used to back stars such as Bjorn Borg and Boris Becker and on its current roster has Mark Philippoussis and teenager Jelena Dokic – the company has decided to focus more on events.

'In the past everything was driven by the top characters,' said Michele Scannavini, the former Ferrari commercial director who was appointed Fila chief executive seven months ago.

'Today it's about more than paying millions of dollars to individual athletes. We like to be associated with something broader than a single player. In terms of value for money, this is the best strategy,' he said.

Mr Scannavini cited professional cycling and the recent scandals about the use of performance enhancing drugs on the Tour de France and the Tour of Italy as an example of how sponsorship can go badly wrong for companies.

Sandy McLennan-Fordyce of International Sponsorship Management, a sponsorships consultancy, said it made sense for companies to move away from costly individual endorsement deals. 'These days companies get a lot more bang for their buck sponsoring a tournament rather than an individual.'

Source: Financial Times, 29 June 1999

19.10 Because of its focus as a company Fila have used sports sponsorship as being the most appropriate public relations vehicle. The changes they are undertaking show a move to a different type of sponsorship. Why would you think they have done this and what other diversifications could they consider?

19.11 Increased sales have clearly been Fila's aim to date. Why might they have undertaken this change and how could they evaluate its effectiveness?

19.12 Identify the role that public relations has played in Fila's communication activities and what benefits might accrue from the change in focus.

19.13 PR has a clear value to a commercial organisation. What limits do you think there should be on corporate sponsorship of public services, if any?

20 Strategic Marketing

So far we have looked at operational marketing activities, those that are in general of a short-term nature. These activities are honed and refined to generate a certain desirable end. Profit may be a desirable end, increased output as a result of increased sales may be another. Increased donations may be yet another. Successful expansion into other markets could be an end. But who says so and why? What dictates the end which we strive to achieve?

Strategy is the driver behind all these activities – it sets the goals and how in general we are to achieve them. Strategic marketing puts up the goalposts and makes the rules for the game. This, of course, is in itself driven by the corporate strategy derived from the mission statement and business plans decided upon as the way forward for an organisation. In practical terms we have to pay attention to all the internal and external forces which are brought into play, our strengths and weaknesses and the opportunities and threats which apply.

Having said all this it is also important to recognise that elements of corporate strategy are heavily influenced by marketing analysis of what is possible and, importantly, what is not possible. The marketing function is the eyes and ears of the organisation, watching the marketplace, the competition and the customers as well as scanning the horizon to anticipate problems of a broader macro-environmental nature. This activity is defined as securing and maintaining the competitive edge of the organisation, the thing which distinguishes us from the rest of the world.

Because we are engaged in a constant 'battle' often military analogies are used in order to give some 'scaffolding' on which to hang notions of strategy. We talk of attacking competitors, of surrounding them or of fighting for market share. But without stretching the point too far, marketing strategy supports and assists the corporate strategy, and strives to give shape to the desires and objectives of the organisation in a way different from, and better than, its competitors. This activity sets the parameters for the operational side.

In order to complete the tasks in this chapter you will need to be familiar with:

- influences on marketing strategy;
- Ansoff's matrix;
- the BCG matrix;
- the Shell Directional Policy matrix;
- defensive strategies;
- integrative growth strategies;
- competitive positioning;
- generic strategies.

Article 20.A   FT

Cold comfort amid a forest of cranes

Lucy Smy explores the forces compelling plant hire companies to diversify beyond their traditional base in construction

A skyline crowded with cranes is sometimes interpreted as a sign of a healthy economy. But construction is a lagging indicator, which can thrive even when gross domestic product growth is slowing. So construction-related businesses at present are drawing little comfort from the thickets of cranes in the UK's cities.

Faced with an approaching economic downturn in Britain, prospects seem poor for plant hire companies, which have traditionally been dependent on rising construction output for profits growth.

Plant hire businesses have been scrambling to convince investors that they are better protected than construction industry customers. But they have had little success.

Since the start of the year plant hirers have underperformed the market by almost 30 per cent, even though the construction sector, where most are listed, has underperformed by less than 16 per cent.

Fans of the UK's handful of listed plant hire companies cite two main reasons to be cheerful about their future.

The first is that the companies have reduced their dependence on construction. They have won new clients by exploiting an enthusiasm for outsourcing equipment supply that has gripped other industries.

As little as five years ago, most plant hire companies were totally dependent on construction.

Today, that dependence has eased to 25–50 per cent of turnover, and they boast client lists that include utilities and petrochemical companies as well as rail maintenance businesses.

'We have gone from having four customers to having more than 30,000 customers in the UK,' said George Burnett, managing director of Ashtead, one of the biggest quoted plant hire concerns. 'In 1990, we were 100 per cent dependent on the UK construction industry, but we've tried to get away from that.'

To attract different clients, companies have had to supply different products. 'We can do large power generators, which could power a small factory, or provide alternative energy for a utility. It is a completely different market from construction,' said Mr Burnett.

The second reason analysts cite for being bullish about plant hire companies is a trend within construction companies themselves to free capital by hiring equipment instead of buying. This gives plant hirers scope to raise turnover even when construction output is falling.

At one time every construction company had its own plant division. Now heavy plant makers sell more than 75 per cent of their machinery to plant hire companies.

'For that reason it is less a commodity business and much more service-oriented,' said Graeme Kemp, an analyst at Collins Stewart. 'Plant hire companies regularly renew their plant, offering their customers a more up-to-date and consequently more reliable range of equipment.'

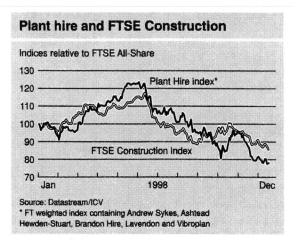

Plant hire and FTSE Construction

Indices relative to FTSE All-Share

Source: Datastream/ICV
* FT weighted index containing Andrew Sykes, Ashtead
Hewden-Stuart, Brandon Hire, Lavendon and Vibroplan

Plant hire companies have, meanwhile, strengthened their grip on the lower end of the construction market, dominated by jobbing builders, by buying high-street tool-hire shops.

In the past six months Hewden Stuart, the Scotland-based heavy plant company, has bought Michael Bowyer, a tool-hire chain in the Midlands, while Brandon Hire has been expanding its coverage of tool hire in the south and west of England.

But if the future for listed plant hire companies is so rosy, why are valuations so low? The average prospective p/e ratio is just 12, compared with 11.2 for the construction sector.

'It may be that the market is too simplistic,' said Andrew Bell, of BT Alex Brown, suggesting that plant hire still looks too close to construction to deserve a better rating, particularly while signals of an economic downturn are growing.

The other question troubling investors that have shunned plant hire companies is whether a broader client base equates to a stronger client base.

The diversity of clients is not in doubt, but whether new customers are any more recession-resistant than the old ones is unclear.

With the economy slowing, 1999 could well help to answer this question.

Source: Financial Times, 30 December 1998

As the outsourcing trend continues, leading to demand for better service deals including such add-ons as specific on-site maintenance requirements, so the pressure for consolidation among plant hire companies will grow. Some analysts predict that smaller, family-owned private companies will feel the squeeze, leading eventually to a smaller number of participants, and improving the pricing power of the survivors.

20.1 A number of influences on the marketing strategy of plant hire companies have been subject to change. What are these influences and how have the companies modified their strategies to take account of these changes?

20.2 In terms of Ansoff's matrix how would you describe Ashtead's current strategy?

20.3 Discuss portfolio analysis with regard to the plant hire industry and construct a BCG matrix to illustrate the actions taken by companies described in the article, and show how they might continue to generate growth.

20.4 Do you think such strategic choices as shown will be successful? Show your argument for such a position.

Battle for readers moves underground

Associated Newspapers is set to launch London daily in an attempt to defend its share of the market, writes Cathy Newman

The 450,000 Londoners who buy the Evening Standard each day will soon have an alternative. Associated Newspapers – the same group that publishes the Standard – plans to launch a weekday morning tabloid in the capital.

The London Metro – which will start appearing in the first quarter of next year – will also carry news, listings and features, and be given out free at London Underground stations.

It may seem odd that Associated should compete with its own publication, but analysts believe it had little choice. Senior executives are believed to have heard that another publisher planned a free daily London launch.

That could have hit sales and advertising revenues for the Standard. 'Associated isn't interested in making money on this. It's interested in preventing others from doing it,' says one observer.

A free subway paper has worked well in other European cities. Modern Times Group, a leading Scandinavian media company, pioneered the concept with its Metro title, now published in Stockholm, Gothenburg, Prague and Budapest.

Robert Braunerhielm, managing director of Metro Scandinavia, says one reason the title was an instant success in Sweden was because it was very cheap to distribute at subway stations. Unlike UK publishers, other Swedish newspaper owners have to spend 25 per cent of their earnings distributing their titles to subscribers' homes.

The Stockholm metro reached break even in its first year, and last year reported turnover of SKr195m (£14.6m), and profits of SKr40m–SKr45m Swedish kroner. After its first week, Mr Braunerhielm says: 'We were the second biggest morning paper in Stockholm.'

But can the success be repeated in London? Rival newspaper publishers argue the market is different from other European territories.

Jeremy Deedes, managing director of Telegraph Group, publisher of the Daily Telegraph, says: 'Our newspaper world is a completely different one. Nowhere in the world are you given as much choice as in the UK at a very low cost.'

Another newspaper executive says London has more news-stands in stations than other European cities, so people find it easier to buy papers to read on the Underground. Distributing a morning paper on the Tube also poses problems. 'Commuters leave from many more points to come into towns than they do to go home,' he says, suggesting a free evening paper would be easier.

Associated, which also publishes the Daily Mail, has chosen a risky time to embark on the project. An economic downturn would hit advertising, and could make the going tough for a title which relies on nothing else for its profits.

But although self-defence may have played a part in Associated's plans, there are several publishers who may find their own papers under attack from the new title.

Kevin Rolfe, managing director of Independent Magazines, publisher of free London weekly magazines such as Girl About Town, says the proposed launch could have an impact on national morning newspapers.

Jim Brown, executive chairman of Newsquest, the regional newspaper group that publishes free weekly papers in London, worries that a new competitor would mean 'another chip off the advertising market'. But he agrees that Associated's paper is 'directly aimed at the nationals'.

He believes Associated has the firepower and experience to make an impact. Other executives, such as Mr Deedes, are less charitable. 'It may be a great success, but potentially if it is, the losers are going to be Associated themselves because of the Evening Standard. The danger is they'll cannibalise their own readers.'

Source: Financial Times, 12 December 1998

20.5 What alternative strategies are available to Associated Newspapers? Describe the action being taken and justify the use of this particular strategy in preference to those others available.

20.6 What dangers may exist because of Associated Newspapers' adoption of this strategy? What benefits can you identify that would outweigh the dangers?

20.7 Consider the position from the point of view of a competitor in this market, and describe what strategy you could adopt to attack such a market leader.

Article 20.C   FT

Liggett raises cigarette output in Russia

Moscow plant will nearly double capacity, writes Andrew Edgecliffe-Johnson

Bennett LeBow, the self-confessed maverick investor who controls Brooke Group, likes the Russian way of doing business.

'You sit there in the steam bath and beat each other with twigs,' he says, recalling his efforts to negotiate distribution deals for Brooke's Liggett cigarette division.

Yesterday, the mayor of Moscow opened a £90m plant for Brooke's Russian tobacco business, Liggett-Ducat, replacing its 19th-century factory and almost doubling capacity to 35bn cigarettes a year.

That will place Liggett-Ducat second only to RJ Reynolds International (which was bought this year by Japan Tobacco) in the world's fourth-largest tobacco market. It will also permit the company to make higher-margin American blend cigarettes, rather than the more pungent domestic blends, without having to pay the 115 per cent duties imposed on imported tobacco.

Brooke bought Ducat from the city in 1991 for just $700,000, but has since poured in $30m–$40m in equity and absorbed five years of losses. It recorded its first profit – of $8.6m – in 1997, but increased this to $13.2m last year, or 30 per cent of Brooke's total profit.

That turnround, coupled with the fact that Liggett broke ranks with other US tobacco companies to settle smoking-related lawsuits, has helped Brooke's share price to rise almost five-fold in the past nine months.

Ron Bernstein, the director in charge of Liggett-Ducat, is confident the growth will continue. Last year's financial crisis in Russia hurt the company's profit margins, he says, but the damage was offset by stepping up production from a planned 17bn cigarettes to more than 20bn – almost double the factory's 1995 output.

It was able to adjust quickly to the crisis, Mr LeBow adds. 'You change your prices daily if you need to.' Mr Bernstein says the absence of a cumbersome corporate hierarchy helped: 'Mr LeBow evaluates our plans and allows us to operate as long as we hit our numbers.'

Liggett-Ducat fared better than some US manufacturers because it sells relatively cheap cigarettes, such as the oval-shaped unfiltered Prima and Papirossi – cardboard tubes with pouches of tobacco at the end – which go for 8–10 cents per pack.

In the new factory, however, Mr Bernstein plans to launch three new brands in higher price ranges, including the 35 cent mid-range Ducat brand.

The company chose a Russian brand name deliberately, Mr Bernstein said: 'There's a belief within Russian consumers that there are now quality Russian products they can consume.'

Mr Bernstein also believes that the Russian market is far from saturated. Officially, 250bn cigarettes are sold in Russia each year, although the real number is estimated at 300bn.

The market has been growing at 2–3 per cent but Liggett-Ducat believes consumption could grow to 400bn. Although 61 per cent of Russian men smoke, just 17 per cent of women do. That latter number is growing rapidly.

Russia is unlike the US, where litigation dominates investors' attitudes towards tobacco companies. 'There is not a litigious atmosphere here,' Mr Bernstein says. Russians understand the health risks associated with smoking, he says, adding: 'It is something they enjoy, such as drinking vodka is something they enjoy.'

The appeal of the Russian market has not been lost on Liggett's rivals: Philip Morris, the maker of Marlboro, is among those expanding, and is expected to open a $300m plant this year.

Liggett-Ducat sells about three-quarters of its cigarettes in and around Moscow, but is looking to capture more of the rest of the country. It has opened an office in St Petersburg and is working on deals to expand its distribution further. Mr LeBow expects to spend much more time in the steam room.

Source: Financial Times, 16 June 1999

20.8   By reference to the Shell matrix, explain why Liggett bases its growth strategy round the Russian operation.

20.9   Although the Russian economy is notoriously unpredictable Liggett are being successful. What particular capabilities do they have which enables this success, and how is their management structure particularly able to exploit the possibilities as they arrive?

20.10   What strategy does the company demonstrate, and where would you place them on Ansoff's Directional Policy matrix?

20.11   Liggett have studied cultural differences to achieve a substantial share of the Russian market against considerable competition. Use the BCG matrix to place their products as mentioned in the article to illustrate where they hold a particularly strong position.

Article 20.D   FT

Let us spray

Almost half of all perfume sales are made in the run-up to Christmas. But how many of this year's best selling fragrances will still be around in a year's time?
By Lucia van der Post

AT THE Manhattan headquarters of Ralph Lauren Fragrances, there is a sense of quiet but palpable jubilation. It is high summer, just a few months after the launch of Romance, Lauren's first major scent for women since 1996 (when Polo Sport Women, which turned out 'not to have a broad appeal', hit the stores). Its last great success was Safari, which dates back to 1990 – aeons ago in fashion terms. The company needs to inject new life into what used to be known as scent, but what everybody now insists on calling the 'fragrance' business. The sales figures are looking good. Later it turns out that, in the US, Romance had hit the number one spot in 98 per cent of the stores it was in. These are only the US figures, but since the US has

40 per cent of the 'prestige perfume' market, what happens there is crucial.

'You can usually tell within a few weeks if you have success on your hands,' says Andrea Robinson, general manager of Ralph Lauren Fragrances (RLF) worldwide. 'The anecdotal stuff – "We can't take it out of the boxes fast enough" sort of thing – starts to filter back, but it takes about a year to know if you've got a classic,' – a classic being the Holy Grail of the fragrance world.

The reason for the high tension surrounding this (and every) launch is that there's a thorny problem at the heart of the fragrance business that it is hard even for a company as hugely successful as Ralph Lauren to resolve. A fragrance takes a couple of years to develop (if it's done properly), costs a fortune to launch and promote (RLF had a war chest of about $20m to get Romance on the road), and yet the fashion cycles during which they can expect to sell are becoming shorter and shorter.

Claudia Lucas, buying manager of perfume and cosmetics at Selfridges, says that 15–20 per cent of the perfume business is now done with new fragrances. And much of that occurs in a narrow window of opportunity: Christmas. Harrods says that 40–50 per cent of all its perfume sales take place in the eight weeks up to Christmas, while one large distributor does 48 per cent of its annual business over this period, and 32 per cent in the last four weeks before Christmas.

Nor is the market growing appreciably. Even at Selfridges – which, in its newly revamped form, has one of the UK's largest and most successful perfumery areas – the perfume side has grown by 9 per cent in the past year, compared with 33 per cent for skincare and cosmetics.

It's the hype and publicity around the launch of a fragrance that catches the interest of the customer – not that the customer needs much urging, for she is primed to look for what's hot and what's new. Department stores need new perfumes to keep their counters alive and kicking and to attract new young punters. 'As the launch market gets more and more aggressive,' says Lucas, 'fewer and fewer fragrances have much longevity to them.' Deborah Nadler, head of public relations for RLF, agrees. 'You used to be able to get a new customer and keep her for 20 years – now you'd be very lucky to keep her for five.'

Here many of the industry watchers point to the fate of CkOne, which was one of the biggest successes in the history of the industry for about two years after it launched; before long, however, many CkOne fans had drifted off to Tommy and Tommy Girl.

But to Ralph Lauren, whose fragrance division is estimated to contribute between eight and 12 per cent to overall profits (you'd need to be an Alan Greenspan to wend your way through the web of holding companies and licensing agreements to get the precise figures), all this time, money and effort will only pay off if Romance becomes one of the handful of new perfumes that are still around in five and 10 years' time.

Then there is the further problem that the market seems to have reached saturation point, so that the only way to make bigger profits is to increase market share. Another worrying factor is that the nose of the consumer has changed in the past two decades.

Firmenich, which developed the new perfume for RLF, worked hard to eradicate any overtly synthetic smell – yet many new younger users have grown up with synthetically based perfumes, and some of them don't know anything else; they will need to be inducted into the subtler pleasures of less synthetic perfumes. John Horvitz, president of Horvitz & Associates, a marketing consultant who specialises in beauty, cosmetics and perfume, is in no doubt that the industry is going through major changes. 'It used to be a very fragmented business with hundreds of players, and it was relatively easy to make and sell a perfume,' he says. 'Saks 5th Avenue or Neiman Marcus would take a punt on a small fragrance maker. Today, four companies – L'Oréal with 15–16 per cent, Unilever with 14–15 per cent, LVMH with 13–14 per cent and Lauder with 10–11 per cent – control about 55 per cent of the worldwide fine fragrance business. Not only that, but department store groups in the US are consolidating, so that newcomers find there are just six main department store groups, and if they say "no", that's a very big "no" and it closes very big doors.'

It is fascinating to see how badly RLF seems to need a new fragrance. Why the endless need for something new (I'm still a devotee of Safari)? Says Robinson: 'We have to refresh the brand, slightly change the look of things if we're going to bring in new customers. The challenge is to be new and different enough to catch the attention and yet have staying power.'

To make it work, it also needs to bring off several difficult double acts – the company sees Romance as a prestige brand but has to sell it in large numbers to recoup its outlay, let alone make a profit. It has to be sufficiently of 'this moment' to seem right, and yet not so specifically of this particular moment as to seem wrong next year.

Then it has to appear 'fresh' to a younger audience and 'sensual' to an older one, and finally, while it obviously needs to be unique, it mustn't be so unique that it won't have this essential quality called 'a broad-based appeal'. Poor little frail things to carry so many hopes and dreams – no wonder few can stand the pressure and so many fall off their perch after two or three years.

What is clear is that behind every successful perfume there is some real synergy which connects with the customer, often at a deep, unconscious level. Perfumers are getting cleverer at tying the bottle, the 'juice' (as it is inelegantly called in industry circles) and the image into a consistent package, and so, this year, the competition for a product like Romance is strong.

Just as Romance is a perfect expression of the Ralph Lauren aesthetic, so many other new perfumes are expert at conveying the essence of their designers. In the same way that Romance – its bottle, imagery, advertising promotion – conveys the classic timelessness that Ralph Lauren has always managed so effortlessly to project, Gucci Rush perfectly captures the mood of Gucci. A funky, modern shape ('almost a block, a bar, but barely a bottle – whose purpose is ambiguous', says the press release with a rare regard for accuracy), it sums up what Gucci is all about, just as Gucci's Envy did so successfully a few years before. Equally evoking the essence of the 'house' is Christian Dior's J'Adore – all classic beauty – while Jean Paul Gaultier's Fragile (gold dust packaged in a snow dome) provides exactly the right note of wacky kitsch that fans associate with his clothes. Then there's Christian Lacroix trying again with a shell-like bubbled glass container in a very nice red box, while Thierry Mugler's Angel has taken his trademark star and produced a star-shaped bottle with a silver star stopper; the liquid itself is pale blue. All these are consistent with the designers' image and all are already showing signs of success.

But besides encapsulating the spirit of the designer, this little bottle and its 'juice' also need to capture the mood of the moment. Gucci's Rush captures the cool, hip, slightly iconoclastic urban culture that Gucci clothes embody so succinctly. Romance caught the mood of summer to perfection – the optimism of the rising stock markets, all the sweet, little girly dresses, the rage for pink (Gwyneth Paltrow at the Oscars), the softer interiors, the sense that people were seeking a refuge from the high-tech world in their homes, that they wanted relationships based on something other than power. As Horvitz puts it: 'Romance isn't a new idea – it was always there historically, but RLF made it work in a contemporary way.'

But there is yet another concept that any new perfumer has to note if he wants global success – and

that is the 'masterbrand'. Ralph Lauren started it, in his instinctive, intuitive way, without really knowing what he was doing, back in 1977 when he launched Polo (for men) and Lauren (for women), each with the same positioning and strategy.

Calvin Klein established the concept in a big way with Eternity and Eternity for Men, Obsession and Obsession for Men, and since then many others have entered the arena – Estée Lauder with Pleasures and Pleasures for Men, Clinique's Happy and Happy for Men, while even the grand house of Chanel has done it with Allure and Allure Homme.

These days, nearly 50 per cent of perfumes are part of a masterbrand, while some 70 per cent of all men's fragrances are masterbrands. It will not surprise you that Romance for Men is being launched in the US and next May it will be here. It may seem an odd concept to sell to men, but RLF believes that the simplicity of the packaging, the fragrance itself which will be given a more masculine edge and the clear heavy glass bottle will diffuse the feminine bias of the name – and, anyway, who said men weren't romantics, too? Time will tell.

Meanwhile, eating away at little bits of the profits of the big boys are the small niche brands. They've always been there – Annick Goutal, the Crown Perfumer, Jo Malone (not so little now), Les Parfums de Rosine, Acqua di Parma (ultra cool now), Boucheron and others but the bigger the big boys get, the more the really fashionable want less well-known scents from little-known names.

Many of them are being snapped up by the big players – LVMH's perfume and cosmetics chain Sephora is buying up anything it can, while Jo Malone was recently bought by Estée Lauder which, like all big fish everywhere, wants to have everything all ways.

What is certain is that it's a volatile difficult world in which to make money from fragrance, and hedging your bets each way seems a likelier route to being a winner than trying to crystal gaze.

Source: Financial Times, Wecherd FT Issue 44, November 1999

20.12 Define the external influences which direct the strategies adopted by the major perfume manufacturers.

20.13 By use of the appropriate portfolio model show how any one of the companies discussed in the article have arrived at their own strategy, and how this reflects the competitive context within which they exist.

20.14 Given that the fragrance market has a low growth status, how does a company achieve growth in such a market? Illustrate your answer by reference to examples within the article.

20.15 How do fashion and design relate to the fragrance industry, and why would the great fashion houses link themselves to a low-growth industry such as the fragrance industry? To broaden your answer discuss the various strategies available to them and why they would choose one above another.

21 Marketing Planning, Management and Control

No organisation can hope to survive let alone develop and grow unless marketing planning and the necessary control and monitoring systems are in place. In general the larger the organisation, the more formal must be the marketing planning process. Sales functions operating independently of the other functions within the organisation lead to disorganisation and failure. How much product will be wanted? When? How do we get it there? How much raw materials, staff, machinery will be needed? Without the benefit of an integrated planning framework disaster is inevitable.

The planning process and especially the marketing plan do not offer solutions in the absence of predetermined targets, goals and motivation. Planning takes time and should be an ongoing process, from the board of directors down. Strategy and targets need to be set. What resources are to be made available? What might government activity be over the next five or ten years? What are the requirements for capital, and what does our risk analysis show us? In the medium term we need to look at functional management, planning of competitiveness, product development and market position. Short-term planning is an operational activity and will concentrate on issues such as stock levels, competitor analysis and market performance.

Decisions such as those related to market share, volume and profitability are marketing department issues, and decisions taken here have a significant impact in other areas such as purchasing, manufacturing, transportation and even recruitment and credit control. It is essential that all those involved both internally and externally, such as suppliers and distributors, should be included in the formulation of planning, not only to maintain a coherent organisational approach but also to give a solid basis for the achievement of any action considered and undertaken.

In order to successfully complete the tasks in this chapter you will need to be familiar with:

- SWOT analysis;
- marketing objectives;
- marketing strategies;
- mission statements;
- control and evaluation;
- market/sales potential;
- sales forecasting;
- sales analysis;
- organisational structure.

Picking at the bones

Companies have performed poorly because their initial sums were wrong or their products are outdated. By Tony Jackson

Picking over Europe's worst equity investments in the past five years might seem a slightly morbid exercise. But there are some consistent themes to be found among those companies which have subtracted most shareholder value in that period.

The first is the triumph of hope over experience. There are two splendid examples of this, both fittingly European: Eurotunnel and Euro Disney.

For a good 10 years it has been apparent that Eurotunnel was an investment disaster: that the banks – let alone the shareholders – had made an expensive gift to the travelling public. On the other hand, the tunnel is in operational terms a distinct success. It seems correspondingly difficult for all those investment types, shuttling between London and Paris, to accept that it will never pay.

When Eurotunnel underwent an £8.5bn restructuring in 1998 – whereby the banks took equity for debt and ended up with majority control – it should not have come as much of a surprise. The previous restructuring had been billed as final: but so had the one before that.

The aim of the latest restructuring is that Eurotunnel should break even in 2004, and start paying dividends thereafter. Well, perhaps. But this reminds us of the second component of total shareholder return – income. If companies pay no dividends, TSR is that much harder to come by.

This brings us to Euro Disney. Again, this is operationally successful – it's the biggest tourist attraction in France – and has been a financial disaster from the outset.

Launched, like Eurotunnel, in 1989, Euro Disney had its restructuring just five years ago. This involved a rights issue and a further financial injection from a slightly improbable source – the Saudi billionaire Prince Al-Waleed bin Talal.

Further warning signs were quick to appear. In August of that year, the chief financial officer left after 18 months in the job. His successor lasted less than three years, quitting in February 1997.

Last November, the company warned of a 'tough 99'. Disney, the former US parent, is apparently starting to charge royalties for the first time. The result will be zero profits and – once more, like Eurotunnel – a receding prospect of dividends.

As we look further down the list of poor performers, some less familiar names appear. Take the East Asiatic Company, the second worst performer after Eurotunnel with a return of –74 per cent over five years. This was once Denmark's biggest industrial company, also taking in trading, shipping, shipbuilding and forestry.

East Asiatic was founded just over a century ago by a Danish sea captain with a hotel in Bangkok. It remained heavily represented in Asia, especially Malaysia, with predictably awkward results when the Asian crisis struck some 18 months ago.

The writing had been on the wall before that. In 1982 the company passed its dividend for the first time since the second world war. But it took until 1992 for outsiders to be brought in to run the business.

Then the disposals started: most of the Plumrose tinned meat business, the shipping division, the Malaysian plantations, the graphics business. When last heard of, the company, a shadow of its former self, was still in loss.

Next on the list comes Philipp Holzmann, Germany's biggest construction company. This has been a more rapid downfall. Five years ago, the company was rated as Europe's most respected construction company in a Financial Times survey.

Unfortunately, the company had expanded aggressively in the late 1980s and early 1990s, incurring heavy debt in the process. Then came a severe recession in the German construction industry. By 1995 Holzmann was making heavy losses.

In 1997 a new chief executive was brought in by Deutsche Bank, and jobs were cut by a quarter in one of Germany's biggest corporate restructurings to date. All the while Holzmann's smaller rival, Hochtief, had been trying to take Holzmann over. This proved fruitless, and as from last December a 25 per cent stake in the company is held instead by Gevaert, the Belgian holding company. So watch this space.

The next two on the list are British: Coats Viyella and BICC, both former industrial giants which have fallen on evil days. Coats Viyella is the UK's chief remaining representative in the textile industry, a business notoriously unsuited to the developed world today.

Again, the past five years have been dramatic. Disposals started in 1994, and then top executives started to leave: the finance director in 1995 – ominously, after only six months in the job – followed by Neville Bain, chief executive, in 1997, and finally this March by the man who had built the company through acquisition over 40 years, chairman Sir David Alliance.

The fate of BICC has been equally dramatic. Five years ago, this was the world's second biggest maker of cables, with a market value of close to £2bn. By late last year its value had sunk to a pitiful £160m, less than a single year's cash flow. Earlier this year it sold its entire cable business in two chunks to American rivals, leaving it only with the construction company Balfour Beatty.

We thus end up with a curious contrast. Two of the worst performers in the table are new, focused companies which got their initial sums wrong.

Most of the rest, though, are precisely the reverse: Europe's industrial old guard. Other examples include Kvaerner in shipbuilding, Leykam and Arjo Wiggins in paper and Pilkington in glass. At least some of these, sadly, are companies which have outlived their usefulness. Their performance in the past five years has accurately reflected a deeper malaise.

Source: Financial Times, 18 June 1999

21.1 The companies illustrated failed to plan effectively, and to monitor and control the effects of this failure. In your work group discuss and list these failures in each case.

21.2 Why do you think these failures occurred? What two elements of the process of marketing planning and control especially might have helped indicate that failure was likely?

21.3 Through outside research identify other companies which have failed due to planning and control issues. How do you recommend other companies learn from those mistakes for future success?

Article 21.B   **FT**

Manufacturer's 300,000 reasons to get the product right

Europe's colostomy-bag users will benefit from efforts of a small company growing through innovation, writes Peter Marsh

The testing station in Germany had seen few items like it: a colostomy bag which dissolves when discarded in the toilet to admit its contents safely into the sewers. Such was the rite of passage for a novel product from a small UK manufacturer that is planning a big rise in exports over the next year.

Welland Medical was set up 10 years ago by Chris Raper, an accountant who had worked previously in the pharmaceutical and engineering industries and is now Welland's managing director.

The company's products rarely hit the headlines but are vital to an estimated 300,000 people across Europe who, as a result of surgery associated with colonic cancer and related diseases, need to attach bags to an opening in their stomachs to receive faeces or urine.

The difficult, not to say messy, process of disposing of these bags and their contents exercised the attention of Mr Raper and colleagues at Crawley-based Welland. Normal colostomy bags – which have to be highly resilient to stop leakages – have to be discarded separately from their contents. Because they would cause blockages, they cannot simply be thrown down the toilet. But just over two years ago, after a three-year research effort, the company introduced what could be described as the ultimate goal of the colostomy bag industry: a bag which stands up to normal wear but which biodegrades when in contact with water.

With the bags certified by special testing stations around Europe – including Germany and Sweden, two countries with strong green credentials, which would be worried by non-degradable materials entering the sewers – the new products have helped Welland to expand exports from virtually zero five years ago to nearly £1m last year. Next year, it is aiming for exports of £1.5m, out of total sales of £4.6m – 15 per cent above this year's sales figure of £4m.

Mr Raper, who owns 4 per cent of the company, with the majority held by Clinimed, a private healthcare group, describes as 'whingers' other UK manufacturers that have complained about the high pound cutting into their overseas business.

He says Welland has progressed partly through a strong focus. 'Colostomy bags tend to be a taboo subject but I view them as a business opportunity.'

Of Welland's 73 employees, 11 are in its technical department. They came up with the specification for the new bag based around an internal biodegradable lining inside a relatively sturdy plastic outer casing which holds the lining in place and can be retained after the lining is discarded. The biodegradable liner is based on a cellulose-like material which looks like paper tissue but whose chemical formula is a closely guarded secret.

Welland has had to pay special attention since the mid-1990s in signing up distributors in parts of the world where the company exports, such as Germany, Italy, the Netherlands and parts of south America. It has also had to invest heavily in new equipment; its latest machine used for automatically making bags cost about £250,000.

Because of its relatively small size, Mr Raper says the company may be able to bring to the market new ideas which would otherwise be buried within the bureaucracy of larger companies, such as the Big Three of the colostomy bag industry – Convatec and Hollister of the US, and Coloplast of Denmark, which control an estimated 75 per cent of the European market.

Source: Financial Times, 3 December 1998

21.4 Suggest a mission statement for Welland Medical, supporting it from information in the article.

21.5 Four characteristics of a well thought through mission statement are stated by Day (1990) as being (a) Future orientated, (b) Reflecting the values and orientation of the leader, (c) Stating strategic purpose and (d) Enabling. Explain these characteristics, and show how far your answer to 21.2 above reflects these.

21.6 Bearing in mind the product discussed what promotional activities might be employed, and how could you judge their efficacy?

Article 21.C

Creating an armoury for all eventualities   FT

Companies will need to adopt a top to bottom approach to ensure that they are able to respond to financial and other risks involved in fulfilling their objectives

Balancing risk and reward is a game of precision that is played in every part of an organisation. It is one that companies regularly lose either through failure to predict the next move or the lack of an adequate rule book. The recommendations of the Turnbull working party aim to change that situation in the UK.

For the first time, companies will have to show they can respond to all the risks involved in the fulfil-ment of business objectives, not just the financial ones. David Davies, director of Aon Business Risk Consulting, says most companies will have to work hard to meet the requirements. 'There are very few companies that live up to the vision embodied within the Turnbull Report,' he says. 'But a lot of companies are waking up to it. The big institutional investors will start to take Turnbull as a given and increasingly even non-listed companies will have to take notice.'

Current thinking dictates that the most effective way to deal with business risk is to take a holistic approach. The idea is to start at the top and drill down into each part of the organisation until every risk is identified, defined and assigned to a manager. Mark Butterworth, chairman of The Association of Insurance and Risk Managers, stresses: 'You can take a holistic approach but the practical day-to-day management must be assigned to real people.'

Risks are divided into categories. These will vary between companies but most will start at the top with strategic risk, including core business decisions such as acquisitions and investment. Of all the categories, strategic risk has the greatest potential for an upside as well as a downside. 'An organisation has to examine to what extent it is prepared to take a risk in order to do better than its competitors,' says Helen Nixseaman, a partner at Pricewaterhouse-Coopers (PwC).

Operational risk is a cover-all term that can apply to both tangible and intangible risks incurred in day-to-day business. Here, risks range from business equipment to environmental liability or fraud. Human resources risks, including the mindset of the existing management, can fall into this category.

Some companies also have a separate grouping for intangibles covering risks such as loss of reputation, intellectual property and commercial espionage. Risks relating to IT can be allocated to a single category or across several.

A strategy to sell via the internet may be a strategic risk while establishing a file back-up would be operational. Finally there are the financial risks – the most feared. Companies are required to disclose the treatment of financial risks under the financial reporting standard 13 accounting rule and have established guidelines and practices.

'Financial risk management is about risk transformation rather than risk mitigation,' says Chris Taylor, European head of the capital markets practice at PwC. This applies mostly to market risks such as currency trading where banking products allow unwanted positions to be transformed into a more acceptable risk.

Credit risk is closer to other forms of business risk and can be mitigated using methods such as credit derivatives, insurance, or diversification. Operating risks relating to the treasury function are fundamentally the same as in other business areas but can be more significant.

'You have to delegate authority to relatively junior people which increases the risk,' says Mr Taylor. 'The controls need to be much stronger and should be preventative rather than for detection.'

Concern over lack of insurance cover

Per cent

Loss of reputation	34
System failure through Y2K	30
Brand/trademarks	25
Intellectual property erosion	21
Fraud	14
Terrorism	9
Climatic	7
Credit risk	7
Class action	5
Currency risk	5
Claims against directors & officers	2
Genetically modified organisms	2
Stress claims against employees	0

Base = all respondents, including no replies

Source: Airmic/Lloyd's

Across all categories the most obvious way to manage a risk is to transfer it and for many risks this still means traditional insurance. As well as regular corporate insurances, a company could have 'key man' insurance for its directors, 'rogue trader' insurance for the dealing room, and 'reputation insurance' to salvage its good name if all else fails.

Alternative risk transfer solutions such as self-insurance or transferring the risk to the capital markets via a range of over-the-counter insurance derivative products are a further option. The recent growth of holistic risk management has also encouraged reinsurers to engineer integrated solutions that offer protection for both business and financial risks.

However, risk transfer may not be the most effective course of action. 'The real management challenges are the uninsurable risks,' says Mr Davies. 'The strategy should be to reduce the risk as much as you can provided it is cost effective to do so.' This task should be assigned to line managers, both to leverage their knowledge of individual businesses and to encourage ownership of the risk management process. Final decisions should be taken within the context of a framework set at the highest level.

The whole process requires considerable scrutiny of internal procedures and controls as well as external risks but, as long as the framework safeguards company assets and enhances shareholder value, it does not have to make the company risk averse.

As Mr Davies points out: 'It is about understanding what the risks are and taking a balanced and informed decision about whether they are acceptable.'

Source: Financial Times, 25 June 1999

21.7 What part should marketing planning and control take in this activity? What particular functions should it perform to reduce risk?

21.8 What particular risks may be addressed by marketing? What tools might it employ?

21.9 What type of organisational structure is most effective in identifying and planning-out risk?

Article 21.D   FT

Safeway chief outlines his vision

By Susanna Volye

Carlos Criado-Perez, Safeway's new chief executive, is expected to flesh out further details of his strategy for the supermarket group in May next year.

The former Wal-Mart executive told a City audience yesterday that he was amazed at the amount of strategic detail his rivals were happy to talk about publicly.

His first comments on the UK market and his plans for Safeway are designed to lure back disaffected shoppers. But he is expected to outline a longer-term strategy at the time of the full-year results in May.

Mr Criado-Perez hopes that this strategy, built around selective deep discounting, will give Safeway a distinctive edge.

He said the new Safeway would be food-based – with an emphasis on fresh food – and value-led. He also promised a push to make the stores more 'presentable and exciting' to shop in. He was optimistic that the changes would bring about 'an exciting new merchant culture which will transform the way we do things'.

He wants all members of staff – from managers to check-out staff and trolley pushers – to feel they can contribute to sales and is to devolve more decision-making to branch level in an attempt to achieve this.

Comment

● Safeway's new chief executive certainly made a splash yesterday. There was a sense of relief that, following Tuesday's muddled presentation from rival J. Sainsbury, at least Mr Criado-Perez has a vision. However, the hopes were tempered by the fact that his gimmicky vision for the future is totally untried and untested. True, it seems to have pepped up the staff – no mean feat after 10 years of underperformance and sluggish management. But that in itself will not be enough – and the group is now in the hands of its customers. It will have to see whether their curiosity gets the better of them and local discounts and promotions lure them into the stores. With full-year profits forecast at £230m, the shares trade on a prospective p/e of 11. In spite of their low rating, and the gap with peers, Mr Criado-Perez did not say enough yesterday to make them attractive in the short term.

Source: Financial Times, 26 November 1999

21.10 Using the 'hints' given in the article and marketing planning and control procedures, construct Mr Criado-Perez's outline report to the board of Safeway indicating how you think he may be intending to proceed.

21.11 What marketing objectives would you suggest Safeway pursue? Justify your answer.

21.12 How will performance be judged and what control techniques might be employed?

22 Services and Non-profit Marketing

Marketing in the service and non-profit sectors, while in every sense making use of the basic theories and practices, presents certain marked differences. These differences reflect the fact that services themselves have characteristics unique to this sector which require special understanding and therefore special treatment in terms of the marketing thinking and activities associated with these characteristics.

At the core of the difference is that in effect we are trying to encourage and persuade people into the purchase or adoption of products which they can never 'own' in the same way that they might expect to 'own' a motor car or a pair of shoes. The product/service for which they are expected to part with good money can never be taken away, it probably doesn't last long, you can't touch it and it cannot be stored for sale or consumption later. If the sale is not generated at the point of contact with the potential consumer, that specific time/place/opportunity is missed forever. Therefore the offering has to be as perfectly designed, placed and presented as possible in order to exploit the window of opportunity to its maximum.

Following the idea that services are different in essence to goods, from a marketing point of view, the realisation that non-profit activities are susceptible to the ministrations of the marketer leads us to the theory that the two activities are markedly similar in their special characteristics and therefore in their marketing management requirements. One area which demands special attention in both sectors is the training of staff who come into contact with the customer. No matter how much money has been expended on building the product/service, no matter how worthy the cause, if the delivery is poor, the remaining impression is one of negative response. This is true in a hotel receptionist, in a fast-food outlet with slovenly or couldn't care less staff, at a charity whose staff treats donors with contempt and at a hospital which fails to handle complaints or questions successfully. We need not dwell long on the treatment of the public by government departments. A case for emergency treatment perhaps?

Having made the transition to service sector marketing, the shift towards non-profit marketing becomes much more straightforward to achieve. The non-profit sector is wholly rooted in the service sector and as such the same techniques apply. Once we can grasp that 'profit' may be interpreted in a different way, and other than money, the opportunities that open up to use marketing in all its aspects become clear. Good marketing is effective communication, and communication is, in general, the lifeblood of any non-profit organisation. The getting and allocation of resources are their means and reason for existence.

Article 22.A **FT**

Tate ready to power into the millennium

In the first of an occasional series leading up to the opening of London's museum of modern art on Bankside, Antony Thorncroft looks at how the project has been carefully marketed as it attempts to make its name

One May morning in 2000 the Queen will declare open the Tate Gallery of Modern Art on London's Bankside. It is one of the few landmark millennium projects about which everyone feels confident: Sir Giles Gilbert Scott's extinct power station beside the Thames is being transformed by Swiss architects Herzog and de Meuron into the capital's much-needed specialist museum of 20th century art, on time and within budget.

There have been scares – over asbestos and the state of the roof – but the £130m development is proceeding remarkably smoothly. This month the new glass roof, which will house the restaurant and provide light for the upper galleries, is being installed, along with the ramp, which will draw most of the expected 2m visitors a year to the gallery, and will double as a performing space and sculpture hall.

The Tate Gallery of Modern Art is very much the inspiration of Nick Serota, director of the mother institution, the Tate Gallery at Millbank. When he took over there in 1988 he told the trustees they had to confront the problem of the 20th century collection. By a quirk of history the Tate housed two very different schools of art – British art and 20th century global art. It was home to both Turner and Matisse, Gainsborough and Picasso. It was schizophrenic.

As a result London was not taken as seriously as it would wish as a centre for modern art. Specialist galleries, such as the Museum of Modern Art in New York and the Pompidou Centre in Paris, had accumulated finer collections. Major exhibitions of modern art, most recently of works by Matisse, bypassed London, mainly because its museums could not contribute key works to the shows. As a perceived leader in the arts, London needed a world-class gallery devoted to the 20th and, also, 21st centuries.

The original idea of Serota and his trustees was to build an extension to the Tate at Millbank, but the space was limited and planning procedures a nightmare. The delay was providential. By the early 1990s John Major, the then prime minister, had been convinced London's leading arts palaces were desperately in need of renovation.

With the government reluctant to provide the money, a national lottery was the ideal solution. The Tate, along with Covent Garden opera house, can claim some of the credit, or blame, for the creation of the lottery.

Bankside was not the first choice – sites near King's Cross railway station, alongside County Hall on the South Bank, and at Vauxhall, opposite the Millbank Tate, were also considered. But the Scott building had architectural merit; it was available from its owners Magnox Electric for £8m; and it was cheaper to adapt an existing structure than to start from scratch.

Bringing the Tate to Southwark had one other inestimable advantage – it would help to revitalise a depressed part of London. The power of the arts to regenerate industrial blackspots – from Glasgow to Birmingham, from Pittsburgh to Bilbao – is well known.

Southwark council was happy to provide £1m towards a feasibility study, and its gamble is already paying off: the area around Bankside is coming to life, with new cafés and art galleries, hotels and apartment blocks. There is also the Globe Theatre, a recreation of Shakespeare's original, as a neighbour, and a planned £17m Millennium Bridge that will link the Tate with St Paul's – and the City.

Serota is adamant that he would have pushed ahead with the idea of a new museum of modern art even without lottery funding, but the £50m from the Millennium Commission, along with £12m from English Partnerships, the urban regeneration quango, made the £130m target manageable. Even so, Serota still had to find roughly half the cost from outside sources, a monumental challenge.

So far, £110m has been gathered, and Serota is confident the remaining £20m can be collected. Most of the money has come from private individuals and trusts, still clinging to their anonymity. This will change when the Tate nears its opening, as many of the dozens of new galleries, stretching over three floors at Bankside, will carry their sponsor's name.

When individuals and trusts were first targeted, Serota let it be known that for the right donation, say £30m, a mega-rich benefactor could secure the kind of immortality which has come to Sir Henry Tate, the sugar tycoon whose money contributed crucially to the creation of the Tate Gallery in 1897.

No such benefactor was forthcoming. In fact, the Tate has been helped by many generous contributions rather than a few enormous cheques. The biggest donation to date is less than £5m, but about 50 benefactors have shown their commitment in a handsome way. Now the corporate sector is being canvassed. Next year the Tate will appeal to the public, starting with the Friends of the Tate.

Serota will be in no way embarrassed if the appeal brings in more than £130m. Bankside will cost about £10m a year to run. The government's recently declared commitment to free access for all national museums will inevitably involve a higher government subsidy, but Serota expects an extra £5m a year will have to be raised through earnings and sponsorship.

Any additional contributions will go towards keeping Bankside open and, more importantly, establishing an endowment, an essential nest-egg for a time when governments are less generous with their grants.

Serota also needs money to improve the Tate's holdings of 20th century art. He expects loans and gifts from collectors and artists, keen to see their work displayed in the new building. But he knows that to rival the Museum of Modern Art in New York and the Pompidou, the Tate must plug gaps in its collection. It is weak in the art of the early 20th century masters, especially the Germans and Russians. It also needs more sculptures, particularly by artists such as Picasso and Matisse.

The first task for Lars Nittve, the Swede from the Louisiana Museum in Copenhagen, who in April was chosen to be the gallery's first director, will be to improve the collection by securing gifts and loans, and to build up a treasure chest so the Tate can buy at the best prices.

One of the main driving forces behind the creation of Bankside was to enable the Tate to show more of its collection. In spite of the success of its BP-financed New Displays programme at Millbank, under which the collection on show is freshened each year, the Tate exhibits less than a quarter of its stock of art.

With the extra 80,000 sq ft of gallery space at Bankside, this will rise to nearer 40 per cent. By constantly revolving the works, Serota hopes that half the Tate's collection will be available to public view within three years.

It was quickly decided that the greatest British artists of the 20th century – Moore, Bacon and Spencer among them – will be on show at Bankside and Millbank, displaying their work in a national and international context. But, of course, Bankside will also free space at Millbank.

While the great appeal continues, the Tate has also been extraordinarily successful in raising most of the £32m it needs to transform Millbank into the Tate Gallery of British Art, a development that will add 35 per cent more gallery space. This transformation will be completed by 2001.

The solid appearance of the Tate Gallery of Modern Art, maintaining much of the power station's bold 1930s brickwork embellished with decorative post-modernist touches, matches the Tate's assured marketing campaign for the new museum.

Not everything has gone to plan. Raising the cash proved harder than at first thought and there was not enough money to complete all aspects of the project – the chimney will not now contain a lift, whisking visitors to a viewing tower. A further £5m is needed to achieve this.

But compared with most other millennium projects, it is proving a politician's dream. A stagnating stretch of London is being transformed, with the likelihood of at least 2,000 new jobs coming to the area. London's status as a centre for art, the equal of New York, will be bolstered by a museum that should attract art lovers and tourists, bringing yet more prosperity.

The notorious Young British Artists will now have a beacon, challenging their aspirations, while the public will see not only more of the best of 20th century art in a British gallery, but also new works, and better travelling exhibitions. (After displaying its own collection in 2000, Bankside will mount a big specialist show in 2001.)

With the Tate Gallery of Modern Art at Bankside still more than 18 months away from opening, it is already hard to imagine how London managed without it.

22.1 Define the special characteristics of a service organisation and explain how these differ from those of a manufacturing organisation.

22.2 The Tate is a multi-million-pound organisation that has neither shareholders nor a profit motive. Why should it then be interested in marketing?

22.3 Define who the stakeholders in the Tate are, and which particular group of stakeholders Nick Serota has targeted and why. How did he achieve his aims?

22.4 What methods are available to the Tate to monitor performance of their staff and what special areas of staff training will need attention?

Article 22.B   FT

A sweeping success at cleaning up

Quality instead of price is the key to growth in the industry, the ISS chief executive tells Clare MacCarthy

With her smart uniform, crisp white shirt and black leather attaché case, the woman cleaning the computers is light years from the usual office cleaner.

It is obvious, as she air-blasts biscuit crumbs from the keyboards and wipes away fingerprints, that she enjoys her work. The wages are fine, she says, and her employer is flexible enough to allow her to juggle job and family.

Her employer is the Denmark-based ISS Group, the world's biggest cleaning company. And the man responsible for transforming Mrs Mop into a high-technology service operative is Waldemar Schmidt, its chief executive.

An affable 58-year-old who has spent much of his working life outside Denmark, Mr Schmidt's declared goal is to turn ISS into the world's leading service company.

In the European Union alone an estimated 2.4m people work for some 54,000 cleaning companies. Small-scale operations that undercut each other from contract to contract, heavy staff turnover and un-skilled workers are the norm.

Mr Schmidt's aim is to build a dominant position through acquisition and by adding expertise in specialist services such as hospital cleaning and high-technology maintenance.

'We are the undisputed leader of the market, and we also want to be the leaders of the consolidation of the industry,' he says.

Motivated full-time employees are part of this move to professionalise the industry. 'If we have people who are well-paid, have smart uniforms and are properly trained, then we can create a quality job at a high level of productivity,' he says.

In the UK, ISS was one of the first big companies to support the idea of a minimum wage. 'Competing on wages makes no sense. It would only give us the image of a cowboy industry,' Mr Schmidt argues.

'We view unions as partners,' he adds, evidently gratified that FIET, the international federation of clerical, professional and technical employees, regards ISS as a model company.

This approach has helped ISS Group achieve an impressive reversal of fortune since a fraud and mismanagement scandal in its US arm in 1996 forced it to spend $100m (£62m) on provisions to cover insurance liabilities and accounting irregularities.

The US arm has since been sold off, revenues and profits are on a steady upward path, and the share price has bounced some 275 per cent to DKr368 (£32) per share from the 1996 doldrums.

The pace of acquisitions is quickening: 27 companies, worth a combined DKr1.9bn, were added in 1998 and another 14 so far were acquired this year.

Last month, ISS bought Netherlands-based Abilis, Europe's second-largest provider of cleaning and specialised services for DKr3.6bn.

The Abilis deal brings the ISS Group workforce to 195,000. And although he has more than 70 companies spread across 32 countries, Mr Schmidt has an appetite for more.

'We are the undisputed market leader in Europe and Asia and our ambition is to become a global company,' he says.

While general cleaning and maintenance services for offices, schools and the like has been the mainstay of the industry, ISS sees most potential in growth areas such as specialised transport maintenance, food hygiene and healthcare.

In 1998 42 per cent of its revenues came from specialised cleaning services; by 2002, it plans to increase that share to 80 per cent.

To achieve this, says Mr Schmidt, training will be more important than ever. At Seagate's disc drive facility in Bangkok, for example, where even the smallest amount of dust can disrupt production, the 1,000 ISS staff 'clean room' operatives are skilled and experienced.

In Finland ISS is funding a four-year part-time MBA programme for 30 employees.

ISS is also introducing extensive management training for outstanding executives. 'Most people would say this is a people-intensive industry but it is also management-intensive,' Mr Schmidt says. 'You have to be on your toes the whole time.'

Mr Schmidt's own career at ISS began in 1973 when, aged 33, he was appointed managing director of the group's operations in Brazil.

By the time he left South America in 1979 to take up an executive position at ISS headquarters in Copenhagen, ISS's Brazilian workforce had grown sixfold to 6,000. Today the company employs 10,000 Brazilians.

He grew up in the same provincial town as Poul Schlüter, the former Danish prime minister and a friend since childhood.

Unusually among chief executives in charge of a global enterprise, Mr Schmidt can genuinely claim to know the business from the ground up. His first four weeks at ISS were spent on the shop floor – mopping it.

Even now, whether passing through an international airport or checking in at a hotel, he will invariably spot an undusted corner or a carelessly wiped window. 'Oh yes, I'll certainly notice when something needs cleaning,' he says.

Source: Financial Times, 8 June 1999

22.5 What particular aspects of the 7P's have been used to such good effect in this example?

22.6 Consider the principal aspects of service-based offerings and explain why staff training is so important.

22.7 What strategic choices are illustrated in this article, and how would you increase differentiation further?

22.8 Discuss what internal marketing efforts can be seen or inferred from this article.

FT

Refreshing the parts a customer seldom sees

Airlines spend a huge amount of time and money on livery designs, but strategies differ, finds Michael Skapinker

A giant beetle crawls across the screen in a hangar in Stockholm airport. Lakes shimmer. A woman swims by in a red bikini. The slogan 'Soft, gentle floors' appears before our eyes. It snows.

The cinema screen disappears, to be replaced by a small live orchestra. Finally, the reason we are here: the lights shine on a Boeing 737, sporting the new livery of SAS, the Scandinavian airline.

'My eyes get wet when I see this beautiful thing,' says Jan Stenberg, SAS's chief executive. Then he rips off his jacket and turns round to show us the black letters emblazoned on his shirt. They say: 'Follow me.' And he marches across the hangar.

'Is this normal?' asks an incredulous colleague, attending his first airline launch. No, it is not. There was something missing.

Where, I ask an SAS official, was the dry ice? He looks abashed. The dry ice had to be abandoned, he says. The air conditioning was blowing it all over the hangar.

After 15 years with the same livery, SAS has recreated itself. It is the second European airline to do so in recent months; just over a year ago, British Airways did the same. But the strategies of the two carriers could not be more different.

BA's new livery, with ethnic tailfin designs from around the world, created a furore which shows no sign of dying down. British newspapers repeatedly report that the tailfin designs are about to be scrapped. BA denies this.

It says the number of designs, originally set at 50, will be reduced. But the basic philosophy remains unchanged: BA is a world airline. A majority of its customers are not British. And while the airline is proud of its UK heritage, its tailfins are meant to show it is at home anywhere from Lithuania to Botswana.

By contrast, SAS, which is half-owned by the governments of Sweden, Norway and Denmark, has decided not to present itself as a world airline. 'We are proud of our Scandinavian heritage,' SAS tells its customers and staff.

Rather than attempting to be all things to all nations, the new SAS livery aims to sell Scandinavia to the world. 'We are perceived as being informal,' says Jan Olson, the SAS vice-president in charge of the redesign. 'Our customers tell us we are honest. They can trust us. We're innovative and fresh.'

Above all, says Mr Olson, Scandinavia is famous for clean design, and the new livery reflects that. The fuselage looks off-white; Mr Olson calls it 'warm grey'. The tailfins are all the same: dark blue, with SAS emblazoned on them in huge white letters.

'Scandinavian Airlines' appears in equally large letters on the fuselage, along with the colours of the airline's three national flags. In a gesture towards modernity, the flags are broken up into boxes, which Mr Olson says look 'digitised'.

The surprise is the engines, which are painted bright red. This is to show that, in spite of their understated elegance, Scandinavians also know how to go mad. 'It's a little bit of a glint in the eye,' chuckles Mr Olson, 'a little bit of "how could they do such a thing?"'

It is a question that occurs to me more than once. On the fuselage next to the front door of the re-designed 737, SAS has painted, in English, what it calls a 'poem'. It says: 'There are many ways to look at travel. All of them are the same – completion.'

The aircraft interior is similarly thought-provoking. The seats have slogans attached to them, apparently at random: 'Think', 'Relax', 'Rest'.

Imagine the arguments at the check-in desk.

'Could I have a Think seat?' a passenger might ask.

'I'm sorry, sir, we're very full tonight, the Think seats are all gone. I can give you a Relax seat or a Rest seat.'

'But I must have a Think seat! I've got a lot of work to do.'

What does Mr Olson think of the BA redesign? 'I was a little bit surprised,' he says. 'If I fly BA, it's because I want to fly British, not because I want a multi-cultural experience. Our customers said they wanted us to keep our national identity.'

Who is right? Should airlines capitalise on their national and regional strengths, and quirks, as SAS has done, or present themselves, like BA, as global companies?

In one sense the question is unfair. BA is already a global company, with a more cosmopolitan clientele than SAS. About two-thirds of SAS's passengers are Scandinavian.

A more important issue is whether BA has created so many designs that, even after reducing the number, people do not recognise its aircraft.

Airlines spend a huge amount of time and money on creating distinctive livery designs. But how many people, apart from airline executives and baggage handlers, get to study the outside of an aircraft?

When we board a flight from a fixed walkway, we see little more than a door. We see more of other airlines' aircraft – out of the window, while we are waiting to take off, or after landing. But these are the briefest glimpses. Airline designs get little chance to make an impression.

Most airlines have a single design, many using instantly recognisable symbols. Air Canada's maple leaf, Swissair's white cross on red and SAS's large tailfin letters leave us in no doubt who they are.

But how many airline passengers around the world say 'Ah, that must be BA,' as some Chinese calligraphy, or a Polish cockerel, or a lurid pink number that could have been scraped off a child's birthday cake, slip past?

Source: Financial Times, 6 October 1998

22.9 What strategic choices are available to airlines to secure growth in this highly competitive service industry? How does BA's decision about its livery reflect the choices it has made?

22.10 Describe SAS's differentiation effort and show how this is illustrated in the article.

22.11 How can an airline turn an intangible service into a tangible benefit? What must they achieve internally as well as externally?

22.12 How do airlines try to overcome the perishability of their service and what problems do they encounter in this process?

Under Granada's spell

Elizabeth Robinson assesses the media and hospitality group's prospects

Ask a geographer about Granada and there is only one answer: it's a Spanish city. Ask a City observer the same question and you can expect a variety of replies about the group which is expanding its media interests while at the same time beefing up its hospitality business.

When Granada presented full-year results this week, the questions coming from the floor to Gerry Robinson, chairman, and Charles Allen, chief executive, ping-ponged between inquiries about the media operations and those about the hotels and food services division.

Although the group is built on two very different pillars, Robinson insists that this is its strength and dismisses any notion that it would be better off splitting itself into separate components. 'Our strength lies in our two main businesses,' he said.

Hospitality, which includes hotels, restaurants and food services, is the larger pillar in terms of profits and turnover, accounting for more than 60 per cent of each, but the balance is shifting: last year, media accounted for 24 per cent of group turnover compared with 19 per cent the year before.

Granada has always been a media leader, from operating a cinema chain in the 1920s to its first commercial television network in 1954 (best known for its long-running soap opera, Coronation Street). It was one of the founding shareholders of British Satellite Broadcasting, which merged with Sky in 1990 to form BSkyB.

Last month, however, Granada sold down its BSkyB holding, leaving it with a 4.3 per cent indirect stake. It can now devote energy to a digital television venture with Carlton Communications, set up to rival BSkyB's digital ambitions.

BSkyB's digital service was first off the blocks, pipping the launch of the Granada/Carlton venture – ONdigital, which began broadcasting on November 15 – by six weeks. But Granada remains unruffled. Certainly, BSkyB has a huge potential customer base, with nearly 7m subscribers to its satellite service, but Granada has its own tactics.

First, it believes the UK is a nation of dish-haters and would much rather receive its television signals discreetly; hence ONdigital's broadcasts from land-based transmitters to ordinary aerials. Second, the company is tapping its small television rental division to offer rental customers free boxes that unscramble the digital signals. Third, it offers what it feels are a more manageable 30 digital channels compared with BSkyB's 140 and, for a lower subscription, viewers can 'pick and mix' their favourites. With all of this, Granada seems disappointed that the market has not recognised what it calls 'the huge potential value' of ONdigital. This week, it claimed the venture would break even in its third year of operation, when it hopes to have 2m subscribers.

Even so, and although analysts were cheered by this year's 17 per cent rise in pre-tax profits and promises of further double-digit growth, Granada's shares have underperformed the market by around 10 per cent since the start of the year.

Part of the reason is that analysts are cautious about how Granada will achieve the growth it expects. This week, the company did receive a £30.9m fillip related to savings from changes to payments for its ITV licences for Yorkshire, Tyne Tees and its share in GMTV, the terrestrial breakfast channel, but not all of this will reach the bottom line.

The greater part of the group is still the hospitality division but profits growth here has slowed, to 19 per cent last year from 41 per cent the year before. On top of this are fears of a consumer downturn which some analysts say will lead to less demand for hospitality.

Growth last year in the division – which spans roadside Little Chefs to the upmarket Le Meridien hotels – was achieved largely by squeezing costs so that margins became what one analyst described as 'phenomenal'. Although the company's three-year plan details new openings, especially of roadside and motorway catering, much progress will depend on rebranding the existing portfolio.

Rooms in the mid-market Posthouse hotels will be upgraded, for instance, while the less corporate-looking Heritage properties will be promoted as the UK's answer to Relais et Chateaux quality hotels. And while more value can be released from the division, the company seems in no rush to sell the Grosvenor House Hotel, in London's Park Lane, which last year contributed £28m to profits.

Possible deals that may inject some energy into the division include a hotel marketing alliance with an Asian group and an acquisition of a contract catering company. Robinson said this week a purchase was likely within a couple of years.

That time scale appears pedestrian compared with the changes Granada is sure to undergo in its media division. No wonder the issue of a demerger remains a topic of debate, for Granada's two pillars are looking less and less parallel.

22.13 Construct an extended marketing mix description for (a) a high-quality hotel in London and (b) a family hotel in a seaside resort. What are the differences and where are they similar?

22.14 Having squeezed out large amounts of costs, what alternative strategies are open to the hospitality part of this group in the light of an apparent slowdown in demand for hotel rooms?

22.15 How is Granada reacting to the changes in communications technology and how can they maintain their position against much larger operators in this area?

22.16 Non-profit organisations do not have as a yardstick their share of a particular market, rather they maintain a profile of their user customers and serve that market to the best of their ability. Discuss this statement and either refute or justify it.

23 International Marketing

As the communications revolution gathers pace and becomes more embedded in the whole fabric of doing business, the old politics of national boundaries become increasingly less relevant in terms of conducting international trade. With this attitude that 'the world is our marketplace' companies are finding compelling reasons for opening up and developing international interests of their own. The reasons may be one or more of the following:

- spreading risk through broader activity;
- entering new markets;
- escaping small or saturated domestic markets;
- seeking or achieving economies of scale;
- engaging in international production;
- responding to competitor moves; and/or
- strengthening the firm's overall competitive position.

There are, of course, varying approaches to 'internationalism', from exporting from a domestic production base to setting up distribution arrangements in other countries right up to establishing autonomous manufacturing operations around the world, either wholly owned or as joint ventures with local companies. Increasingly firms are choosing to adopt a position further along this chain as an initial attack, rather than feeling their way forward from the 'a bit of export and see how it goes' attitude of the past. Time is much more the crucial factor in success or failure.

But beware. Just because business is conducted in a particular way in the domestic market it is almost positively not a guide as to how the same business may be carried out elsewhere. A clear understanding of all the issues, economic, political, regulatory and cultural, that come into play when contemplating such a move is essential to any degree of success. What are the motives of any joint venture partners? Do we all clearly understand the how's and *why's* of what we are doing? Assume nothing, find out the facts and learn the language in both the literal and the broader sense.

The changes in the international scene are immense. Trading blocs are becoming less powerful, currency exchange and movement of staff, materials and information are becoming easier. With this opening up of new markets, and the means to access them, comes the increasing realisation among companies that they can do it too.

In order to successfully complete the tasks in this chapter you will need to be familiar with:

- types of investment;
- joint venture;
- market entry options;
- market selection factors;
- product adaptations/standardisation.

Carrefour's revolutionary

Peggy Hollinger, in a continuing series, talks to the hypermarket chairman who had an idée fixe about globalisation before it became fashionable

It is hard to tell if it is vision or obsession, but Daniel Bernard, chairman of hypermarket operator, Carrefour, has been preaching the gospel of globalisation for ages.

In future, he says, 'we will have local companies or global companies but not much in between. Globalisation will lead those who are not in the first team, or who are national retailers, to make alliances.'

Mr Bernard's views have been forged by years of globe trotting, first as head of international operations at Germany's Metro, Europe's largest retailer, where he was tipped to succeed former president Erwin Conradi.

Then, when a falling out between Carrefour's family shareholders led to management changes, the emigrant Frenchman was tempted back home to run the group in 1992.

Even then Carrefour was arguably furthest down the road, among Europe's top retailers, to being a global company, having introduced the hypermarket concept to Spain as early as 1973.

By the end of this year it will have operations in 20 countries, which are expected to generate about FFr187bn (£20bn) in annual sales. While other retailers may have greater total sales, few food retailers have been pursuing international expansion with the determination of Carrefour.

Even fewer have opted for Carrefour's approach of building stores from scratch – albeit with joint venture partners – rather than buying into existing operations.

Mr Bernard has had only six years at the helm of Carrefour to put his beliefs into practice. But in that time he has significantly stepped up the pace of expansion, adding 12 countries in the last five years alone. Last year the group invested FFr13bn in opening new stores abroad.

'There is a race and a lot of companies are qualified for the race,' he says. But 'to go global you need to be early enough. Generally in new countries you need to be the first in for the first win. When you arrive as number three or four it is too late.'

For Mr Bernard, there is no other option but to go global for a company such as Carrefour. 'You *have* to enter the race,' he says, citing the three forces which are pushing modern retailers to pursue global expansion.

First, the growing sophistication of consumers means retailers must be able to offer better and wider choices.

'The big move is the maturity of the consumer,' he says. 'They want it now and they want it with the best service and the best quality. Not only in mature markets, but in emerging markets the customer is more demanding. They have money, so they have power.'

Second, food retailing, particularly in the maturer markets of northern Europe, is more capital intensive than ever.

Retailers are being forced to fight off international competitors with investments in service, systems, technology and price. For those with international ambitions, the stakes are even higher, given the increased competition for prime positions in new markets.

'Before you could grow slowly,' says Mr Bernard. 'You did not need too much capital. But now, to be global, you need money.' And not only to invest in new markets, but to keep up with the competition at home.

Finally, retailers have to be able to extract the best price from their suppliers to stay competitive. Mr Bernard, like many of his rivals, believes market share and volume are the keys to winning bargains.

'You need good market share to negotiate with suppliers,' he says. 'If you are good globally, but weak locally, you are weak. If you are strong locally, but not globally, then you are weak for the future.'

Mr Bernard is clear about what he believes to be the real issue for retailers in the next century.

'When you mix the customer evolution with the other factors, we are facing a new revolution in retailing,' he says. 'You need huge volume, not for the volume, but to have the right know-how.

'We have to learn to be global. We have to learn global sourcing and how to manage capital intensity, the needs of our customers, our market shares and the war of formats. Because the format [the type of store or the services a group offers] must adapt every day.'

These are complex issues, but there is at least one area where retailers might find life easier in future, he suggests. Mr Bernard has been an outspoken supporter of European monetary union, and has advocated rapid introduction of a single currency. 'It is stupid for companies to have this financial difficulty [of operating in different currencies],' he says.

But if companies think it will make pan-European expansion any easier they should think again, he warns. Retailing, even global retailing, must be firmly focused on the local customer. 'Europe is a market where you have cultural differences,' says Mr Bernard. 'Italy is a specific country as far as development and politics. Spain, France and Belgium are all different.'

The real effect of the Euro will be to give more power to retailers with significant market share. But he remains vague as to whether that power will be measured in terms of individual markets or on a pan-European basis.

However, there are signs that Carrefour – like its Dutch rival on the international stage, Ahold – may be coming round to the view that it needs a stronger presence in the mature markets of Europe in order to be a truly global retailer.

Hitherto firmly focused on hypermarkets, Carrefour recently acquired Comptoirs Modernes, a leading French supermarket operator. The acquisition may open the way for Carrefour to tackle maturer markets, where trends are for smaller, local stores.

'There are a lot of new markets and everywhere there is still a lot to conquer,' he says. 'Even in France, where we have been very limited by law. There is no market where we are satisfied.'

Mr Bernard's brand of restless enthusiasm has clearly helped to transform Carrefour into a standard of global retailing. But he acknowledges that maintaining that standard depends to a large degree on his ability to cultivate an outward-looking corporate culture. More importantly, he cannot control everything from the centre. 'As long as you do that it means that the international operations are appendages to local operations,' he says.

But Mr Bernard is not too worried. Carrefour, he says, has been successful precisely because management is not done from the top down. 'Luckily enough,' he says, 'we have a permanent volcano under our feet.'

Source: Financial Times, 4 December 1998

23.1 How does Carrefour create overseas expansion? What issues are raised in terms of similarity and dissimilarity of the markets Carrefour have entered or intend to enter?

23.2 Investigate the French regulatory framework to explain why expansion has been restricted there.

23.3 How might Carrefour differentiate their offering as between more and less developed consumer maturity situations?

Article 23.B   FT

Pernod-Ricard hopes to cheer spirited Czechs

French drinks group sees exports as key to success in republic, writes Robert Anderson

When Pernod-Ricard added the liqueur Becherovka to its portfolio of brands last year it could not have anticipated the storm of protest the acquisition would arouse in the Czech Republic.

Rival bidders in the privatisation tender for Jan Becher, the distiller, complained that the Kč2bn ($64.8m) offer by the winning consortium – in which the French drinks company holds 40 per cent – had not been the highest and that its business plan was the worst.

Newspapers hinted of a deal stitched up between the three parties in the governing coalition and speculated about the political influence of Karl Schwarzenberg, the Czech aristocrat who owns 20 per cent of the consortium.

The incoming Social Democrat government has also indicated that it wants to take a closer look at the company's privatisation.

'Our privatisation came when the atmosphere was pretty heated,' says Alan Walden-Jones, chairman and chief executive of Jan Becher and former business development director at Pernod-Ricard.

He says that last September's sale was caught up in the backlash against other unpopular privatisations and in mounting speculation about cabinet corruption which eventually led to the fall of the government.

But he admits that the privatisation was bound to be sensitive because 'Becherovka is to some extent national property'. Although the drink has only 10.5 per cent of the domestic spirits market, it is the only liqueur with a big export demand and it has a long history and a well established place in Czech life.

The herb-based drink was first made in 1807 by an apothecary as a gastric medicine to accompany cures at the elegant west Bohemian spa town of Karlovy Vary, then known as Karlsbad.

The '13th spring of Karlovy Vary' is now drunk as an aperitif, digestif or used as a mixer, and the secret combination of herbs, local spa water and maturation in oak barrels is still believed by Czechs to aid digestion and ward off colds.

Its international reputation is such that the bittersweet liqueur could even be sold during prohibition in the US because it was classified as medicinal.

'Becherovka is one of the world's most solidly established local brands,' says Mr Walden-Jones. It therefore fits Pernod-Ricard's strategy of acquiring local brands with regional export potential and whose distribution networks can be used to sell Pernod-Ricard's global brands.

'We purchase networks which are leading brands in their own countries,' says Alain-Serge Delaitte, head of communications.

Last year, Pernod-Ricard bought Larios, the Spanish gin maker, and in June, the Yerevan brandy company in Armenia. Its plan for the new brands is to match its success with the Italian liqueur Ramazzotti, which now sells more in Germany than at home.

Since it bought Jan Becher, Pernod-Ricard has concentrated on improving the production flow and marketing, restructuring the finance departments and creating its own distribution network.

Plzensky Prazdroj, the country's biggest brewer, lost its exclusive distribution contract and is now only one of the distributors the company uses. Pernod-Ricard was also able to close its own distribution company and merge it into Jan Becher's new network.

The company's net profit rose 8 per cent last year to Kč149.6m on revenues up 12 per cent at Kč848m. Domestic sales increased 3.7 per cent to 8.6m litres, but are weaker in this year's first quarter because Czechs are spending less and imported brands continue to make inroads thanks to big advertising campaigns.

Mr Walden-Jones says a 20 per cent rise in excise tax is not helping and that it threatens Pernod-Ricard's ability to meet the secret sales targets in the privatisation tender.

'The privatisation targets are perfectly reasonable and achievable if the Czech market remains the same size it was in 1997,' he says. 'But it hasn't.'

The company hopes exports, using the Pernod-Ricard network, will make up the difference. Exports rose 5.7 per cent last year but are still only 12 per cent of unit sales and 9 per cent of revenues.

Pernod-Ricard wants to increase sales in western and eastern Europe, although it says low incomes and high import duties will hold back sales among the Czech Republic's neighbours.

It has restarted exports to Russia, where, like other Czech brewers, the company sees great potential as Czech products have traditionally had a good reputation.

Becherovka used to be well known in Russia before former President Mikhail Gorbachev killed sales with his anti-alcohol campaign in the mid-1980s.

However, the company faces a serious problem in Germany – the liqueur's biggest market after the Czech Republic and Slovakia – owing to a trademark dispute with Underberg, a German drinks company.

Underberg obtained the secret recipe from a member of the Becher family and its exclusive right to the trademark has been supported by German courts.

Talks have yet to start between Jan Becher's new owners and Underberg, but Mr Delaitte says: 'Germany is certainly one of the countries we would like to export to.'

Pernod-Ricard says that it plans eventually to double last year's sales of 9.75m litres by expanding exports.

'I see no reason why we could not sell 2m cases [18m litres],' says Mr Walden-Jones. 'It is achievable in well under 10 years.'

Such a level of success might allow Czechs to forgive it for buying their national liqueur.

Source: Financial Times, 8 September 1998

23.4 What type of investment have Pernod-Ricard made?

23.5 How will this investment benefit both parties?

23.6 Describe the overall marketing strategy revealed by the article. How should they deal with the political issues arising from this involvement?

23.7 Given the Czech sensitivity to foreign purchase of a national institution, how can the company overcome this reaction? What other strategies might they have adopted?

Article 23.C   FT

Tyremaker pumps up business with plant in China

By Chris Tighe

Bicycle tyre manufacturer Colin Scarsi is preparing to tap the world's biggest potential market for his product – China.

Green Tyre, Mr Scarsi's Teesside company, which exports puncture-proof recyclable polyurethane tyres to 28 countries, has forged a joint venture with Chinese businesspeople to set up in Shanghai. Its first phase, under construction and due to open in April 1999, will make more than 1m tyres a year.

There are more than 500m bicycles in China, a figure growing by an estimated 36m a year.

The Green Tyre project, which has taken two years of negotiation, is based on the belief that there are now enough Chinese cyclists who can afford a stylish puncture-proof tyre. It will cost, in initial outlay, twice as much as the old-style rubber variety though it lasts three to four times as long.

Mr Scarsi's Chinese products will be badged Greentyre, but marketed under the name Dong Fang – a strong sun rising in the East. 'Western products are chic, and coloured tyres will make them stand out,' he says, adding that the business market – delivery bikes are very common in China – should also help sales.

Mr Scarsi, managing director of Green Tyre, founded the Middlesbrough business in 1992. Current year turnover will be nearly £2m, 40 per cent up on last year.

Green Tyre, which claims to be the world's biggest producer of puncture-proof tyres for bikes and wheelchairs, has focused heavily on research and development and robotics to enhance its product and production processes.

Mr Scarsi's partners in the Chinese venture, who run media and computer businesses, have put up most of the £4m cost of the Shanghai plant's first phase; Green Tyre is investing its technology and expertise.

The Middlesbrough company will take a percentage of profits, and Mr Scarsi says the venture could be worth up to £15m to Green Tyre over the next 15 years. After that his company will own the plant and have sole rights to the market developed in China.

Praising the project, announced this week, Mr Brian Wilson, trade minister, said: 'This success should be an example to other exporters and demonstrates what can be achieved by developing a reputation for quality.'

The Shanghai plant will initially employ 34 Chinese. It has also created four new jobs in Middlesbrough to allow employees to go to Shanghai to train their Chinese counterparts.

Mr Scarsi said the issue of human rights in China, raised in connection with the recent visit to the country by Tony Blair, the prime minister, was a 'can of worms'. He added: 'It's very difficult for us in the west to understand their culture. I don't know if it's right that we sit in judgment on these places. It's for their people to change if in their society they wish to make such a change.'

Source: Financial Times, 16 October 1998

23.8 How robust do you think the venture discussed in the article might be? What factors lead you to this conclusion?

23.9 What other options might be available to Green Tyre?

23.10 What other markets could be available to Green Tyre, and what factors would make such markets of interest?

23.11 Should Green Tyre undertake any product adaptation? If so what and on what basis? Should they standardise and if so why?

Index

7 P's, 70
7 P's, 155, 158
Acquisitions, 13, 165
advertising, 17, 105, 107, 108, 109, 110, 125
advertising ban, 111
advertising message, 105, 111
advertising radio, 105, 107
advertising TV, 105, 111
advertising, government controls, 111
Ansoff's, 140, 141, 144

BCG matrix, 140, 141, 144
brand, 17, 49, 102, 112, 132, 133, 134, 135, 136
brand equity, 5, 45
brand extension, 59
brand management, 53
brand value, 49
branding, 2, 5, 37, 43, 45, 46
BS 5750, 55
budget setting, databased, 96, 102
budget setting, judgemental, 96, 102
buyer behaviour, 22, 26, 27
buying criteria, 23, 26

campaign planning, 105, 110, 111
celebrity endorsement, 101
channel design, 84
channel strategy, 81, 83, 84, 85, 86
communication, 95, 97, 99, 101, 102, 123
communication models, 96, 99, 101
competition, 49, 76, 77, 89, 97, 121, 128
competitive positioning, 140, 142, 146
competitive/comparative advertising, 105
consumer behaviour, 16, 19, 21, 43, 61, 66, 71,
    73, 83, 85, 100, 109, 113, 165
consumer information, 127
consumer segmentation, 21
consumerism, 20
control and evaluation, 148, 150, 152
corporate hospitality, 131
corporate strategy, 139, 140, 142
creative department, 105, 111
culture, 164, 165
customer, 16, 17, 28, 56
customer loyalty, 89
customer loyalty schemes, 115, 117
customer orientation, 44, 46

customer price assessment, 69, 70, 71
customer satisfaction, 89
databases, 124, 130

defensive strategies, 140, 142, 146
demand curves, 69, 70
development capital, 64
direct marketing, 124, 127
discounting, 88
distribution, 81, 87, 129, 130, 135
distribution channels, 81, 83
distributors, 126

e-commerce, 39, 40
economy of scale, 26
employee satisfaction, 89, 91
endorsements, 101
environmental analysis, 45
environmental influences, 17
environmental lobby, 64
environmental scanning, 2, 7, 8, 11, 43, 92, 105,
    111
environmentalist/ism, 19, 20, 21
ethical public relations, 131, 138
Europe, 91
European regulations, sales promotion, 115,
    118
European Union, 8, 9, 11, 15, 31
European Union regulations, 126, 130
exhibitions, 131
exporting, 26
external influences of pricing, 69

generic strategies, 140
geodemographic segmentation, 28
global marketing, 43
globalisation, 163

information filtering, 40
innovation, 60
intangible benefits, 157
integrated marketing, 105, 109
intensive growth strategies, 140, 146, 147
internal marketing, 158
international, 82, 98, 99, 132, 133, 134, 135, 136,
    143, 145, 158, 159, 162, 163, 165, 166, 167
International Trade Sanctions, 11

Internet marketing, 4, 38, 92, 93, 94, 102, 104, 107, 108, 122, 124, 125, 126, 127, 128, 130
ISO 9000, 56

joint ventures, 128, 163, 166

Kaizen, 23
knowledge management, 41

logistics, 82, 83, 85
loyalty marketing 11P's, 115, 119

macro-environment, 8, 61
mail order, 124, 128
mailing lists, 124, 130
market dominance, 74
market entry, 163, 166
Market orientation, 1
market potential, 148, 151, 152
market selection forces, 163
market share, 66
marketing analysis, 7
marketing channels, 81
marketing control, 148, 150, 152
marketing define, 1
marketing information systems, 36, 42, 86, 90, 122
marketing management, 148
marketing mix, 2, 5, 27, 28, 31, 70, 91, 109, 161
marketing objectives, 148, 151
marketing orientation, 22
marketing plan, 31
marketing planning, 148, 150, 151, 152
marketing research, 36, 42, 40, 41
marketing strategies, 148, 150, 157, 158, 159, 160, 161, 169
marketing strategy, 49
Maslow's hierarchy, 17, 21
micro-environment, 61
mission statements, 148, 151
monitoring, 115
monitoring performance, 121
motivation, 17, 19
mystery shoppers, 37

new product classification, 61
new product development (NPD), 60, 61, 62, 65, 66
new product introduction, 118
niche markets, 33, 74, 76, 77
not for profit, 59, 136, 155, 157, 161

OFTEL, 130
organisational buying behaviour, 21, 22
organisational buying decision models, 23, 24, 27
organisational markets, 85, 119
organisational structure, 148, 152

packaging, 60
perceptual mapping, 53, 54
perishability, 159
personnel selling, 121, 122, 123
personnel selling, ethical practice, 121, 122
Porter's Five Forces, 23, 26
portfolio analysis, 28, 58
price, 68, 73
price adjustments, 74
price elasticity, 69, 71
price, elasticity of demand, 69, 71
pricing methods, 74
pricing policy, 70, 73
pricing strategies, 74, 76
primary research, 37
privatisation, 165
product, 44, 45, 54, 89
product adaptation/standardisation, 163, 165, 167
product depth, 45
product development, 40
product innovation, 23
Product Life Cycle (PLC), 52, 58, 59, 61, 66
product line, 45
product line extension, 53
product management, 52, 53, 58, 59, 97
product mix, 45
product orientation, 1
product width, 45
production orientation, 1
profit, 46
promotion, 33, 151
promotional mix, 95, 99, 104, 113
promotions, 38
psychographic segmentation, 28
psychological influence, 17
public relations, 131, 132, 133, 134, 135, 136, 138
purchase decision, 21
purchasing decision, 45
push pull strategies, 96, 101

quality, 55, 157, 158

re-branding, 19
relationship life cycle, 23, 26
relationship marketing, 23, 24, 26
relationships, 121
Research and development, 61, 62, 65
response hierarchy models, 96
retailers, 87, 89, 91, 94, 130, 163
risk assessment, 151, 152

sale orientation, 1
sales analysis, 148, 151, 152
sales forecasting, 148, 151, 152
sales management, 121, 122, 123

sales potential, 148, 151, 152
sales promotion, 114, 116
sales promotion evaluation, 115
sales promotion objectives, 115, 117
sales promotion, European regulations, 115, 118
sales team management, 121, 122, 123
sampling methods, 37
sampling size, 37
secondary research, 37
segmentation, 19, 21, 28, 29, 31, 33, 35, 43, 77, 84
service sector pricing, 74
services, 88, 89, 126, 155, 157, 158, 160, 161
services marketing, 4, 38, 86
SERVQUAL, 155
Shell Directional Policy Matrix, 140, 144
sourcing, 23, 164
sponsorship, 131
STEP analysis, 8, 13, 15, 28, 35, 73
strategic marketing, 137, 142

strategies, defensive, 140, 142, 146
strategies, generic, 140
strategies, intensive growth, 140, 146, 147
subscriber information, 124, 130
suppliers, 126
supply and demand, 68
supply chain relationships, 88, 91
SWOT analysis, 28, 35, 92, 148, 150

Targeting, 31, 33
Tariffs, 13
Telemarketing, 124, 130
Telesales, 121, 122
training, 155, 157

USP, 87

VisCAP, 96

wholesaler, 87, 92